The Crisis of Global Capitalism

The Crisis of
GLOBAL CAPITALISM

*Pope Benedict XVI's Social Encyclical
and the Future of Political Economy*

EDITED BY

ADRIAN PABST

 CASCADE *Books* • Eugene, Oregon

THE CRISIS OF GLOBAL CAPITALISM
Pope Benedict XVI's Social Encyclical and the Future of Political Economy

Cascade Books
An Imprint of Wipf and Stock Publishers
199 W. 8th Ave., Suite 3
Eugene, OR 97401

www.wipfandstock.com

ISBN 13: 978-1-60899-368-0

Cataloging-in-Publication data:

The crisis of global capitalism : Pope Benedict XVI's social encyclical and the future
of political economy / edited by Adrian Pabst.

xii + 290 p. ; 23 cm. — Includes bibliographical references and index.

ISBN 13: 978-1-60899-368-0

1. Catholic Church. Pope (2005– : Benedict XVI). Caritas in Veritate. 2. Catholic
Church—Doctrines—Papal documents. 3. Love—Religious aspects. 4. Social justice—
Religious aspects—Catholic Church. 5. Christianity and justice—Catholic Church.
I. Pabst, Adrian. II. Title.

BX2347 .C3873 P30 2011

Manufactured in the U.S.A.

Contents

Contributors

Jon Cruddas MP is Member of Parliament for Dagenham, London, UK. A member of Compass, he is a leading figure in the British Labour Party and a major voice on the political left in Europe.

John Hughes is Chaplain of Jesus College, University of Cambridge, where he obtained his PhD in Philosophy of Religion in the Faculty of Divinity. He is the author of *The End of Work: Theological Critiques of Capitalism* (2007) and numerous articles in international journals, including *Modern Theology* and *New Blackfriars*.

Eugene McCarraher is Associate Professor of Humanities at Villanova University. His research is in the fields of cultural and intellectual history, social and economic theory, and political theology. In addition to numerous articles and essays, he is the author of *Christian Critics: Religion and the Impasse in Modern American Social Thought* (2000). Currently he is writing *The Enchantments of Mammon: Corporate Capitalism and the American Moral Imagination*.

John Médaille is Adjunct Instructor of theology at the University of Dallas, Texas. He is the author of *The Vocation of Business: Social Justice in the Marketplace* (2007) and the editor of *Economic Liberty: A Profound Romanian Renaissance* (2009). His latest book is *Toward a Truly Free Market: A Distributist Perspective on the Role of Government, Taxes, Health Care, Deficits, and More* (2010).

John Milbank is Research Professor of Religion, Politics and Ethics at the University of Nottingham and Director of the Centre of Theology and Philosophy. One of the world's leading theologians, he is the author of *Theology and Social Theory* (1990), *A Word Made Strange* (1997), *Truth in Aquinas* (2001, with Catherine Pickstock), *Being Reconciled* (2003), *The Suspended Middle* (2005), *The Future of Love* (2008) and *The Monstrosity of Christ* (with Slavoj Žižek, 2009). Together with Catherine Pickstock and Graham Ward, he is the co-editor of the *Radical Orthodoxy* volume (1999). He is currently completing *Philosophy: A Theological Critique.*

Adrian Pabst is Lecturer in Politics at the University of Kent, Canterbury, UK, and a Visiting Professor at the *Institut d'Études Politiques de Lille* (*Sciences Po*), France. Previously, he held a Leverhulme Early Career Fellowship at the University of Nottingham where he is a member of the Centre of Theology and Philosophy. He has published numerous book chapters and articles in international journals, including *Modern Theology, American Catholic Philosophical Quarterly, Telos,* and *New Blackfriars*. His first monograph, *Metaphysics: The Creation of Hierarchy*, will be published by Eerdmans in late 2011/early 2012. Currently, he is writing *The Politics of Paradox*, a book on a new political economy after the demise of left/right and state/market that have been dominant since the secular settlement of the French Revolution.

Tracey Rowland is Associate Professor and Dean and Permanent Fellow of the John Paul II Institute, Melbourne, as well as a Fellow of the Centre of Theology and Philosophy in the University of Nottingham. She is the author of *Culture and the Thomist Tradition after Vatican II* (2003), *Ratzinger's Faith: The Theology of Pope Benedict XVI* (2008) and *Benedict XVI: A Guide for the Perplexed* (2010).

Jonathan Rutherford is Professor in Cultural Studies in the School of Arts and Education at Middlesex University, and editor of Soundings Journal (http://www.soundings.org.uk). His latest book is *After Identity* (2007). He is chair of Compass's Good Society working group and a frequent contributor to *The Guardian* and *The New Statesman*.

David L. Schindler is Edouard Cardinal Gagnon Professor of Fundamental Theology at the Pontifical John Paul II Institute and the Catholic University of America, Washington D.C. One of North America's leading Catholic theologians, he is the author of numerous books and articles. He is also the editor of *Communio: International Catholic Review* that was co-founded by Joseph Ratzinger.

Stefano Zamagni is Professor of Economics at the University of Bologna and Vice director of the Johns Hopkins University SAIS Bologna Center where he is also Senior adjunct professor of International Economics. One of Europe's leading political economists, he has published widely on capital theory, theory of consumer behavior, social choice theory, economic epistemology, ethics, economics, and civil economy. Among his most recent books are *History of Economic Thought* (co-written with E. Screpanti, 2005), *Civil Economy* (co-authored with L. Bruni, 2007), *L' economia del bene comune* (2007), *Avarizia. La passione dell'avere* (2009), *Cooperative Enterprise: facing the challenge of globalization* (co-written with V. Zamagni, 2010) and *Dizionario di Economia Civile* (co-edited with L. Bruni, 2010). He is a member of the Pontifical Council for Justice and Peace that advised Pope Benedict XVI on the encyclical *Caritas in Veritate*.

Mark and Louise Zwick are the Editors of the *Houston Catholic Worker* and founder of Casa Juan Diego Houses of Hospitality for Immigrants and Refugees in Houston, Texas. They are the authors of *The Catholic Worker Movement: Intellectual and Spiritual Origins* (2005).

Acknowledgments

THIS COLLECTION IS PARTLY based on a conference held at the Centre of Theology and Philosophy in the University of Nottingham on July 9 and 10, 2009. The conference was the first extended theological discussion in the UK of Pope Benedict XVI's social encyclical *Caritas in Veritate* (published just two days before, on July 7, 2009). With speakers and participants from around Europe and the U.S.A., the engaging debates on the significance of the encyclical persuaded me to publish parts of the proceedings as a book.

I am very grateful indeed to the speakers for making their papers available for publication. I would also like to thank those who did not participate in the conference for their contributions to this collection.

I owe a special debt of gratitude to my colleagues at the Centre of Theology and Philosophy and the Department of Theology and Religious Studies at Nottingham for their support, in particular Professor John Milbank and Dr. Conor Cunningham. It is with immense appreciation that I would like to acknowledge the extensive financial support by both institutions that made this event possible.

Finally, I am most grateful to the publishers Wipf and Stock, in particular Charlie Collier for his immediate support and Diane Farley for her patience and assistance.

July 7, 2010, on the first anniversary of the
publication of *Caritas in Veritate*.

ADRIAN PABST

Introduction

The Future of Political Economy

Adrian Pabst

"This Time Is Different": Capitalism and Secular Modernity

In a sense, the global recession of 2007–2010 is just another remind-er that capitalist economies suffer periodic crises but that capitalism does not collapse under the weight of its own inner contradictions. Instead, it always reverts to the "normal" cycle of expansion, contraction, and recovery. This reversion is linked to over-accumulation and falling profit rates that prompt capital owners to cut the real wages of la-borers in order to generate new surplus value, as both Adam Smith and Karl Marx recognized.[1] But whereas Smith evaded the issue of "primi-tive accumulation," Marx followed Sir James Steuart in arguing that this is the condition of possibility for the genesis of capitalism. What Rosa

---

1. Smith, *Wealth of Nations*, vol. I, chap. 9; Marx, *Capital*, vol. 3, chs. II and XIII. A contemporary example of this is "wage restraint" in Germany over the past decade. While it has significantly improved the competitiveness of German exports, there can be no doubt that it has also magnified the unsustainable imbalances between surplus and deficit countries within the eurozone and beyond.

Luxembourg and Hannah Arendt later add to Marx's account is the idea of the permanent need to renew this process of enrichment based on expropriation—hence their theory of imperialism.[2]

Neither Marx nor his disciples could however explain how and why the capitalist commodification of land, labor, and social relations based on the repeated, cumulative process of "primitive accumulation" through dispossession requires a redefinition of the sacred and the subordination of the sanctity of life and land to the quasi-sacrality of the market—aided and abetted by the state, as Karl Polanyi has shown.[3] In this manner, free-market capitalism—increasingly unconstrained by the shared moral codes of civic culture and civil society—tends to exacerbate both income and asset inequality, as exemplified by advanced economies in the U.S. and the UK over the last thirty years or so.[4] In different ways, the gap between capital owners and wage laborers also widens in fast-growing, emerging markets like China and India where hundreds of millions have been lifted out of abject rural poverty, only to join the new underclass of the "working poor" who face a lifetime of urban precariousness.

In the ongoing process of "primitive accumulation," money and the everyday market economy are superseded by layers of financial capital, which is marked by ever-greater abstraction from the real economy and makes money out of money—value in search of surplus value. At the top of this inverted pyramid sits global finance, seeking short-term returns that neither produce long-term prosperity nor trickle down to the masses. Instead, disembodied capital inflates and subsequently deflates the real value of physical assets by using them as collateral in credit-fuelled and debt-leveraged acts of speculation that assume rising asset prices which are in reality unsustainable. That's why recessions and depressions on Main Street only ever occur in the wake of financial crises on Wall Street.[5] Such crises are caused by careless lending, excess borrowing, debt default, and market panic—exactly the sequence of the 2007–8 global "credit crunch." One can say with the economists Carmen

2. Marx, Capital, vol. 1, ch. XXXI, "Genesis of the Industrial Capitalist." Cf. Perelman, *Invention of Capitalism*, 13–58, 92–195; Harvey, *New Imperialism*, 137–82.

3. Polanyi, *Great Transformation*.

4. The negative impact of both income and asset inequality on economic growth and the well-being of societies (in terms of better physical and mental health, less crime, less family breakdown, higher educational levels, etc.) has been documented by Wilkinson and Pickett, *Spirit Level*; and Rajan, *Fault Lines*.

5. Kindleberger, *Manias, Panics, and Crashes*.

Reinhart and Kenneth Rogoff that this time seems no different from the past "eight centuries of financial folly."[6]

In another sense, however, the current crisis is unprecedented in its magnitude, intensity, and nature. Not only is this the first global recession that hit the developed economies at the core with greater severity than the emerging markets at the periphery. But compared even with the Great Depressions of 1873–1896 and 1929–1933, the extent to which finance has pervaded and dislocated the real economy is unprecedented. Following President Nixon's *de facto* abolition of capital controls and the end of managed exchange rates in the early 1970s,[7] capital was globalized as international money markets sucked in savings from around the world and made bumper profits on exchange rate speculation, culminating in a series of financial crises and sovereign debt defaults (Mexico in 1994, East Asia in 1997, and Russia in 1998). Reinforced by successive waves of liberalization, deregulation, and privatization, easy credit was increasingly poured into new services such as finance, insurance, and real estate (or FIRE). Thus the "new economy" was born. After the dot-com crash in 2000 when over 7 billion dollars was wiped off technology shares, central bankers across the globe opened the money tabs and injected mass liquidity into the financial system in order to stave off recession, paving the way for the global financial bubble that burst in 2007 and plunged the world economy into the worst recession for at least seventy years.

Fuelled by the sovereign wealth and foreign exchange reserves of Asian countries and the Gulf States, private and corporate debt was secured almost exclusively against the increasingly inflated value of residential and commercial property. That, in turn, provided the basis for the infamous instrument of "mortgage securitization" that encapsulates the concentration of capital and financial speculation on short-term nominal exchange value—rather than long-term productive investment in the real economy that spreads wealth through income and asset distribution.

Crucially, stagnant or declining real wages in advanced economies like the U.S., the UK, and even Germany reduced the purchasing power of lower- and middle-income families at a time when the rise in the cost of living by far outstripped official inflation rates of 2 percent per annum. The fall in purchasing power not only exacerbated inequality but also generated a growing demand for consumer credit and home mortgages

6. Reinhart and Rogoff, *This Time Is Different*.

7. Eichengreen, *Globalizing Capital*.

that could only be met by new financial vehicles speculating on asset inflation instead of monitoring the ability to repay debt. Thus, credit-fuelled and debt-leveraged consumption and speculation supplanted income-based saving and investment. Here one can suggest that the link between financial abstraction from the material world and its necessary reconnection with the real economy constitutes a dialectic that is entirely internal to the logic of late modern capitalism.

But given that the nominal value of capital must be reinvested in real material processes, the living universe is supplanted by a virtual reality that is grounded in a vacuous generality—the capitalist fetishization of idealized commodities and the notion that the worth of material objects lies in their status as exchangeable commodities instead of being somehow both intrinsic to things and added to them by human labor. Like all ideologies and political economies, capitalism is predicated on an ontology that makes philosophical and theological claims about the nature of the shared world we inhabit. More than any other economic system, free-market capitalism weakens real relations among actually existing things because it privileges discrete, individual objects at the expense of the social, cultural, and religious structures and arrangements that bind them together, as R. H. Tawney and his Christian socialist friend Karl Polanyi first argued.[8]

By separating materiality from symbolic meaning and subjecting everything to standards of abstract value, the capitalist mode of production and exchange subordinates the sanctity of nature and human life to the secular sacrality of the free market and the sovereign central state that have colluded from the outset of the modern age.[9] For just as the market requires state support to extend contractual proprietary relations and nominal exchange into ever more areas of public and private life, so the state needs the market to expand its powers of surveillance and enforcement to hitherto self-regulating organizations of civil society. For this reason, the birth of capitalism in early modern Europe is inextricably intertwined with the rise of the national state that subsumed civic culture and civil society under the central authority of the sovereign ruler.[10]

8. Tawney, *Religion and the Rise of Capitalism*; Polanyi, *Great Transformation*.

9. Pabst, "Modern Sovereignty in Question," 570–602.

10. Tilly, *Big Structures, Large Processes, Huge Comparisons*, esp. 147; Arrighi, *Long Twentieth Century*.

Nevertheless, throughout the development of urban society and modern economic life in the long European transition from the late Middle Ages to the Enlightenment and beyond, the life of households, communities, and intermediary institutions was governed by principles and practices of reciprocity and mutuality as part of "economies of gift-exchange" that were indissociable from the Church and Eucharistic celebrations.[11] Broadly speaking, medieval Christendom and its Renaissance-Byzantine legacy in East and West viewed both the economy and politics as penultimate, embedded in human and social relations, as well as regulated by civic virtues of sympathy and fraternity. Those religious traditions that promoted or endorsed the increasingly disembedded capitalist mode of production and exchange were also those that deviated from creedal Christianity. This applies to the Calvinist sundering of contract from gift, as John Milbank argues in chapter 1, and to the Baroque scholastic separation of "pure nature" from the supernatural, as Tracey Rowland shows in chapter 2. Since capitalism emerged with the approval and connivance of actual religion, it can only be fully understood as part of the theological shifts that brought about modernity. By focusing on work ethic, Weber was less than half-right.

Religion is indispensable to political economy for another reason. In the past and the present, capitalism has faced resistance from more orthodox faith traditions (both within and across different world religions) that defend strong notions of gift exchange, ethical limits on exchange (like anti-usury laws), and the sanctity of life against contractual-proprietary relations, capitalist commodification, and bio-politics. As such, the capitalist system requires for its very operation (and not just as mere ideological obfuscation) the re-conception of the sacred and the institution of secular simulacra like fetishized commodities and market utopia—with the collusive complicity of religion.[12]

The secular logic at the heart of capitalism is also the mark of the intellectual traditions that have been dominant in the modern age, chief of all political liberalism and its roots in late medieval nominalism and

11. Bossy, "Mass as a Social Institution," 29–61; Black, *Guilds and Civil Society*, esp. 12–43 and 237–41. For a critique of Black's definition of civil society, see Milbank, "Real Third Way," this volume, ch. 1.

12. On the complicit collusion of Protestant liberalism and unfettered capitalism in the U.S., see Frank, *One Market Under God*; Connolly, *Capitalism and Christianity, American Style*. Cf. Pabst, "Modern Sovereignty in Question," esp. 585 n. 60.

voluntarism.[13] This late medieval legacy, which the Hobbesian-Humean and Lockean-Kantian strands of liberalism carry forward, translates into the modern univocal poles of left and right, the binary poles of individual and collective sovereign volition as well as the institutional poles of state and market (as John Milbank suggests in his contribution to this collection). All three poles underpin liberal market democracy, which has conspicuously failed to deliver universal freedom and prosperity. It is therefore surely no coincidence that the crisis of global capitalism occurs at the same time as the crisis of secular modernity. This time is different after all.

In what follows, I will not summarize or assess each contribution to this collection of essays. Instead, my aim is to reflect more broadly on our present geo-economic predicament and on the contribution of *Caritas in Veritate* to contemporary debates on economics, politics, and society. The account that is presented in this introduction in no way reflects the views of all the contributors, but I have drawn on their work in order to substantiate some of my own arguments. What I will suggest is that Pope Benedict's call for a civil economy represents a radical "middle" position between an exclusively religious and a strictly secular perspective. His argument is that faith can lead to strong notions of the common good and a belief that human behavior, when disciplined and directed, can start to act more charitably. There can also be secular intimations of this: the more faith-inspired practices are successful even in secular terms (e.g., more economic security, more equality, more sustainability and greater civic participation), the easier it will be for secular institutions to adopt elements of such an overarching framework without however fully embracing its religious basis. Indeed, intellectuals and decision-makers across the political spectrum have recognized that there is a clear convergence between visions for a progressive stakeholder society and Catholic alternatives to unbridled capitalism.[14]

13. See André de Muralt's genealogy of modern philosophy and political thought from John Duns Scotus and William of Ockham via Suárez and Kant to John Rawls, in his seminal book *L'unité de la philosophie politique*.

14. See, for instance, Hutton, "What I Told the Pope."

THE SPECTER OF DEPRESSION AND THE IMPASSE OF SECULAR SOLUTIONS

Both state and market responses to the global crisis show just how intellectually defunct and morally bankrupt secular political economy now is. Three years after the onset of the credit crunch that unleashed the biggest economic bust since 1929, the U.S. economy teeters on the brink of a double-dip recession that could not only drag down much of Europe, Latin America, and Africa but also mutate into a full-scale depression (similar to Japan's lost "double decade" in the 1990s and 2000s). Even if the fledgling recovery of the U.S. economy continues, austerity programs in the eurozone and the rest of the EU will for the foreseeable future have a strongly deflationary effect beyond Europe's borders that cannot be offset by expansionary monetary policy, with baseline interest rates near 0.5 percent and central banks wary of the inflationary implications of further quantitative easing (increasing the money supply by printing money to purchase public bonds or private assets). Even if the worst-case scenario is averted, large parts of the world economy will face years of sluggish growth, mass unemployment, social dislocation and environmental degradation.[15] Of course religion is no panacea, but the principles and practices of Christian social teaching (and cognate ideas in other religious traditions) offer an alternative path that outflanks the binary logic of state and market and of left and right that has prevailed since the secular settlement of the French Revolution.

Secular solutions have failed to overcome the fractures of the world economy because they have treated the symptoms of the crisis rather than its causes. Following the disastrous decision on September 15, 2008, to allow Lehman Brothers to go bankrupt, a concerted effort to

---

15. As a recent UN report documents, the escalating destruction of nature and the unprecedented decline in bio-diversity present a far greater risk than the excessive emission of carbon dioxide and climate change (though the latter have an impact on the former). On narrowly economic terms, the costs of mitigating climate change are approximately 1–2 percent of annual global output, with longer-term benefits of around five to twenty times that figure. By contrast, the value of saving "natural goods and services" such as crops, pollination, medicines, fertile soils as well as clean air and water will be between 10 and 100 times higher than the costs of saving the habitats and species which provide them. For example, establishing and operating a worldwide network of protected areas would cost 45 billion dollars a year, but the benefits of preserving the diversity of species and landscapes could amount to 4–5 trillion dollars per annum. See UNEP, "Dead Planet, Living Planet."

bail out banks and other systemically important institutions like AIG averted a meltdown of the international financial system (with a total rescue package amounting to 9 trillion dollars in cash injections, lending guarantees, and funding lines, according to IMF estimates). But since then, the world's leading economies have failed to reform global finance and reduce the fiscal imbalances that fuelled the credit and asset bubbles. Nor have political leaders taken action to reduce financial speculation in commodities, which was responsible for the price hike in the first half of 2008[16] and continues almost unabated. While the immediate panic that erupted in September 2008 has subsided, the near-meltdown of the world's financial system has bequeathed a loss of trust in the workings of markets themselves.[17] Absent wholesale reforms, most of the conditions for another economic crisis are still firmly in place.

At the international level, the G20 is deeply divided between developed economies, emerging markets, and developing countries. Since it first met in November 2008, it has proven to be a useful instrument of crisis coordination (financial bailout, monetary expansion, and fiscal stimulus). However, it has failed to bring about significant changes to the global economy, let alone launch a process of systemic transformation. The group has neither begun to implement basic financial reform (capital requirements, bank levies, or transactional taxation) nor made progress on new growth models (re-localizing global capital, promoting green technologies, etc.). The summit in Canada in June 2010 where the U.S. and Europe disagreed on austerity programs confirms that the

16. See UNCTAD, "Global Economic Crisis." As with financial services, the core problem of commodity trade is an unprecedented concentration of ownership and under-regulated futures trade. At the height of the 2008 commodity bubble, the Chicago CME Group—itself the product of a merger of the Chicago Mercantile Exchange with the Chicago Board of Trade—witnessed more than a million contracts per day. Hedge funds and other financial institutions not only engage in future trading (involving, for example, the daily contracting of 30 million tons of soybeans for future delivery) but also acquire the companies that stock commodities. Such and similar speculation is highly distortive and destructive of the actual market precisely because these traders never take delivery. Instead, they make gigantic gains on both soaring and falling prices: futures contracts serve to drive up current prices and enable speculators to unload their holdings onto a distorted market, hurting both producers and consumers in the process. Crucially, speculators bet that artificially inflated prices will eventually collapse, at which point they can once more snap up cheap assets and repeat the process.

17. This is evinced, for example, by the "flash crash" on May 6, 2010, when equity prices gyrated on an unprecedented scale—an unusual pattern of fluctuations that remains unexplained by rival schools of economics.

power of the G20 to modify the relations between states and markets has already peaked and is now waning.

At the national levels, governments and central banks have offset some of the worst effects of the recession through a combination of fiscal stimulus packages and unorthodox monetary expansion. But with both households and corporations de-leveraging, a recovery led predominantly by private sector investment and consumption looks increasingly unlikely. Paradoxically, this is particularly true in countries like the UK where massive public spending cuts—coupled with a substantial increase in sales (or value-added) taxes—further depresses aggregate demand and private sector activity that is highly dependent on public sector contracts. Nor have parliaments or presidents had the courage either to enforce existing laws or to put in place new anti-monopoly legislation aimed at breaking up financial and retail conglomerates that represent a form of casino-cum-cartel capitalism.[18] Even banks that have had to be taken into part-public ownership have not restored lending to cash-strapped businesses or households. How in these circumstances the recovery can possibly be sustained by private sector spending has never been explained by the "deficit hawks." Thus, both globally and

18. Johnson and Kwak, *13 Bankers*. The authors document how the assets of the six largest banks grew from 18 percent of national output in 1995 to 60 percent in 2009 at the height of the financial crisis and that they have access to money at significantly lower rates than smaller banks. This confirms once more that free-market capitalism does not avoid private cartels and monopolistic practices. While governments collude with banks that are "too big to fail," there is evidence that breaking up such conglomerates has economic benefits. When Standard Oil was broken up in 1911, for example, the individual parts became more valuable than the whole and no longer threatened to bring down the entire sector. Moreover, the objection that neither Lehman Brothers in the U.S. nor Northern Rock in the UK were universal, integrated banking conglomerates (the former was a pure investment bank and the latter a mortgage bank) but nevertheless went bankrupt is misguided because both were inextricably intertwined with the global financial system. Lehman, in the form of counter-party, was deeply linked to mainstream banking, while Northern Rock could only leverage itself to such an unsustainable degree because investment banks like Lehman bought its securitized mortgage packages and sold them on. A Glass-Steagall divide between commercial, retail banking, and investment banking would have allowed Lehman either to go into administration without bringing down the entire financial edifice or to be taken over (like Bear Stearns). Likewise, Northern Rock could have been taken into public ownership at a much lower cost to the taxpayer. Failure to ban certain speculative instruments enables both types of banks to engage in similar practices and thereby spread systemic risk throughout the world economy. This undermines the argument that the uncorrelated and asymmetrical cycles of investment and retail banking serve to reduce risk and make a division of different types of banking unnecessary.

locally, the world economy remains fractured along the same pre-crisis fault lines and risks a repeat of the financial crisis.[19]

Ideologically, neither the left nor the right has fully repudiated the shared neo-liberal consensus that prevailed for most of the post-Cold War period. The left has bailed out global finance without reforming it, while the right has slashed public spending on which the private sector depends. Both have relied on central banks printing money to buy up the toxic debts of banks and corporations, but neither has helped individuals or households restructure their debt and thereby avoid personal bankruptcy and home foreclosures. Left and right argue over fiscal sustainability, but neither has developed a credible growth strategy that reduces debt while also creating employment.

By not breaking up banks "too big to fail" and creating incentives linking finance to productive investment, both left and right are propping up a system that privatizes profits, nationalizes losses and socializes systemic risk. Neither left nor right has so far launched a genuine redistribution of power and a re-balancing of wealth in favor of citizens, communities, intermediary associations, and small businesses. Both left and right are scaling back statist welfarism but fail to institute asset-based welfare. As a result, benefits and other entitlements provide little more than income redistribution at the margin and some meager compensation for the proletarianization and de-professionalization of the workforce that is denied mutual self-organization as part of corporate guilds. With widening asset and income inequality, the polarization and fragmentation of society will continue to proceed apace (as Jon Cruddas and Jonathan Rutherford argue in chapter 9). This endangers the social bonds of trust and reciprocity on which vibrant democracies and market economies surely rely.[20]

MORAL SENTIMENTS AND POLITICAL ECONOMY: KEYNES, MARX, AND SMITH

So what is to be done? Since 2007, critics of the neo-liberal "Washington consensus" and the underlying intellectual orthodoxy have looked to three different traditions for alternatives: Keynes, Marx, and Smith. Keynes has inspired the fiscal stimulus packages to prevent the global

19. Rajan, *Fault Lines.*
20. See Pabst, "Crisis of Capitalist Democracy," 44–67.

recession from turning into another Great Depression. Keynesian principles are also shaping current efforts to reform the international financial architecture centered on the Bretton Woods institutions which he helped design in 1944. According to this much-needed revisionist reading, the contemporary return of Keynes is a late vindication for the most important economist of the twentieth century. Not only is his theory not to blame for the crisis of the post-war "Keynesian settlement" in the late 1960s and 1970s. It was in fact the neo-classical, monetarist revolution that abolished Keynesian capital controls and thereby helped unleash the forces of global finance which condemned the world to the worst crisis since 1929–1932.[21]

Aspects of Marx have been rightly reclaimed, not just by sections of the secular left but also by religious thinkers—most prominently the Archbishop of Canterbury Rowan Williams. In particular, he has defended Marx's critique of unbridled capitalism as a kind of mythology that ascribes reality, power, and agency to money and commodities that have no life in themselves.[22] This has the effect of turning such and similar fetishes into idols and transforming the unreality of debt into an independent force that is nevertheless increasingly abstracted from the real economy (as I have already indicated). Indeed, the global economy dominated by disembodied finance represents an edifice built on sand, as the patriarchs of Rome, Moscow, and Canterbury have consistently argued throughout the crisis (a theme to which I will return below).

The legacy of Adam Smith has been championed by a number of economists and historians, chief of all, Amartya Sen. He hails Smith as a theorist of the market that is governed by non-profit values like prudence and generosity that serve social justice rather than simply private profit.[23] Read in conjunction with his *Theory of Moral Sentiments*, Smith's *Wealth of Nations* seems to show that the "invisible hand of the market" is not in or of itself sufficient but requires mutual trust and confidence in order to operate efficiently. Absent a shared framework of moral sentiments, human self-interest mutates into excessive risk-taking in a search for profits that turns the fellow feeling of responsible agents into the ruthless speculation of "prodigals and projectors." Far from licensing the

21. Skidelsky, *Keynes*; Clarke, *Keynes*; Davidson, *Keynes Solution*.

22. Williams, "Face it."

23. Sen, "Open and Closed Impartiality"; Sen, "What Do We Want?"; Sen, "Adam Smith's Market."

domination of capital, Smith's morally embedded market economy—so Sen's argument goes—uses production and exchange in order to foster intellectual emancipation, social progress, political enlightenment, and civil society.

The ideas of Smith, Marx, and Keynes differ significantly from one another, but what they share in common is an attempt to overcome classical political economy (as developed by Mandeville, Hobbes, and Locke) in the direction of social philosophy and moral theory. In different ways, all three seek to replace the idea of private vice and arbitrary divine power with enlightened self-interest and human agency. (Indeed, Smith's "invisible hand" involves the theologically dubious idea of human cooperation with the regular and immediate intervention of divine providence.[24]) However, the "progressive" moral economy of Smith, Marx, and Keynes is grounded in a shared denial that the exercise of virtues requires a transcendent common good that alone can direct individual self-interest to communal, public well-being and bind together both moral and civic virtue. Linked to this is a divide between moral sentiments and virtues, on the one hand, and the operation of the market, on the other hand. Indeed, the logic of gratuitousness and the practice of reciprocal giving are sundered from the logic of contract and the processes of production and exchange. As such, none of these three intellectual traditions represents a compelling alternative to the prevailing economic ideas and policies.

Skidelsky is right to credit Keynes with a "third way" beyond statist communism and free-market capitalism that is based on a critique of utilitarian-hedonistic ethics.[25] Keynes's critique does not just focus on economic aspects (for example, treating money as an end rather than a means) but also extends to moral questions like the nature of the good life. He rejects the acquisitive spirit of utilitarianism and argues for an economic system that is rooted in locality and serves human needs and desires: "So, in conclusion, ideas, knowledge, art, hospitality, travel—these are things which should in their nature be international. But let goods be homespun whenever it is reasonably and conveniently possible and above all let finance be primarily national."[26]

24. For a critique of recent attempts to rehabilitate Smith along these lines, see Pabst, "From Civil to Political Economy."

25. Skidelsky, *Keynes*, 133–53.

26. Quoted in Skidelsky, *Keynes*, 187.

However, Keynes never fully repudiated his earlier embrace of G. E. Moore's *Principia Ethica* that shaped the moral thinking of the influential Bloomsbury circle of intellectuals and artists. Moore claims that the good is a "non-natural" and non-teleological property that escapes rational judgment and is best experienced through personal affections and aesthetic enjoyments.[27] As a result, friendship and the contemplation of beauty (whether in nature or in art) are the only morally justifiable ends of human action. That sets Moore—and Keynes—apart from the hedonistic utilitarianism of Jeremy Bentham and James Mill. But by the same token, the individual pursuit of wealth (goods rather than money) is not framed by a substantive notion of the shared public good that can blend private prosperity with the public commonweal. For Keynes the good is a purely nominal property that is confined to the mind and has no discernible presence in the material world. As such, goods are nothing more than those things that provide us with some emotion, not simply pleasure (as Bentham and Mill claimed) but also pain (being in love always involves both). For all the talk about goodness rather than utility, Keynes's moral vision remains wedded to the utilitarian, nominalist denial that good things reflect and intimate a transcendent source that endows everything with a share of the good.

Unlike Keynes, Marx is no residual utilitarian but his social theory is caught in the irreconcilable, modern *aporia* between notions of unalterable nature and notions of human artifice.[28] Accordingly, human behavior and collective action are best explained by law-like generalizations whereby material conditions and class structures of power are the ultimate causes that bring about ideology and beliefs. But to reduce ideas and beliefs to mere immaterial effects of material causes reveals a dualistic ontology that is both nominalist (denying the real existence of universals in things) and voluntarist (giving priority to the power of volition rather than ideas in the intellect). For Marx, the highest form of individual liberation and collective self-emancipation is the imprinting of individual will on society or nature. And by rejecting any teleological account in terms of a hierarchy of goods that provide the ends of human action, Marx's social theory sunders facts from values and proposes an instrumentalist view that collapses "ought" into "is."

27. MacIntyre, *After Virtue*, 6–21.
28. Latour, *Nous n'avons jamais.*

Smith's moral theory is neither proto-utilitarian nor non-teleological, but his political economy is no less problematic than Keynes's or Marx's. His account of virtues and pre-rational, moral sentiments eschews the idea of private vice and arbitrary divine power in favor of notions of enlightened self-interest and human agency (as I argue in chapter 6). But for Smith, market production and exchange is not constrained by the strong bonds of moral virtue and interpersonal ties. The only values that regulate the market are liberty (freedom from coercion) and equality before the law (absence of hereditary privileges, etc.). Since market relations are characterized by weak ties and serve self-interest rather than the common good, Smith divorces the quest for happiness that involves a hierarchy of goods from the exercise of civic virtue like justice.

By the same token, he also separates private, moral virtues such as love and benevolence from public, civic virtues like prudence or justice. As such, he departs from the emphasis in the Neapolitan and the Scottish Enlightenment (Paolo Mattia Doria, Antonio Genovesi, and David Hume) on the mutual sympathy that binds together what we now call civil society and the market—a civil economy wherein market exchange is embedded in relations of mutuality and reciprocity. It is precisely this tradition of civil economy that Pope Benedict XVI retrieves and extends in his encyclical *Caritas in Veritate* (as Stefano Zamagni shows in chapter 5).

Re-Imagining Political Economy

Building on Catholic social teaching since the groundbreaking encyclical *Rerum Novarum* (1891), Benedict's call for a civil economy is the most radical intervention in contemporary debates on the future of the economy, politics, and society. Against apologies of free-market fundamentalism or statist solutions to get us out of the recession, the Pope seeks to chart a Catholic "third way" that combines strict limits on state and market power with a civil economy centered on mutualist businesses, cooperatives, credit unions, and other alternative models at the grassroots level, as chapter 4 by Mark and Louise Zwick vividly illustrates. By arguing for an economic and a political system that is re-embedded in the reciprocal relations and civic virtues of civil society, Benedict's vision of political economy transcends the old secular dichotomies of state and market, left and right, and the secretly collusive voluntarism of the individual and the collective. As such, *Caritas in Veritate* develops the Catholic Christian "third way" in the direction of a virtue economy that re-embeds not just the market but also the state within the bonds of society, as John Milbank argues in his wide-ranging chapter.

Like previous interventions on economics by Joseph Ratzinger,[29] *Caritas in Veritate* rejects the secular logic of separating the market from morality. This would imply that only market freedom and the unfettered interplay of supply and demand can secure economic efficiency, social progress, and individual emancipation. But the sundering of ethics from economics opens the way for a crude deterministic utilitarianism that equates liberty with the negative freedom of negatively choosing individuals. Linked to this is a second secular illusion—that the natural laws of the market are good and work for the good of all, irrespective of the intentions of individuals in pursuit of their own self-interest.

In the light of these illusions and internal contradictions, the Pope deconstructs the foundational assumptions of modern economics. First of all, he rejects the idea of a "value-free" and pure science of economics with the argument that market production and exchange requires the social bonds of reciprocal trust in order to function efficiently—otherwise the costs of social control can outweigh the benefits of unconstrained market anarchy (even if the current system fails to price in these and other externalities). Here chapter 10 by John Médaille is key: he shows how economic efficiency depends on the equity of distributive justice, which in turn is largely determined by the distribution of assets (not just incomes). Médaille's argument resonates with Pope Benedict's conception of theology as the queen of all sciences that orders lower sciences to higher ends but also learns from them and speaks to each science in terms that are intelligible to it.

Second, Benedict opposes the secular logic of scarcity of resources with an alternative logic of producibility and creativity,[30] whereby natural riches are multiplied by patience, human labor, and ingenuity. In such a supernaturally infused economy, scientific discoveries and technological innovation are at the service of enduring human needs and aspirations—rather than fabricating false desires that distort our natural outlook on the supernatural Good in God.

29. See Ratzinger, "Church and Economy."

30. These ideas have also been developed by economists, e.g., Baranzini and Scazzieri, *Foundations of Economics*.

Third, the Pope dismisses instrumental rationality, perfect and asymmetric information as well as rational expectations as questionable conceptions of human knowledge that deny any mediation between *a priori* reason and *a posteriori* experience. On the contrary, Benedict views reason in terms of trust (*pistis* or faith) in the reasonableness of reality and in our ability to apprehend it both with our senses and with our mind. As such, reason is much broader than instrumental rationality supposes. On this account, our faculty of reasoning is also linked to our pre-rational, moral sentiments in ways that Adam Smith failed to recognize—namely that our capacity for sympathy (rather than merely empathy) binds us to other individuals, society, and even the natural universe as a whole. Thus, reason is far more embodied and related to our senses than empiricists (whether in economics or other disciplines) acknowledge. All this calls into questions the theoretical foundations and conceptual commitments of the "dismal science of economics." By contrast, Stefano Zamagni explains in his chapter how *Caritas in Veritate* contains the seeds of an alternative conception of political economy wherein fraternity as the reciprocal giving and receiving of social benefits replaces pure profit making. Zamagni also demonstrates the far-reaching implications of the notion of fraternity not just for the science of economics but also for national and international policymaking.

In line with his entire theological *œuvre*, the Pope's alternative to modern political economy blends the metaphysical theology and theological anthropology of the Church Fathers and Doctors with the Romantic Orthodoxy of nineteenth- and twentieth-century theology, notably *nouvelle théologie*.[31] Central to his vision is the symphonic synthesis of faith and reason (as outlined in the 2006 Regensburg address) and the Neo-Platonist account of natural law that is always already supernaturally infused by divine grace. Taken together, these two elements of Ratzinger's theology represent a powerful repudiation of the dualistic separation of "pure nature" from the supernatural which we owe to both Calvinism and Baroque scholasticism and which underpins the modern capitalist economy: specifically, the twin assumption, first of all, that markets are "value-free" and do not require the exercise of virtue and, second, that contracts are sundered from gift (and works from faith, as the followers of Calvin wrongly claimed). Tracey Rowland's chapter demolishes attempts by neo-liberal and neo-conservative U.S.

31. Rowland, *Ratzinger's Faith*; Rowland, *Benedict XVI*.

Catholics to dismiss the Pope's critique of unbridled free markets and also social-democratic or Marxist Liberation voices to ignore Benedict's repudiation of centralized statist solutions to the recession.

The Pope's compelling critique of religious *apologias* for capitalism, coupled with an unequivocal indictment of the moral relativism that characterizes the late modern secular age, strongly resonates with the other Christian traditions, in particular Eastern Orthodoxy[32] but also Anglicanism, as chapter 8 by John Hughes clearly shows. Anglican theologians have indeed been at the forefront of recovering St. Augustine's notion of charity as reciprocal gift-exchange, most recently the work of Archbishop Rowan Williams. Likewise, contemporary Anglican reflections on Christian universalism in a world characterized by value-pluralism holds many important insights on how to promote the Christian social and moral teaching that is shared by the episcopally based churches. This pan-Christian consensus is certainly true of the current patriarchs of Rome, Moscow, and Canterbury who rightly associate the dominant forms of social and economic liberalism with aggressive secularism and militant atheism. All three are also critical of the hegemonic power of state and market and in its stead seek to affirm the autonomy of civil society upheld by the Church and all the intermediary institutions it supports.

By proposing an alternative modernity that combines a liturgically ordered high culture with gift economy, *Caritas in Veritate* has the potential to advance both the reunification of the episcopally based churches and promote new economic models that transcend the old divide between the purely religious and the exclusively secular. The chosen ground for Benedict's intervention is the twin thematic of humanism and anthropology. Against the ancient and modern focus on the individual (whether fixed substance or atoms in flux), he contends that human beings stand in mutually irreducible relations with each other and their transcendent source in God, as David L. Schindler argues in chapter 7 on the anthropological unity of *Caritas in Veritate*. Remarkably, the Pope's most recent encyclical tackles head-on the common objection

32. One indication of the growing convergence between Roman Catholicism and Eastern Orthodoxy on matters of social and moral teaching is the glowing endorsement of Cardinal Bertone's book on the common good by the then Metropolitan Kirill. Since then Kirill has been elected the Patriarch of Moscow and All Russia—the head of the Russian Orthodox Church. See his preface on the Christian notion of the common good as a corrective and alternative to economic globalization and the secular social consensus, in Bertone, *Ethics of the Common Good*.

that Catholic social teaching is nostalgic and utopian, looking to a past golden age and ignoring the reality of human sinfulness. However, as Schindler demonstrates, Benedict's theology is more orthodox than that of conservative traditionalists and more radical than that of modern progressives because he rejects their shared dualism in favor of an over-arching unity—the universal human vocation to love that translates into practices of reciprocal giving. It is this logic of gratuitous gift-exchange that is more fundamental to human nature and social life than either state law or market relations.

Compared with a centrally imposed social contract (Hobbes and Locke) or vague, pre-rational moral sentiments (Smith), the Pope argues for a more organic polity governed by bonds of reciprocal trust, mutual assistance, and gift-exchange. Concretely, this is reflected in mutually intertwined networks of intermediary institutions and associations such as guilds, universities, and local "economies of communion," with over-lapping jurisdictions and multiple membership. As such, political and economic activity is re-embedded within the institutions and practices of civil society. In this manner, the social contract of the central state and proprietary relations in the marketplace are transformed and directed towards the common good in which all can share. Anthropologically and economically, the relational nature of human and social life cuts across the horizontal, binary poles of secularism upon which global capitalism is founded. Thus, *Caritas in Veritate* is a quest for a virtue politics and economics that cannot be charted on our current conceptual map.

The Unfulfilled Promise of 1989: Associative Economy and Civil Democracy

Why does Pope Benedict's call for a civil economy matter? Well, twenty years after the collapse of state communism, the ongoing crisis of "free-market" capitalism provides a unique opportunity to chart an alterna-tive path. Now that the dominant secular orthodoxy of neo-liberalism has been shown to be intellectually dead and morally bankrupt, both politics and business must look to genuinely fresh ideas and transfor-mative policies.

While in some Western countries the center-right has switched from a neo-liberal to a more communitarian discourse, it is unclear whether ruling parties have either the political will to curb the power of global finance or the determination to improve the lot of workers, families, local communities, and underdeveloped regions. Meanwhile, the center-left (both in Europe and the U.S.) looks to Keynesianism and Green movements for new economic and political inspiration. Notwithstanding the important insights that the Keynesian and Green traditions offer, both remain in the end wedded to a social-liberal, utilitarian creed that privileges personal choice and individual emancipation at the expense of communal interest and the wider public good.

This ideology of social liberalism is entirely compatible with the ideology of economic liberalism that has failed so spectacularly. Indeed, the dominant language of "choice" legitimates the extension of free-market mechanisms (aided and abetted by the regulatory state) into virtually all areas of socio-economic and cultural life—including education, health, the family, and sex. Today's scale and intensity of commodified labor, social relations, and our shared natural habitat is beyond Polanyi's worst fears. Thus, much of the contemporary left and right remains caught in a fundamental contradiction between calling for more economic egalitarianism, on the one hand, and advocating ever-greater social liberalization, on the other hand.

Moreover, older civic virtues of justice, mutuality, and reciprocity have been sidelined and supplanted by the new economic values of fairness and aspiration. Worse, these "progressive" values represent a new, cozy consensus that endorses the logic of capitalist democracy that tends towards an ever-greater centralization of power, concentration of wealth, and financial abstraction from the real economy and the common natural universe on which we all depend, as I have already indicated.

These failures underscore the (unrealized) potential of Christian social teaching. Crucially, the principles and practices of Christian social teaching should not just be heeded by the churches and Christians at their workplace or in their communities. Much rather, these principles and practices have appeal for policy and decision makers as well as grassroots movements and community organizing (as illustrated in the chapters by Jon Cruddas and Jonathan Rutherford as well as Mark and Louise Zwick).

Indeed, at a time of fiscal austerity, ageing populations, ballooning budget deficits, and long-term unsustainable public finances (social security and pension systems), both politicians and business leaders must look beyond income redistribution to asset distribution, asset-based welfare, and decentralized models that foster human relationships of communal care and mutual help—rather than state paternalism or private contract delivery. For example, there are successful examples that combine universal entitlement with localized and personalized provision, e.g., by fostering and extending grassroots initiatives like "Get Together" or "Southwark Circle" in London that blend individual, group, and state action. Both initiatives reject old schemes such as "be-friending" or uniform benefits in favor of citizens' activity and community organizing supported by local council—instead of central target and standards. The overriding "logic" underpinning such and similar initiatives is that of mutualism, reciprocity, and civic participation in accordance with the twin Catholic Christian principles of solidarity and subsidiarity (action at the most appropriate level to protect and promote human dignity and flourishing).

Likewise, Christian social teaching can help devise a series of economic reforms. Pope Benedict's vision for an alternative economy, which is re-embedded in politics and social relations, offers a refreshing alternative to the residual market liberalism of both left and right. In practice, an embedded model means that elected governments restrict the free flow of capital and create the civic space in which workers, businesses, and communities can regulate economic activity. Instead of free-market self-interest or central state paternalism, it is the individual and corporate members of civil society who collectively determine the norms and institutions governing production and exchange.

Concrete policies discussed in this collection include (in no particular order), first of all, introducing anti-usury legislation and putting in place measures aimed at breaking up banking and other financial conglomerates that are "too big to fail." As Mark and Louise Zwick document in their chapter, transforming the food industry is absolutely crucial to a civil economy. Second, neither prices nor wages should be determined by global capital or the iron law of international demand and supply. Instead, a combination of free guilds and political corporatism can provide a more autonomous, stable framework within which workers are also stakeholders and owners look to their employees rather than the top management and shareholders.

Third, policies that go beyond old-style income redistribution include, but should not be limited to, paying public-sector workers a "living wage" and opening up more areas of the entire economy to social enterprise that reinvest private profits in public-interest activities such as local regeneration, housing associations, and educational projects. Campaigns to implement such and similar measures can be led either by grassroots organizations like London Citizens (bringing together local communities and different faith groups under the umbrella of Catholic social teaching)[33] and the Chicago-based model of community organizing championed by Saul Alinsky or by governments in concert with other stakeholders. Linked to this is a greater emphasis on mutuality, reciprocity, and gift-exchange in the running of welfare programs.

Fourth, greater civic participation in the decision making of business and local politics, coupled with a wider distribution of assets, must be encouraged and promoted by national and global institutions. Fifth, the world economy requires new forms of capital control and limits on certain speculative practices; otherwise banks and other institutions will continue to build up bubbles of fake financial wealth that undermine and destroy real value in the economy. The overriding aim must be to preserve the sanctity of natural and human life and to promote human associations that nurture the social bonds of trust and reciprocity on which both democracy and markets depend.

Finally, Pope Benedict debunks the dominant anthropological myth since Adam Smith's *Wealth of Nations* that we are economic, "trading" animals with diffuse moral sentiments who follow their "propensity to truck, barter and exchange one thing for another," as I have already hinted at. Instead, the pontiff contends that we are fundamentally gift-exchanging animals who primarily seek to protect and enhance the well-being of ourselves and our neighbors in mutually augmenting ways instead of merely maximizing individual material gain. Throughout *Caritas in Veritate*, he contrasts the modern, secular idea of a universal commercial society dominated by abstract formal contracts and proprietary relations with a more Romantic vision that is neither nostalgic nor utopian but blends political idealism with economic realism. Fundamentally, he rejects both market liberalism and state socialism, arguing that they destroy the autonomy of civic culture and the freedom of civil society. By calling for a program of political and economic decentralization, Benedict's civil economy is far more radical than right-wing privatization and left-wing nationalization.

33. Ivereigh, *Faithful Citizens*.

Nor is Christian social teaching a nostalgic vision that is stuck in the past. In addition to the civil economy tradition of the Neapolitan Enlightenment or the English distributism of Hilaire Belloc and G. K. Chesterton, Christians should look to other figures, as Eugene McCarraher rightly suggests in chapter 3. His point that the pontiff does not go far enough in condemning capitalism is contestable, but his critique of the collusion between Christians and the capitalist system is as apposite as his reading of the long tradition of Catholic socialism—from the pre-science of Carlyle via the radicalism of Ruskin to the eclecticism of E. F. Schumacher and the socialist Dominican theology of Herbert McCabe.

Moreover, all those currently interested in alternatives to global capitalism could also look to the more recent past, notably 1989. The events of 1989 saw the triumph of civil society over totalitarian states. And behind civil society stood the churches and religious organizations that defended and promoted workers' associations, professional guilds, intermediary associations, educational establishments, and communal welfare. As such, 1989 marked an unprecedented opportunity to overcome the bipolar order of the communist East and the capitalist West, building a genuine "third way" beyond centralized, bureaucratic statism and unbridled, free-market capitalism.

We now know that the end of the Cold War was followed by a new unipolar world order based on essentially secular values of individual freedom, value-pluralism, and liberal democratic capitalism. Arguably, the parallel rise of religious fundamentalism is largely a reaction against the triumphalist arrogance of the secular West and the new ideology of militant atheism. However, the post-1989 secular consensus is already unraveling, as I have already suggested. The ongoing economic crisis once again highlights that the primacy of individual freedom over communal justice is undesirable and unsustainable. Similarly, value-pluralism alone can neither secure the integration of religious minorities nor solve ethical questions like assisted suicide because it negates universal principles such as cultural cohesion around religion or the sanctity of life. Finally, the spread of capitalism has produced regimes that are neither liberal nor democratic. In Central Europe and beyond, communism mutated into ethno-nationalism, supported by fundamentalist Christians and Muslims in the Balkans and elsewhere. In countries as different as Russia and China, global market democracy evolved into authoritarian state capitalism.

Even in the West, we have entered a post-democratic phase where democracy remains formally in place even after actual democratic practices like voting and party membership dramatically decline and power reverts from the masses to small elites and new classes. After thirty years of neo-liberal capitalism, nominal differences remain in place but real distinctions between the secular categories of state and market, "left" and "right" as well as democracy and authoritarianism have begun to dissolve. Indeed, we have seen the fusion of state and market at the expense of civil society autonomy, as more and more civic institutions are subject to the administrative and symbolic order of the post-democratic, authoritarian market-state.[34] That's why religious support for civil society is so crucial.

By emphasizing human relationships within the institutions and practices of civil society, *Caritas in Veritate* proposes a radically communitarian and associative virtue politics and virtue economy that outflanks both the left-wing adulation of the central state and the right-wing fetishization of free, unregulated markets. Since neither offers a credible exit from the current crisis, what is required is a genuine "third way." By offering an account of political economy that cuts across the divide between purely religious and exclusively secular perspectives, Benedict is proposing a vision that has universal resonance.

34. Pabst, "Crisis of Capitalist Democracy," 44–67.

PART I

Christianity and Capitalism

I

The Real Third Way

For a New Metanarrative of Capital and
the Associationist Alternative

John Milbank

THE PRIMACY OF MEDIATION

A COMMON VIEW ABOUT Christianity and politics is that Christians
divide up over politics in much the same way as other people.
But this is only superficially true and only true of Christians who have
thought about politics superficially and in disconnection from their faith.
For if one examines the writings of Christian thinkers who have thought
long, hard, and theologically about politics, then the consistency of their
emphases ever since the dawn of the Industrial Age is extremely striking.

This is most of all true of Catholic thinkers, but the conclusions of
Anglican and Orthodox thinkers have been remarkably similar. With
some qualification one can extend this consensus to Calvinist thinkers

also. Moreover, there are strong resonances with Christian conclusions in the ideas of some Jewish, Islamic, Hindu, and Buddhist social theorists. If one can speak of a Christian political consensus, it is even possible to speak of a certain religious political consensus.

What is this consensus? It has to do with thirdness, or with mediation. This takes two forms: first of all, politically speaking, the modern doctrine of absolute sovereignty is rejected as linked both to secularity and to a perverse voluntarist theology.[1] Instead, a "pluralist" distribution of sovereignty is recommended: a distribution which more respects both human fallibility and the mere penultimacy of political purposes. This gives rise to the theme of the importance of civil society (meaning here the agglomerate of associations which are neither for economic contractual nor for state administrative purposes) and of "intermediate associations" which the current patriarchs of Rome, Moscow, and Canterbury would all endorse, along with so many of their predecessors stretching back over two hundred years.

Such a favoring of "group rights" renders Christians and other religious people suspicious at once of an idolatry of the State and of the absolute autonomy of the sovereign individual.[2] Hence a "third way" is advocated between statisms of the far right or the far left, on the one hand, and ultra-liberalism, on the other. Yet this is no mere matter of compromise. To the contrary, religious thinkers tend to diagnose a hidden mutual complicity and reinforcement between the voluntarism of the absolute state and the voluntarism of the self-governing, negatively choosing individual. This gives rise to the thematic of the "radical center," a three-dimensional exiting from the horizontal poles of left and right which belong to the secular consensus ever since the French Revolution, and a re-polarization along a vertical axis between the paradoxical "rule of the middle," on the one hand, which is the rule of human relationships, and the left/right rule of the secretly collusive collective and individual wills, on the other.

The Religious Nature of Association

The "rule of human relationships" implies the primacy of the associative body in the most general sense over both state and market. Here one can

1. See Elshtain, *God, State and Self*.
2. Milbank, "On Complex Space," in *Word Made Strange*, 268–92.

follow Augustine in defining the basic "political" body in terms of any sort of human association defined by "the object of its love." This permits us to see (against the entire normal run of modern political theory) that any human association (*including* in reality the state and market) is always at once hierarchical and democratic, involving what antiquity referred to as a "mixed constitution" of the one, the few, and the many. For initially an association is in some historical fashion "set up" by the single force of one person or more likely many in combination. This single force must then hierarchically instill the principles of the logic of the operation of the association through a "teaching process" that is the work of those "few" (however many they may be in reality) who understand this logic. But right from the outset, the association can only exist at all if it enjoys the "democratic" consent, however tacit or explicit, of the many who compose it.

But there is also one final and crucial component. An association must "justify" its existence in order that it have some principles of "just ordering" which it can continuously effect.[3] And most naturally and fundamentally, this justification must be in terms of how the association is supposed to reflect some "given" cosmic order that precedes its composition. It is only modern liberal modernity that tries to evade this mode of justification and discover one that is purely immanent either to mere material nature or to the association itself.

It follows that any human association naturally has a hierarchic component insofar as it continuously remembers and repeats its origins. It has a democratic component insofar as it continuously assents to these origins, thereby perhaps also continuously modifying its own constitution. Together, these two components compose the association as "traditioned," as a passageway of "handing over" through time. And any association also has a third, religious component insofar as it must "justify itself" in order to achieve either initial establishment or continuing consent.

From these conclusions a further, seemingly astonishing one must follow. Modernity assumes that religions are mystificatory and that secular liberalism is candid about itself. However, just because any natural human association, as religious, can and must own up to its "mixed" character, it is able to be honest about its own historical self-constitution. It can and will tell the story of its origins, even if this be taken as the story

3. See Boltanski and Thévenot, *On Justification*.

of its initial subscription to its own myth. But by contrast secular liberalism, because it pretends to be non-hierarchical, cannot tell the truth that the state was "once" set up in an inevitably hierarchical way. It commits a *non-genetic fallacy*, which tries to wipe out origins. It is for just this reason that liberalism was from the outset linked to the necessary political *fiction* of original contract between equal parties. To sustain the illusion that a polity can be the sole and unique non-hierarchical result of equal individuals assembled in a perpetual present, liberalism requires some sort of "noble lie" regarding a primordial moment impossibly without a past, without influence, and so without the inevitable work of the one and the few.

Secular liberalism and not religion is therefore necessarily mystificatory and self-concealing, for it cannot tell the story of its own origins. The price of refusing religious justification because one pretends to non-hierarchy and formally immanent self-constitution is always subscription to a secular myth. And whereas religious mythology, since it regards the extra-temporal and must insist upon the historical event of the cultural imagination of the extra-temporal (as recorded in Scriptures, for example) need not obfuscate human processes in time, secular political mythology *necessarily* must do so, precisely because the object of its mythologization, being secular, must be human history itself.

The same pattern of secular obfuscation applies to the form of association which is contractualist market exchange, on the liberal model. This also has to resort to fictions: of the "hidden hand," of the perfect equilibrium of supply and demand, of perfect self-regulation in an eternal present. In this case, what is concealed from view is that this market serves the hierarchical precedence of a social and economic inequality that inaugurates it and that is established by various modes of "primary accumulation." Equally, this economy conceals from view its continuous repetition of this hierarchy in terms of the unequal bargaining positions of capital as compared to either the worker or the consumer that is rendered invisible by the fiction of a supposedly free and equal contract. The "justifications" offered here, whether in terms of a supposedly pre-associative natural humanity (another fiction) or of the formal logic of association itself, that is supposed to permit the emergence of order despite the hopeless relativity of different substantive opinion and so the apparent absence of "common love" (yet another fiction, because something substantive will always secretly rule, even if this be mere arbitrary power), necessarily preclude any telling the truth about actual histori-cal origins. Hence it is the "enlightened" refusal of both religion and hierarchy that is inevitably obfuscatory and, for a certain vocabulary, "ideological." And one can say that while Marx exposed the fictions of liberalism for what they were, he merely proposed instead the setting up of a more perfectly "emancipated" and so fictional and self-obscuring society in the future. In this respect "actual communism" fulfilled and did not betray Marxist logic.

One can conclude therefore that religions as they exist in the world today should regard themselves both as more basic and more honest modes of association than either the sovereign state or the liberal market. This is rigorously to invert the existing dominant view that religions are both self-deluded and socially and rationally aberrant. On the contrary, religions need now to assert themselves as the *primary* "political" forces (in the broadest sense, going beyond the narrow concern of properly "secular" politics with coercive authority). As such they are able con-tinuously to expose the fictions whereby merely secular state and market claim to be able to justify themselves in terms of a (usually aporetic) mix of appeal to nature and to collective artifice.

And because they understand that their apparent anomaly of be-ing neither statist nor economic modes of association is in reality not anomalous but archetypal, they also understand that all other "mediat-ing" associations between state center and market periphery are not re-ally secondary but actually fundamental. It follows (and this could soon prove to be the crucial political factor of the new century) that there is a natural alliance between the quest of religious bodies to seek their own power and their support for a politics of the intermediary, or of the as-sociation (the "big society" in a real and not party political sense).

And to protest here that religions should not be seeking power is to miss the point. For in the case of the Church supremely, what is in prin-ciple sought is a space of peace and of the power of weakness, the kenotic power of non-power. Yet paradoxically to attempt to increase the scope of this space, to achieve more human "salvation," is itself a war, a power struggle—as the New Testament so explicitly teaches, again and again. More power must be given to the space of powerlessness if there is to be peace and justice. So the fictional powers must be resisted and over-come, and state and market (coercion and contractual consent) reduced to their more modest and *properly secular* roles of serving the good of society which is the good of association. For there is no secular without the sacred contrast: a purely self-referring secular has to sacralize itself according to the merely democratic fictions of immanent justification.

The implications of such "associationism," which as we have seen is necessarily "religious," for political economy is the subject of this chapter.

BIO-POLITICAL ECONOMY

As Michel Foucault argued, liberalism comes fully into being in the eighteenth century with the invention of the science of political economy which proposes the novel idea that governments can rule more by ruling less.[4] Instead of trying to "police" every aspect of their subjects' lives, they can leave much to the operation of the market whose workings are seen as "natural." In this way, through the supposedly natural balancing of supply and demand, wealth and population are increased, while peace and order are spontaneously maintained. The interests of a controlled and strong population, ready to fight wars, are achieved by stealth. It is for this reason that Foucault argued that we must understand liberalism to be the "biopolitical." Apparently, and by its own lights, it releases the economic sphere as natural, as biological. In reality, however, it politically produces this sphere and tries through the educative and cultural processes of "civil society" (in a new and specific sense) to create subjects who are negatively choosing and self-governing, relatively disembedded from family, locality, tradition, and artisanal formation (and so from civil society in an older more generic sense).

In fact, such subjects could well be seen as *less* "natural," but this is disguised from view by Adam Smith's redefinition of humanity as *homo economicus*, disposed mainly to truck and to barter. Karl Polanyi long ago pointed out how absurd this anthropology is and how exploded by, precisely, anthropologists.[5] During most of human history human beings have been so radically and immediately dependent upon each other that the first thing they have looked for is social recognition as the pre-condition of both status and security. For this reason they have usually been content with economic arrangements of reciprocal balance (whether these be egalitarian or hierarchical). For any too-marked seeking of personal advantage has always risked ostracization. The realism

4. Foucault, *Birth of Biopolitics.*

5. Polanyi, *Great Transformation*; Glasman, *Unnecessary Suffering.*

of the past was different from the realism of the present which political economy has decisively shaped.

Once one has this bio-politics, there arises, nonetheless, a certain dualistic tension between the bio and the political. The former factor is vastly accentuated in the course of the nineteenth century. As Polanyi also argued, when the economic sphere is sequestrated, it is bound to become *fundamental,* because it concerns our most vital human needs and functions. The irony is that in all earlier human societies, including the most supposedly "primitive," the biologically basic was *not* socially basic, because reciprocity and redistribution tended to guarantee the biological survival of the individual which was thereby subordinated to the biological survival of the social group. Hence the lower was mediated by the supplement of something higher, the economic was not so much "embedded" (to use Polanyi's phrase) as planted upwards in the heavenly soil of social gift-exchange, itself rooted in celestial sanctions of cosmic reciprocity and divine grace. Only *modern* political economy treats the biological as basic for human beings. And this was greatly accentuated in the nineteenth century through the view—entirely alien, it must be said, to Adam Smith—that only the threat of poverty and the spur of hunger will force people to work in a world of lazy sinfulness and constitutive material scarcity. In point of fact, just as the idea of the supposedly "free market" is in reality politically produced, so, also, scarcity is nearly always something artificially engineered by both monopolization and the neoclassical assumption that all desires are equally valid and so without limit. Indeed one should note here that ecological disaster results from both a fantasizing and an artificial production of scarcity and not at all from people imagining that the world's resources are infinite—as pseudo-pious, liberal politico-economic "ecologism" would have it. For the resources of nature *really are* infinite, if we have patience, as religious people should know. This applies also to the question of population—demanding its limit is always an anti-human, anti-vitalist move, on the side of political economic technocracy and bio-political control. In opposing this mode of demographic fascism the papacy has always been radical and not conservative.

If, however, the nineteenth century accentuated the supposedly "natural" character of the *economy,* it also increased the supposedly "artificial" and "scientific" character of the *political.* The "police" aspect of the pre-politico-economic mercantilist state did not after all go away, even if it was now exercised with more subtlety. From Adam Ferguson onwards, political economy concluded that the state must continue to create an environment within which the market can flourish by attention to education, the arts, sanitation, crime, poverty, and demography.[6] If the market was concerned with a supposed release of free choice, undergirded by property rights, then the civil or political aspect of civil society had to do with material interests at the point where this is also an inescapable aspect of the economic sphere. As Foucault points out, an economic contract is free, but it is assumed that people enter into it in order to secure their material interests or welfare. The freedom of the politically economic subject is indeed a spiritual freedom rooted in rights, but this is paradigmatically linked to the self-government of mere animality which takes into account only utility and sympathy for the material needs of others. Hence, as Foucault again puts it, "interest" in the liberal model always overflows rights.

Nevertheless, one must add in qualification here that Hume, Smith and Ferguson's "utile," a mere different pronunciation of the Latin *utile*, was not as yet quite the reduced "utility" of Bentham and still had Ciceronian and Horatian overtones of the "convenient" and "fitting" that retained its ancient pairing with aesthetic *dulce*. Indeed for Ferguson especially (but in a Humean lineage), the cultivation of social civility helps to *compensate* for that destruction of familial, clan, local, and artisanal solidarity which he saw the market economy as undermining in ways which had dangerous implications for the cultivation of virtue.[7] In this way Scottish (and Italian) eighteenth-century "civil society" still retained something of the sense of a "third space" which had earlier been supremely cultivated and sustained by the presence of the church.

Yet quickly, after Bentham, the notion of the cultivation of civility degenerated into a government-sponsored but socially diffuse promotion of a sheerly sensory "greatest happiness of the greatest numbers" by educative and disciplinary programs more designed to induce a regularity of behavior than any specific spiritual insights.[8]

So where it might appear that liberalism is primarily about individual freedom, on account of its bio-political character it turns out in the long run that it is more fundamentally to do with material interest or

6. Ferguson, *Essay on the History of Civil Society.*

7. See ibid.

8. See Bauman, *Legislators and Interpreters*, 68–80.

with "welfare." Indeed the duality between the political and the biological means that, in the end, it is the freedom of the state which is primary for liberalism, once it has been deconstructed. For the liberty of the subject is only allowed as a device of governmentality in order to increase the power of governance. This liberty of the subject is then really, as far as the state is concerned, ironically an aspect of the *animality* of the subject. The market promotes first of all his *welfare,* and therefore secondarily the welfare of the entire political body. And so it is logical that later, with the advent of the economic doctrine of marginalism, the always latent assumption of political economy that the economic operator is a *utilitarian calculator* is explicitly recognized, beyond even Bentham's perception. Later still, with the neoclassical ideas of Kenneth Arrow and then the Chicago school in the twentieth century, this calculation is extended to the working of bureaucracies and finally even to things like sex and procreation—thereby economizing the entire social field.[9]

At this point the overturning of all inherited human wisdom is complete. No longer is the economy embedded in society regarded as reciprocal gift-exchange; instead, all of human life is supposedly natural or economic. But the economic concerns entirely material interest or welfare. It is this primacy of welfare which allows us better to understand and to deconstruct the duality of market and state. In a first historical phase, a still mercantilist concern with the welfare of the entire body of the nation-state caused the deliberate construction through primary accumulation—via enclosures, abolition of guilds and privileged corporations at home, and colonization abroad—of the sphere of the "natural" market governed only by the price mechanism in the balance of supply and demand.[10] And then after the interval of classical political economy which ostensibly stressed freedom, in a second historical phase during the nineteenth-century, the still-lurking shadow of human freedom gives way more and more to the evolutionist fantasy of an animal humanity. But this means that it is "economism" itself (the doctrine of material accumulation as the fundamental socio-political reality, rather than Polanyi's seeking of social recognition) which returns us *full circle* to the primacy of welfare and so to the primacy of the state as the creator of the capitalist market in the first place.

9. See Screpanti and Zamagni, *Outline of the History of Economic Thought*, 380–455.

10. Perelman, *Invention of Capitalism*.

For if market choice is gradually acknowledged as utilitarian calculation, it remains the case that the market cannot fulfill the whole of utility or of welfare even from a dogmatically liberal point of view. Thus we have already seen, with Adam Ferguson, that the Scots philosophers supplemented the free market with state attention to civil society. And as Polanyi notes, the arrival of an unlimited market in human labor, in land and in money in Britain in the 1830s coincided with an unprecedented extension of state power in terms of the collecting of statistics, of policing and of promotion of scientific education, civic sanitation, and national transportation.

At a later stage, as Polanyi further pointed out, the emergence of state welfare structures in the second half of the nineteenth century was not primarily a reaction against *laissez-faire* but rather an aporetic extension of it. First, the tendency of capitalism towards monopoly required either anti-monopoly legislation or else the quasi-institution of corporations in order to direct them towards the public good (or else both at once). This shows that the state could not now entirely allow market processes to take their course, because what mattered to it was either the ultimate outcome of a free *agon* in terms of the generation of national wealth and strength, or else deliberate organization towards the same end (or else once more, both at once).

Secondly, an unrestricted market in labor implied that workers might logically persist in striking until the very interest of capital owners as appropriators was undermined. This capitalistic—because sheerly self-interested—aspect of trade unionism had then to be interrupted by a state socialism which balanced anti-strike or industrial relations legislation with compensatory welfare measures intended to resign workers to a proletarian status and to inhibit their mutual organization which naturally tended to revert towards the human norm of reciprocal benefit. In this way the subversive thrust of mutualism was suppressed.

And as Polanyi remarked, resistance to capitalism has always come either from classes who sustain this more antique social habit—either semi-feudal classes or interdependent proletarians (besides intellectuals who support mutuality). Almost *never* does it come from the middle classes. For their support for state welfare on generally utilitarian grounds is in reality an endorsement of the principles that underlie the free market which, as we have seen, are inseparable from the principles which undergird the modern secular state. As Anthony Giddens explicitly put it in his book *The Third Way*, the crucial aim of welfare is to produce the freely choosing reflexive and risking individual removed from the relational constraints of nature, family, and tradition.[11] It would seem that the welfare state is generated by capitalism and only subserves capitalism.

STATE, MARKET, AND THE ORIGINS OF CAPITALISM

Yet that is an exaggeration. Polanyi is here more subtle. Crucial here is the fact that one cannot, after all, simply say that the state invented the market. A capitalist market has always hovered in the background and was prophesied by Aristotle. Within traditional localities, human beings exchange gifts—even if this is eventually regularized in terms of money and commodities. With very remote strangers, with whom we share no common language, again the only language which they share in common is that of gift—one strange thing exchanged for another strange thing: transistor radio for rare coral.[12] But in the middle, with *known strangers across the sea,* as for example in the antique Mediterranean, humans tend to operate more in terms of contracts, loans, and mercantile self-seeking. *All* maritime trade in the "mid-sea" has always approximated to a kind of piracy, as Polanyi and Maurice Glasman have emphasized.[13] Hence city-states at the margins of nations have tended to "diagonalize out" of those nations in a freebooting fashion.

However, Polanyi also argued that the function of maritime states was strangely to keep separate reciprocal inland trade from reciprocal remote trade as well as from more zero-sum accumulative overseas trade. An example of this is London in the seventeenth century. As Robert Brenner has shown, the London East India Company remained pro-monarchic and Cavalier because it engaged in a traditional remote reciprocalist trade.[14] But the unofficial and guild-excluded merchant class were Roundhead parliamentary supporters because they engaged in a more piratical mode of enterprise and furthermore joined this up with Calvinist agricultural capitalists who invested in it. Thereby, as often in the past, material landed assets tended to be subverted in their stability

11. Giddens, *Third Way.*

12. Seneca, "On Benefits," III, xvii–xviii, 158–59.

13. Polanyi, *Primitive, Archaic and Modern Economies,* esp. "Aristotle discovers the economy," 78–115; Glasman, "Landed and Maritime Markets."

14. Brenner, *Merchants and Revolution,* 3–37.

through their connection with a more abstract and (as it were literally) fluid form of maritime wealth linked to more speculative fortunes.

For the Marxist theoretical legacy, colonization and globalization are later extensions of capitalism: a response to falling rates of profits leading to sagging demand; hence the need for further primary accumulation.[15] But Marx saw capitalism as inevitable, and so offered an insufficient explanation as to how primary accumulation permitting the absolute commodification of land, labor, and money got going in the first place. Polanyi, Glasman, and Brenner by contrast see (from diverse theoretical perspectives) how it has to do with an always present diabolically "middle" sphere of relatively anarchic international relations escaping the reach of any *ius gentium*. However, Brenner and others realize that the full incursion of the sea into the land engendering capitalism only occurred in England because of the unique capitalization of territory in terms of a free market in property and the establishment of the agricultural laborer as a dispossessed wage-laborer. Both of these things were consequent upon the disappearance of the English peasantry at the end of the Middle Ages and the later dissolution of the monasteries, both of which events vastly increased the amount of land held by the gentry in purely absolute, economic terms, with no social or political duties attached. The gravitation of a segment of the English gentry towards Calvinism, which sharply separated human contract from the divine gift of grace, is in this respect unsurprising.[16]

However, another dimension of the emergence of capitalism concerns the breakup of Christendom. Once there exist competing nation-states linked to different religious bodies, then material organization for war and self-defense becomes a priority. Mercantilism is the inevitable consequence. So the complete invasion of the land by the sea in England produces also for the first time a comprehensive internal market organized upon contractual and competitive rather than reciprocalist lines. This internal *agon* is seen, in line with an economic version of Machiavelli's martial logic for republics, as increasing internal power both through a trial of strength and through a resulting greater size of national wealth.

Yet at the same time Polanyi argued that the state was at once active and passive, encouraging and resisting in relation to these processes. It is at this point that one has to recognize, after his nuanced analyses, that

15. Arendt, *Imperialism*, 3–37.
16. See Hénaff, *Le prix de la verité*, 351–80.

state welfare is ambivalent. Yes it is utilitarian, but it is also conservative and humanitarian in purpose. Both in England and in France, with the decline of guild organization and local charity, the state tried to reproduce their functions at the national level with measures that survived up to the end of the eighteenth century. In England Elizabeth, the earlier Stuarts, and most notably the Laudians tried to resist enclosures and the humanist disciplining of the poor: the Commonwealth reversed these measures and Charles II and later kings continued this reversal—while the rebel Jacobite faction (as with Dr. Johnson's political thinking) intensified the radical dimension of earlier Stuart traditionalism.

In the end though, Polanyi argues, welfare merely disembeds individuals and reinforces capitalism. This happened most of all with the Tory socialism of the Speenhamland acts in the early nineteenth century. Here a living income was distributed to all regardless of labor. The result was both a tendency to laziness amongst workers and a lowering of wages which led eventually to further impoverishment by letting employers off the hook of their responsibilities for justice. So in relation to this crucial example Polanyi provides both liberal and radical arguments against welfare. Conservatively speaking it is true that it undermines a society based on the market—even though he wants to oppose this foundation. Hence he argues with remarkable balance that though the rise of the welfare state in the late nineteenth century was inevitable *on market grounds themselves*, that economic liberals are still right to argue that it tended to undermine the market by reducing the money available for consumption and investment and reducing the incentives for employers to provide work. The most subversive aspect of *The Great Transformation* for conventional social democracy is the way in which Polanyi admits a general "Speenhamland effect" with respect to welfare.

He is even, at his rigorous best, prepared to apply this insight also to some forms of non-State socialism: arguing that attempts to organize industry on socialist lines, following the legacy of the Quaker John Bellers in the late seventeenth century, with his Baconian "colleges of industry," also tended problematically to disturb market equilibrium of prices and wages because they did not question the operation of the capitalist market at the inter-business level. Moreover, all too often they were in effect making money out of poverty itself, and still regarding dispossession as an economic resource of available labor. All this is true of Owenism, which furthermore espoused an essentially utilitarian attitude towards human well-being. So despite Robert Owen's explicit exaltation of the primacy of the social, this in the end comes down to a necessarily collectivist support for individual material well-being. And in general, except where it has espoused a religiously grounded view of fraternity and solidarity, *most* socialisms, even most associationist socialisms, are at bottom liberalisms, because they give ontological status only to freedom and happiness—not to teleological human flourishing. And as liberalisms they remain inadequate genealogies and critiques of capitalism.

Hence we can see that if, in modernity, the economy has replaced society as the basis of human existence, nonetheless attempts to achieve a balance, to re-assert society by the state or even by socialist association of certain types, tend to disturb the operation of the market and finally to produce further impoverishment. Then we get extreme solutions offered instead: the total marketization of neo-liberalism or else total communist state control. The latter ignores the Hayekian problem of the impossibility of perfect knowledge at the center, while the former runs into two *aporias*. First, one cannot really let economy undermine society entirely without resulting anarchy. Secondly, a purely competitive market in the long run, as we have seen, destroys competition. Hence even though social democracy tends to subvert the market, the drift of market capitalism towards social democracy is endlessly recurrent and not an aberration. This is precisely where Polanyi outthinks Hayek.

Towards a Real Third Way

At this point, we can say that most people are agreed in wanting some sort of "third way." No one (save scoundrels) likes unlimited market greed and anarchy. No one (save psychopaths) likes the prospect of total state control, mismanagement, and surveillance. Thus secular solutions search either for a social democratic balance of state and market, or for an ordo-liberal location of a pure and so eternally limited market, or yet again for a New Labour-style oligarchic fusion of state and market processes.

Christian economic thought would appear simply to go along with this modern secular desire. It too has tended to search for a "third way"—not just, in the first place politically, between state and individual in terms of group rights, but also, in the second place, politico-economically, between the dominance of state and the dominance of market in terms of the function of civil society, mutual, and non-profit organizations, as well as the role of religious bodies themselves in the sphere of welfare. Yet does that simply mean that Christians agree as to principles but differ as to means? Hence some will be social democrats, others will be Christian democratic supporters of the ordo-liberal "social market," while others again will be unrepentant New-Labourites?

I do not think so. The Christian economic difference is not simply a matter of principles, though neither is it a matter of magical technical devices which will supposedly restore social reciprocity—like Major Douglas's social credit or Henry George's land tax beloved of old. It is rather a matter of different virtuous *practices*, different habits: something that hovers halfway between principle and structure but tends to generate all sorts of new reciprocalist structures in different circumstances. However, this different habit *really can* solve our politico-economic conundrums, whereas the secular solutions cannot.

How can one make this claim? Well, as we have seen, the secular solutions are unable to unlock the *aporia* which results when one tries to found the society on the economy. The economy cannot be allowed to destroy society and yet any re-assertion of society tends to undermine the economy. Hence the abandonment of reciprocity is inherently *unstable*. But as Pope Benedict XVI argued in his encyclical *Caritas in Veritate*, the point is *not* to modify an inherently immoral or amoral market through welfare measures, but rather to produce not merely a just but also a charitable market in the first place.[17]

This is then to re-invoke gift as both free gratuity and reciprocity. But it is also—in a way that might well have shocked Ratzinger's still somewhat neo-scholastic predecessors and will also shock the conservative Rahnerian neo-scholasticism of the liberation theologians—to invoke the supernatural virtue of charity within the supposedly secular sphere of the economy. Indeed it is to say that for Christians the material economy in the end belongs within the space of the theological *economia* of salvation. So instead of the economy being something produced by the state as pseudo-natural, one now has the idea that the entire "economy" of human give-and-take exceeds the political and belongs in the *ecclesial* sphere, because how we give and how we take affects our *supernatural* destiny. The material sphere does not lie beneath the willfulness of law and politics. Rather it transfiguratively exceeds them, just as our bodies which will be resurrected are also involved in deification.

17. Benedict, *Caritas in Veritate*.

Ratzinger, therefore, suggests that we must bring the economic back within the bounds of social reciprocity, which is ultimately the ecclesial sphere of charity. Is this merely reactionary and nostalgic?

No, because he proposes a relatively more egalitarian mode of reciprocity—even if, as he knows (in accordance with the ontology of the association outlined in section 2 above) the hierarchy of educative guidance by virtue can never be expunged if democracy is to release people's best rather than their worst instincts. No again, because the forces tending to promote the mercantile were already emergent within the Middle Ages and were promoted by some canonists. Indeed the modern voluntarist oscillation between the collectivist and the individualistic was anticipated by some Franciscan theologians who promoted both a comfortable and somewhat hypocritical "communism" for themselves as university teachers and the beginnings of a non-reciprocal contractualism, forgetting the common good for society as a whole,[18] as the following section suggests.

EXCURSUS ON SOME MEDIEVAL ANTECEDENTS OF CAPITALISM: FRANCISCANS VS. DOMINICANS

Despite my overall endorsement of their truly profound ideas about contract and sympathy, I therefore somewhat dissent from Luigino Bruni and Stefano Zamagni's tracing of a reciprocalist approach to the economy back to the Franciscans.[19] To my mind such a stress is far more characteristic of Aquinas and the Dominican tradition. This is because, in general, the Franciscans saw love in unilateral disinterested terms which tended to separate *agape* from *eros,* whereas Aquinas saw love as always a reciprocal sharing between human beings as well as being a "participation" in the divine love. Here "interested" *eros* and "disinterested" *agape* are always fused, because this contrast is transcended in terms of mutual linkage: this is why Aquinas stressed that we must always love the "closest" most of all, reading "neighbor love" in a way that stresses our finitude.

The Franciscan legacy, by emphasizing to the contrary disinterestedness, tended to render any mutual bonding merely a contractual guaranteeing of a mutual fulfillment of fundamentally separate interests.

18. Villey, *La formation de la pensée juridique moderne,* 202–19.

19. See Bruni and Zamagni, *Civil Economy,* 33–42; and Bruni, "Common Good and Economics."

In this manner ontological bonds are sundered in the economic sphere and the way is opened to an all-too-modern contrast between pure contract on the one hand and sheer "altruism" on the other. Even the *Monti di Pieta* arguably too much tried to solve urban poverty by extracting a surplus value from it (somewhat anticipating Robert Owen) insofar as these institutions were in effect "charitable" pawnbrokers. Hence Bruni and Zamagni underrate the degree to which the Franciscans really did pre-invent a (theologically dubious) capitalist notion of contract, as argued by Oreste Bazzichi (whom they nonetheless cite). And perhaps they overrate the continuity of the more reciprocalist currents in humanist economics with the Franciscan legacy.

It follows that on my reading their own ideas are really far more "Dominican" than they allow, since they are so emphatically reciprocalist. It is also perhaps the case that they fail to realize the degree to which the mutualism of *agape* is also "erotic." (Bruni tends to line up the latter with "separate" fulfillment of needs, but such a gloomy post-Cartesian view of *eros* is not that of either Augustine or Aquinas.) In addition, their "distributism" as regards property also connects more to Aquinas, since the Franciscans tended to exalt a sheer "communist" non-ownership for themselves, which dialectically cast an aspersion on ownership as pure "domination"—whereas for Aquinas *dominium* could be good if linked to good usage and orientated towards common usage.

This disagreement is nonetheless in a real sense trivial, because so purely historical in character. Perhaps, though, it makes a real difference when it comes to the question of *usury*, where I would tend to defend Aquinas's greater caution in the face of this practice compared to the position of Duns Scotus and other leading Franciscans. The anti-Aristotelian Franciscan endorsement, in the case of Scotus and Peter John Olivi, of *lucrum cessans*, or compensation for profit foregone in terms of money lent, amounts to treating money unnaturally, not as a medium of exchange, but as a kind of pseudo-thing that has "fertility" in its own right. Thus Olivi declared that "that which in the firm intention of its owner is ordained to some probable gain does not only possess the character of money or a thing straightforward, but beyond this a certain seminal reason of profitability which we usually call 'capital.'"[20] One theoretical building block of "capitalism" is indeed in place here.

20. Olivi, *De Usuris*, Dubium 6.

This shift was compounded by the assertion of another fourteenth-century Franciscan, Gerald Odonis, that the lender retains the abstract property ownership of the sum of money which he lends, rendering usurious interest after all a legitimate "rent."[21] This further contradicts Aristotle and Aquinas by abandoning the distinction between use of things that are not used up by usage, like land, and things that are so used up, like food and money. The crucial shift here is in terms of a disregard for qualitative difference of content between different kinds of things and the beginning of the definition of an economic *res* in merely voluntaristic and nominalistic terms of subjective regard and subjective control.[22] (On the defense of Aquinas's position on usury, see below.)

Aquinas's "distributism," by contrast, ties property entitlement to good use. Linked to this is his limitation of the practice of money-lending to real proper interests foregone and to the benefits of investment, and also his promotion of the just price beyond the mere canonical market current price in terms of both the measure of labor and the comparative measure of right desire. As such, "distributism" for Aquinas was already an act of theoretical *resistance* to a pure market society, to the already faintly observable germs of a capitalistic practice.[23]

Here a further explication is required. As regards the just price, Aquinas assumes, first of all—despite so many modern American denials of this reading—that things have a natural value in terms of their place in the scale of values of the usefulness of things for realizing true human ends and that economic value should have some relationship to this. One American theologian, Christopher A. Franks of Duke University, gets this exactly right: "Thomas certainly relies on a common estimate [in the market] that is variable and based on appraisals of human usefulness. But the usefulness Thomas envisions is not whatever usefulness buyers and sellers can agree to, but the true usefulness of things as such things are intended by God for the sake of human flourishing."[24] In other words his "market value" is also a "moral value."

---

21. Odonis, *Tract.* q. 13; f.91. v.

22. Bazzinchi, *Alle Radice del Capitalismo*; Rousselot, *Problem of Love*; O'Donovan, "Theological Economics," 48–64; Belloc, *Essay on the Restoration of Property*.

23. *Summa Theologiae* II.II qq. 77–78; *De Malo*, q. 13 a. 4. See de Tarde, *L'idée de juste prix*.

24. Franks, *He Became Poor*, 93.

Secondly and in addition, the just price takes desire into account in terms of the value of a thing to the seller and the general "going market rate." Statements by Aquinas to the effect that there is "no usury" involved when this rate is charged do not at all prove that this is all he means by the justice of price: for, as Franks indicates, the market is itself "embedded" in social norms that establish the relative values in relation to human usage—such that, for example, the really important in the sense of "fundamental" like food, shelter and raiment should be readily affordable, while the important in the sense of rare and exemplary, like an exceptional artifact, should properly be expensive.

Thirdly, it is wrong to sell a thing for more than one has paid for it—though this does not apply to added value in terms of making, transport or convenience of rendering goods widely available, as with respectable shopkeeping. Fourth, all third-party mercantile trading tends to be morally tainted but is redeemable if directed towards the general human good and charity. Profits must go to public benefit apart from reasonable rewards to the merchant himself.

The main points of Aquinas's teaching on usury are in accordance with these general considerations on price: first, money is a usufruct entirely "used up" in exchange and therefore one cannot charge rent on it. Second, *damnum emergens* is permitted, i.e., compensation if a loan is not paid up in time—for then the lender has suffered a material inconvenience which he would not otherwise have undergone. This contrasts with *lucrum cessans* (as discussed above) where he is compensated for a possible profit through investment that he might have made out of the money lent. The problem that Aquinas rightly sees with this is that it treats money as an abstract thing in itself and assumes that sheer profit-making (taken alone) is a valid activity outside the context of entering into a commercial association for the attainment of some specific economic and social good that in the end serves the common good. In this respect, *lucrum cessans* implicitly endorses mere private abstract gain (since the gain foregone is a totally abstract "any old gain") and so breaks the circle of reciprocity in a way that Bruni and Zamagni fail to recognize—for all that the entire tenor of their thought runs in the direction of linking all lending back to investment and all profit to mutuality and conjunction of economic with social benefit.

Third, Aquinas defends investment in business and distinguishes this from usury. The key here is that when you loan money you "transfer ownership." (The sharp contrast with the Franciscan Olivi is evident.) But when you invest, you enter into a *societas* with business partners, such that the money invested remains yours, because it is connected to a shared purpose and thereby remains according to its nature a *means*. Hence on anything this money allows to be traded or made or sold you are entitled to reward for risk entered into, because you have actually used your money to buy something—a real product, a genuine good—whereas, in the case of loaning money you have not bought anything and so money remains in the limbo of its unrealized exchange function. Fourth, a grateful borrower may add a gift to the loan repaid without interest, in an acknowledgement of the possibility of gain foregone by the lender which does not treat money as an abstract potential for sheer abstract and isolated personal gain, as implied by *lucrum cessans*. Later in Catholic countries, especially on the Iberian Peninsula, the gift associated with return of a loan became semi-formalized.

All the same, in the fifth place, a lender *can* agree to receive a compensatory interest from the borrower if (a) he has thereby undergone "a real loss," i.e., if by lending he lacks for a time what he *should* have—this shows that Aquinas thinks in terms of what is owing to whatever social status in terms of natural justice; (b) if the borrower by borrowing avoids a loss greater than that undergone by the lender then here, too, interest should be paid. This appears to be seen by Aquinas as an extension of the situation of investment in enterprise: the implication is that here the borrower has undergone such a big positive reversal of fortune through investment that the lender should in effect be retrospectively regarded as a co-investor. One can note here that the justification for lending at interest offered by the Neapolitan political economist Antonio Genovesi in the eighteenth century, as cited by Bruni and Zamagni, would appear to be within this Thomistic trajectory, since he declared that legitimate interest is "the price for the convenience and utility it gives to the person who takes the loan." He explicitly *refuses* the "Franciscan" idea that it is a payment for the "use" of money regarded as still belonging to the lender.[25]

Hence to appeal back to these subtle considerations on price and money is not to appeal to an ideal previous social order free of the taint of usury, which in fact never existed. It is rather to appeal to a critique of a capitalistic market society already faintly emergent. Likewise, to appeal to guild organization or a medieval corporatist blending of the social,

25. Cited in Bruni and Zamagni, *Civil Economy*, 38–39.

economic and the political is not to appeal to a bygone feudal order—which incidentally, historians tell us never existed in the contractualist terms later fantasized, since it was rather a kind of hierarchized gift exchange partly created by the Church in order to reign back knightly violence through a cult of knightly honor.[26] It is rather, in parallel to the invocation of Aquinas, to appeal to past creative ecclesial efforts to *resist and qualify* "free market" tendencies which were already emergent. In this light, the considerable commercial success of the guild and corporate organization, and the medieval/renaissance civic humanist market spoken of by the Pope's key advisors, Bruni and Zamagni, which assumed reciprocal balance as governing *both* contract and gift—such that the market here *required according to its own norms* the material restoration of those who had sunk beneath the level of normal economic and social participation—remain as examples to us precisely because of their *modernity*.[27]

CAPITALISM AS DESACRALIZATION

This fact suggests that if one refuses to surrender to whiggish inevitablism, then one cannot declare that a new re-plantation of the economy upwards in social transcendence is impossible. Perhaps the biggest problem here, as Ratzinger so astutely acknowledges, is the technological. In agreement again with Polanyi, one can say that there is a certain affinity between the market and the machine. There is something Faustian, diabolical about the released forces of electricity, the light wave and the sound wave, etc. whose possibilities seem to re-organize us rather than being subordinate to our social needs and aesthetic preferences. This was already noted by Romano Guardini in his *Letters from Lake Como* where he rightly says that up to modern times there is an "organic" quality to human cultural construction even though this was always adding artifice and sign to nature.[28]

But like the Pope, Guardini was not engaging in mere nostalgia here. He refused to *give up* on the idea that we can find a more organic, sustainable, human, and beautiful way to deploy the huge powers of technology.

26. I am indebted to the ideas of my son Sebastian Milbank here. See also Reynolds, *Fiefs and Vassals*.

27. Bruni and Zamagni, *Civil Economy*, 45–75.

28. Guardini, *Letters from Lake Como*.

But presumably the prime key here would be to unlock technology from the power of the economic regarded as foundational. Then we would start to see that most of the apparently "inevitable" uses of technology are *not* dictated by technology itself, but by market interests. But Ratzinger's hope is realistic finally *because* it is a religious and not a secular hope. To allude to Polanyi once again: if the sea was first capitalized, then this was because it was relatively unknown, and so unsacred, or if sacred, then demonic, as for the Hebrew Scriptures. The enclosure of land and the commodification of people are all to do with *desacralization*. One buys, sells, and exploits without reference to tradition, association, duty or end because things and people are now secular and neutral and so the objects of exploitation. But although Polanyi is basically right here, one does need to cut and paste him with Marx.[29]

Polanyi's genealogy of capitalism is more searching than the latter's insofar as he treats capitalism as ideological because it is the *survival* of religion, the scene of fetishization. In this way, though, he is himself the victim of a politically economic perspective and does not understand the contingent generation of this perspective itself. For, as Bruno Latour argues, humans *cannot* escape from fetishisms because we always give material content to signs and we always see material things as signifying.[30] The politically economic idea of a dualistic sundering between merely "given" material things and equally "given" reasons or artificial constructions which we are supposed to be utterly in command of is a fiction—as the political economists themselves half saw by recognizing the heterogenesis of ends. All material things come marked and valued by us, while all our ideas are specifically embodied in ways that render their import unpredictable. Hence we are always commanded by fetishes—or "factishes" to deploy Latour's neologism—which remain in some sense "divine."

So Marx was naïve in imagining a merely "given" use-value on the one hand and a truly demystified rational control of things on the other. In reality we never step outside religion, and anti-religious structures are basely perverted cults. Secularism itself is such a cult, that is doomed to worship, as Marx saw, the most abstract fetish of all: money, which tends to run speculatively out of control and equally to worship purely physical power which we have now unleashed in such a fashion that we fear

29. Marx, *Capital*, Vol. I, Part I, chap. 1, 43–88.
30. Latour, *Pandora's Hope*, 266–92.

its ultimately destructive powers for the whole planet. Sign as pure sign disconnected from matter threatens us as free-floating finance; matter as pure matter disconnected from sacred signification threatens us as pure force. At this point Marx is, like most socialists, as we have seen, only another liberal after all.

On the other hand, Polanyi's apparent view that it is all right to commodify things in general, but not land or person, lags behind Marx's denunciation of the fetishism of the commodity as such. For to some degree persons and land *must* enter into exchange and so within exchange-value in order that human society be constituted in the first place. The point is that these exchanges should respect true ends and true desires. Yet the same is true for every exchanged commodity. And since persons only exist at all in their use of many things and since land is useless apart from the things that it contains, we cannot abuse most things as commodities without also abusing both land and persons.

All this is to say that Polanyi fails to see that the sacredness of land and persons requires that they be seen in a certain sense as fetishes. He too much sees them in secular terms as after all merely "given." As to his third insistence that money itself should not be commodified, this again interestingly contrasts with Marx. Polanyi says that money as a pure means should not in itself be *used* to make a profit like a usufruct: here he agrees with the medieval critique of usury. He sees corruption as the reduction of exchange to use, where Marx in general sees corruption as the reduction of use to exchange—such that ideally the exchange function of money should disappear in favor of the individual and general technological satisfaction of supposedly given needs. Polanyi is more fundamentally right, and yet both are in a way right: we cannot abolish the exchange function of money, but this also means that we cannot avoid entirely its commodification precisely insofar as it acts as an indispensable measure of the real worth of things which can only be *comparative*.

This is exactly why the issues of just price and of usury are *not* for Aquinas fixed norms but matters of prudential judgment, as D. Stephen Long has rightly stressed.[31] In Aquinas, after Aristotle, money concerns the *contrapassum* of distributive geometric justice which compares like with unlike (via the measure of our rightly ordered desire) even though it apparently belongs to commutative justice which restitutes according

31. Long, "Usury," 133–57.

to a fixed arithmetic scale, given pre-established distributive value.[32] (Though one can recall from Dante's *Inferno* that *divine* retributive justice is contrapassive.) Hence monetary exchange or *chremastike* for Aristotle (*oikonomia* meaning for him "household management" on any scale from literally domestic to civic) is precisely the process of *re-distributive justice* which hovers between political distribution, on the one hand, and criminal or civil restitution, on the other.[33] In this way, as Catholic social teaching sees, the economic is "the middle" between politics and the social because it is that space where we *must continue to perform justice and to revise justice under the impulse of charity which looks for everyone's well-being.* The state should not be the prime redistributor because the economy should itself be precisely that. This is why the Pope, after Bruni and Zamagni's re-invocation of the medieval/renaissance civic humanist economy, calls for a new market that would somehow offer a level playing field between enterprises seeking reasonable profits, merely mutual-trading companies and entirely charitable but still reciprocalist enterprises.

CYNICISM, ETHOS, AND HISTORY

This is an astonishingly radical demand, but is it merely naïve and, as it were, modestly utopian? Bruni and Zamagni gloss papal teaching by suggesting that we need an economic variant of subsidiarism which would demand that whatever can be achieved through non-profit organization should be so achieved, and that this principle should be reapplied along the whole non-profit to shareholder profit spectrum: what can be achieved by the co-operative should be so achieved, with the average modern, profit-seeking company only performing tasks as pragmatically necessary and even then only through the pursuit of a "reasonable" profit-share.[34]

One can basically endorse this principle, while remembering that subsidiarity implies "the lowest level that is most appropriate" rather than simply "the lowest possible lower level." In the economic case this would suggest that sometimes it would be overly dogmatic to rule out a modest pursuit of profit as providing an additional level of spur to enterprise

32. *ST* II.II QQ 77–78.

33. Aristotle, *Ethics* 1130b32–1134a6

34. Bruni and Zamagni, *Civil Society*, 231–32.

and discrimination of effort, alongside more purely social motivations and modes of assessment of working performance. It could be arguable on a case–by–case basis that some social enterprises would not be impaired in their primary goals if some profit-seeking was also involved. (Whether or not this is applicable to educational institutions remains, I think, debatable.) Moreover, the advantage of sometimes conjoining profit to social purpose is that one thereby prevents the operation of the dire "Franciscan" dialectic as already described. For just as a purism that refuses all ownership tends to leave behind a more sordid and negatively pure idea of ownership as a residue, so also an overly strict separation of charity from profit-seeking helps further to render profit-seeking an acceptably legitimate exercise in itself.

But Bruni and Zamagni are basically in accord with this point, since they insist on the beneficial "leakage" of ethos that can occur between not-for-profit and for-profit enterprises. Indeed they argue that this is already occurring and, like many other commentators, give evidence for an increasing hybridization between the two sectors. It is this very hybridization which the Pope seeks to support and hopes can be taken further.

Yet this prompts the inevitable question: just *why* should hybridization be taking place? What are the *economic* reasons for this? And surely, in order to be economic reasons, they must be cynical and not ethical ones? Answers here are very difficult to supply, but one can suggest the following. Not exactly cynical but at least ethically neutral reasons for this increase in hybridization can be: 1. the problem of what to do with increasing excesses of unrealizable capital; 2. the relative security of investment in charitable enterprises; 3. the profitable enhancement of one's image through association with charity; 4. the informal and friendly contractual bonds which charitable activity involves tends to engender an increased making of formal and profitable contracts.

Yet having admitted all that, it should also be allowed that the view that human beings, even as economic actors, are entirely or even primarily motivated by self-interest is an unwarranted dogmatism, for reasons already set out. And at this point the "cynical" and the "ethical" viewpoints can be mediated. Given the way in which, for a considerable segment of Western society, material flourishing can now be taken for granted, it becomes likely that other markers of prestige will have to be sought out by the relatively successful in order sufficiently to establish criteria for social success and social ranking (which can never conceivably be absent in any society whatsoever).[35] And indeed there is some evidence for this taking place: witness at the trivial level, which is often indicatively crucial, the new "camping culture" or vogue for a rugged outdoor and ecological lifestyle amongst the British well-heeled. The new predilection for charity and for volunteer work (exponentially increasing) fits precisely with such a tendency.

To this set of hybrid "cynico-ethical" considerations can be added the way in which (as I shall describe below) an extreme level of erosion of trust is itself counter to a business ethos and therefore tends dialectically to encourage a compensatory bias towards activities purely dependent upon mutual trustworthiness.

Yet finally and most crucially it is indeed merely cynical to suppose that there can be no shift, even within the economic realm, towards a different ethos for sheerly imponderable reasons of shift in moral climate. Clearly at present, we have no such decisive shift, but we might have the beginnings of a certain contestation of ethos amongst businesspeople and financiers themselves between a more neo-liberal and a more communitarian mode of economic practice. In fact a struggle and a competition between two different conceptualizations of competition itself: the one purely for abstract wealth; the other also in moral excellence in terms of the production of high-quality social goods of diverse sorts.

For no genuine historicism imagines that history is the history of cynical reason rather than the variety of ethical reasonings. Always the operation of both are in evidence, since humanity itself is a hybrid animal and characterized by the interweaving of the real with the ideal. The relative dominance of material interest or spiritual ethos is itself a result of historical production. But today the problem with much of the left is its implicit ontological cynicism and consequent practical pathos. It is supposed to be the political right that is pessimistic about human nature, and yet because the political left's Rousseauist optimism has indeed been too merely naturalist, it has tended to be cynical about the "artificial" processes of history itself, imagining by contrast that an innocent glory of true humanity will be unveiled once these processes have finally unraveled. But today, when few of the left really preserve any faith in such ultimate unraveling, a cynicism about history amounts to cynicism *tout court*. In consequence, social democratic thought, no longer

35. I owe this point to my daughter, Arabella Milbank.

hoping to displace capitalism, assumes that the market must *always* take a sinisterly immoral and capitalist shape (meaning a market where the interests of capital are dominant over those of workers and consumers and so of most people, or even every person *qua* person). As a result, the bureaucratic state is seen as the only virtuous, qualifying factor, which often results in the *ultra*-cynicism of substituting regulation and surveillance for the supposed naivety of trust in the worth of individual actors, thereby half-committing us all to the far greater naivety of imagining that we can dispense in such trust in virtue altogether.

And hence the extreme pathos of social democracy: all that can ever be achieved is some qualified defense against the economic and social ravages of the market. But as has been seen, this position cannot escape or resolve Polanyi's *aporia* whereby such state interference on the one hand really does sometimes inhibit whatever human benefits the sheerly capitalist market might bring, and on the other hand only protects capitalism from the social protests to which its own excesses might give rise and therefore helps sustain it in being, whilst preventing the emergence of an associationist alternative.

What the left now misses is therefore the possibility that today not the workers, nor the intellectuals (stuck in passive observational cynicism) could potentially be the main agents of social justice, but rather businesspeople, the half-repentant villains themselves. (The involvement of workers would also be crucial here, but given the level of disempowerment of the proletariat achieved by late capitalism, it is hard to see how they could ever become again partially prime social actors, as they were in an earlier industrial era.) Yet in the case of this possibility a priority to the ethical need not ideologically gloss over inherent differences of material interest, which should not, however, be ahistorically and cynically hypostasized.

To do the latter is indeed once more to commit to "left individualism" and to suppose that individuals always finally act out of material and so lonely and private reasons—given that collective interests of a merely material sort, even if mutually sympathetic, can only ever be provisional and expedient. (After the revolution, we will all go our separate self-satisfied ways.) By contrast, the material interests of owners, managers, investors, and workers can truly be materially fused only when there is a common ethical commitment to certain social purposes of production and exchange and then a division of material spoils is re-organized in accordance with that commitment. This would generally involve a far greater overlapping of these different economic roles in the future.

It should also be said that the appeal to business interests themselves by no means implies an end to all struggle against "cynical" interests of dominant capital. Of course, realistically speaking this will remain until they are defeated by struggle. But the more plausibly effective alliance against these interests is not now the mass of workers and the dispossessed, working through the agency of the "compensatory" state (the aporetic problems with this mode of resistance have been sufficiently outlined) but rather the growing union of all ethical businesses and corporate bodies, uniting in shared purpose workers, managers and owners.

It can therefore be argued that the alternative to social democratic cynicism and pathos is an associationist advocacy of a "moral market." The arrival of the latter alone would free us from the political Manicheanism of cynical reason, which, needless to add, is theologically as well as humanly unacceptable. Once we have identified and genealogically accounted for the ontological cynicism of the current left, it becomes clear that the real source of radical change today would be (and perhaps already is) "religious" *repentance,* and not yet more materialist "analysis," however searching and sophisticated.

To gain greater clarity about this practical and theoretical demand for a just and charitable market, it is worth setting out (a) a brief typology, (b) a resumé of our current predicament, and (c) a sketch of concrete proposals.

A Typology of "Third Ways"

The typology distinguishes between modernist (somewhat to be distinguished from "modern"), postmodern and religious variants of the third way.

The Modernist Variant

We have already characterized the modern. In knowledge it involves a duality of given fact and equally given reason or artificial proposal. In political economy it involves the fantasizing of a natural economy supplemented by artificial political contract and promotion of utility.

Modernism (in philosophy as in the arts) tried to mediate this gulf through a nonetheless still modern and subjective given immediacy of reasoned identity. Husserl is here paradigmatic because of the way in which he argued that we have absolute intentional access to the essences of things. In his *Krisis*, he tried to root the scientific endeavor back in a real experienced intention and to show that it was but one of many authentically intentional relations to reality.[36] Directly under Husserlian influence, the German architects of the post-war social market, the so-called Ordo-Liberals, similarly tried to heal the breach between nature and reason through a better use of reason that would half-restore the organic past. Just as Husserl tried to authenticate and yet limit science, so Wilhelm Roepke tried to authenticate and yet to limit economics in his Husserl-echoing *Social Crisis of Our Times*. Written during the war almost at the same time as Polanyi's *The Great Transformation*, this book is asking the same question about why the long nineteenth century peace had led to twentieth century unprecedented mass war, and answering it like Polanyi by blaming nineteenth-century political economy.[37] Like Polanyi also he wanted to re-embed the market in society, but unlike Polanyi he thought, following Husserlian phenomenological methods, that the market has a pure isolated essence. Hence while the state should prevent monopolies, promote craft guilds, and so forth, the price mechanism of the market merely left to itself will tend to generate local reciprocal exchanges which are not capitalist in character. A natural market will be a confined market—one can see why one should not confuse this with Hayek's neo-liberalism, even though the latter itself never reached the egotistic extremities of the Chicago school.

But Roepke only thinks this for two reasons, theoretical and historical. Theoretically, he sees the market as second-best to pure self-sufficiency, as if reciprocal exchange were historically secondary, which it is not. He is here all too Rousseauian. Historically, he argues with total implausibility that the main reason for monopoly is lingering feudal inequality, rather than it being something which the market itself tends towards. Because he espouses a pure market, for all his admitted kinship with Catholic thought and with English Catholic distributism (a kinship also acknowledged, though far more one-sidedly, by Hayek with respect

36. Husserl, *Crisis of the European Sciences*.

37. Roepke, *Social Crisis of Our Times*; see also Rüstow, *Die Religion der Marktwirtschaft*.

to the way in which socialism can combine with capitalism to produce the monopolistic and oligarchic "servile state"),[38] he rejects ideas of the just price, the just wage and any corporatist political role for the guilds.[39]

The Postmodern Variant

Roepke thus articulated the modernist third way imagined through a fantasized immediacy of essence. What is the postmodern third way? First of all, what is the postmodern attitude to knowledge? It is one of admitted mediation, but of skeptical mediation. Against Husserl, Derrida said that there is no immediate grasp of essences because of the intervention of *semiosis* which is indeterminate. Historically speaking, the algebraic forgetting of original intention in science—whereby we come to manipulate formulae without understanding how they were first produced—is inevitable and always already begun.[40] Here, however, Derrida is far more Cartesian than Husserl, since he exalts a skeptical *mathesis* that itself forgets the mediation of subjective material constitution of signifying practices which Husserl was rightly anxious to disinter. Real mediation would need to split the difference. Our knowledge is always intentional, but as it is also always signifying we never quite know what we intend and must always render a merely provisional judgment upon our own activity.

In political economic terms, it was New Labour which first enacted the postmodern *mathesis*, the skeptical mediation. (In the U.S. this was first done by Clinton and continued by George W. Bush, but to a considerably lesser extent.) Under this continued *regimen* no longer are the political and the economic discrete, but they totally invade each other while yet only accentuating and not abolishing their separation. All businesses are to grow bigger and be more impersonally managed; government is to encourage an internal market in the public sphere and yet all the more to police these with targets and inspections.

Is this really for the sake of modern order? No, from the outset with Giddens' manifesto *The Third Way*, it was for the sake of increasing postmodern risk. Risk most of all encapsulates skeptical fusion: for risk is seen as positive: we must release the nihilistically dangerous, uncertain

38. Hayek, *Road to Serfdom*, 13n.1.

39. In these respects the criticisms of ordo-liberalism made by the Jesuit Oswald von Nell-Breuning are pertinent. See von Nell-Breuning, *Kapitalismus—kritisch betrachtet*.

40. Derrida, *Edmund Husserl's* Origin of Geometry.

and unknown, make everyone more aware of unlimited choice and their sophistic right to choose the uniquely and un-groundedly "different." The market depends upon risk, not of course because of its moral responsibility (that rather accrues to the collective sharing of risks within firms) but rather, from its eighteenth-century outset, because risk led to reward, deserved or not. On the other hand, the more risk increases then the more *unacceptable* risk is also engendered. Hence the ever-increased need for both governmental surveillance and business self-surveillance. The new market state encourages us to be as dangerous to each other as possible, but then it also considers that almost everything we do might be excessively dangerous and so must be stopped. Belloc's "servile state" has here already been reached.[41]

The Catholic Christian Third Way

The third possibility of a third way, is a religious and especially a Catholic Christian one. In terms of knowledge this means a faithful, participatory mediation. As Edith Stein asserted against Husserl, only God enjoys completely immediate knowledge of anything.[42] Any true knowledge that we have must be through faith that we remotely participate in this. Hence our knowledge is thrice mediated: by divine illumination, through the forms of material things that arrive by abstraction in our mind and inform our understanding (thereby allowing a relatively sure phenomenological intuition of essence, without either *epoché* or perfect reduction), and through our knowledge of one thing always in terms of another and so through signs *ad infinitum*.

---

41. Belloc, *Servile State*. The comment of the late Tony Judt in his book *Ill Fares the Land* that it was the old-fashioned "pure state" which had to come to the rescue of the banks after the recent crash and not the supposedly mythical "market state" totally misses the point that what is indeed the market state had to rescue the banks precisely because its own indebtedness was so tied up with theirs. This was self-rescue by an oligopoly, not rescue of the banks by a political force transcendent to the economic. I would argue for the reasons set out in this chapter that Judt's continued advocacy of social democracy does not sit coherently with his extremely accurate castigation of the left for under-appreciating the importance of conserving what is good in the past and so effectively placing a modernist futurism before the quest for social justice and environmental beauty. He correctly remarks that Burke's political ontology, which stresses the primacy of the passage of time for human existence, should be taken as true by all sides of the political spectrum.

42. Stein, *Knowledge and Faith*.

What then, is finally the Catholic "third way" in terms of political economy? I have already adverted to Guardini's search for an organic use of technology and that must be our clue. Humans as natural beings use signs, yet remain entirely animals in doing that. It is crucial at this point to return to Aristotle and Aquinas: we are rational and political animals. *Not,* as for bio-politics, a bit animal with reason and politics tacked on, but entirely *as* animals rational and political and yet in our reason and "politicality" *wholly still animal.* Animals inconceivable to Darwinism who possess the *telos* of reason, politics and the paradoxical end of the reception of supernatural grace which causes us always to exceed the political and justice in the direction of the ecclesial meta-space of charity.

So human beings always add the mediation of signs and the reciprocal exchange of gifts to nature. But they do not thereby leave nature behind, nor is this grounded in a nature "before" our humanity, as for political economy. Nor also, are these additions merely random and subject to no judgment, as postmodern atheism must conclude. No, for human society to be possible we must trust in a paradoxically fundamental middle of habit, ungrounded in either nature or reason, which nonetheless we must believe conducts us towards our true *telos.* This means that, in order to restore the primacy of society over the economy, we must have faith in God and in our participation in God and must be able to "read" certain habitual practices as truly tending in this direction.

Our Current Predicament

How does such a reading relate to the recent and ongoing financial crisis (2007–)? Clearly the latter does not foreshadow the end of capitalism. However, it both reminds us of something and reveals something new. It reminds us that capitalism is subject to a peculiar sort of economic crisis: a crisis of speculation, not of natural disaster or human ineptitude.[43] But it also reveals that globalization has so expanded and speeded up the processes of capitalist change as to engender something qualitatively different. Unrestricted movements of international finance now severely curtail government freedom of action in a way that puts political democracy itself into crisis. The way in which excess capital from one part of

---

43. See Harvey, *Enigma of Capital.*

the world can be so quickly transferred to another has in part generated the recent severe economic destabilization. In response, governments had to bail out the banks by taking over their debts in a manner which locks politics itself yet more into a sheerly economic logic which has less and less regard for the specifically political ends of human well-being and interpersonal communication.

But this supposedly pure economic logic is not the logic of economics as such; only of one particular economic system which acts out certain theoretical assumptions as already described, which can be summarized in the following way. First, there is the accepted dominance of material reality by abstraction: even the bankers themselves scarcely knew what was going on, because they were speculating in terms of ciphers about ciphers and of guesses about other people's guesses concerning the future. By these means they were increasingly entangling us all in the shifting rules of their own game. Secondly, there is the assumption that the well-being of the firm takes second place to that of the individuals who run it, as best illustrated by the "bonus culture." The third assumption is the most fundamental. This is that human beings are at bottom self-seeking animals and that a free market depends upon recognizing this reality.

These three assumptions demand the interrogation which I have already tried to undertake. The dominance of abstraction is rooted in tearing material things apart into a sign-aspect on the one hand and an object-aspect on the other. This is unnatural, because the house I live in, for example, affords me at once material shelter and emotional significance. We naturally see everything in this integrated way. Yet our inherited capitalism depends for its very operation upon the sundering of thing from sign. Thus material things without meaning can be treated always as objects to be manipulated. When the land itself is treated like this, the surface of the earth threatens to become as naturally desolate as it is culturally desecrated. Equally, when human beings are reduced to bodies without souls, they can be regarded as simply sources of labor supply. Even money itself, as Polanyi realized, is treated over-abstractly. Instead of being regarded as an instrument of exchange that measures economic comparative value in accord with moral value, it is seen as something one should try to accumulate in its own right, and as something that can be validly bought and sold and used to constrain people's natural freedom of choice. In this way, genuine meaning floats off into the ether of sheer quantification, while material reality is cruelly wrenched away from all affective attachments.

However, the world goes round and round: if globalization encourages this nomadic abstraction, it also increases the way in which abstraction must in the end relate back to the real material economy. For if you live on one globe, there is eventually nowhere to hide and even Dubai affords no refuge. This is because the total sundering of sign from thing does not make sense even in market terms. Since we are embodied creatures, disembodied capital must in the end be securitized against material resources, else we have no way finally to guarantee its value, without which it loses its purpose.

If our current economic system divides sign from thing, it also, in the second place, tries to divide the individual from the group. But there are limits to this. After all, even bankers do not operate as lone rangers, but within firms. Why also firms and not just markets? Neo-classical economics was simply about markets: it concerned market equilibrium and the idea that markets automatically record exact information. But today a more postmodern economics recognizes that no system is in the long run stable; that rational individual acting can sometimes produce irrational general results, and that the feedback of market information often arrives too late for the benefit of the individual speculator. This is where the role of the firm comes into play. People have to get together and cooperate under both horizontal and hierarchical consensual norms, precisely because within a firm they can create for themselves a niche market that becomes relatively predictable and that supplies reasonably reliable information in sufficient time. *Most* economic activity operates in this institutional space and *not* through patterns of exchangist negotiation. As Bruni and Zamagni put it, we work far more than we shop.[44]

Yet despite recognizing the necessity of collaboration, economics for a while tried perversely to understand even the firm in individualistic terms. This encouraged an appeal to "public choice theory" (with its roots in Condorcet and advocacy by Kenneth Arrow and Amartya Sen in recent times), which has influenced New Labour and has been applied to governmental as well as private organizations. For the crudest version of this theory, employees and civil servants remain utility-maximizing creatures whose main aim is to cream-off benefits of prestige and wealth

44. Bruni and Zamagni, *Civil Economy*, 159–252; Screpenti and Zamagni, *Outline*, 456–519.

for themselves. But even in the subtler variants individual actors are seen as trying to realize their own goals in accordance with their own diverse capacities, no objective shared teleology being regarded as conceivable.[45] In consequence, firms cannot trust their employees, giving rise to our current culture of targets, incentives, bonuses and endlessly employing new employees to check up on other employees.

At the same time, an anti-corporatist theoretical individualism itself reflects the increased individualism in practice of "disorganized capitalism" or "neo-capitalism" ever since the 1970s. In this model, partly encouraged by new technologies and partly by a reinforcement of the inherently individualist logic of capitalism itself, an older managerialist "Fordist" model of production has been replaced to a considerable degree by outsourcing from central to satellite companies and networking between apparently more independent individuals and parties. Yet in reality, as analysts have shown, this has disguised an ever-increased agglomeration and dominance of monopolistic firms, often at the global level.[46] The apparent but actually superficial disaggregation itself permits a greater control by a center whose power benefits from the very fluidity and more evanescent nature of its parts. At the same time, the preponderance of "networking" ensures that a contractualist logic, fundamental to capitalism, increasingly operates at the intra-firm as well as at the inter-firm level, often with apparent interactions at the latter level being in reality covertly manipulated interactions within the former. And the supposedly greater scope for individual initiative which the new system seems both to encourage and to thrive upon is to a degree but another screen of delusion: for in reality what drives the system, and what it benefits from, is the attraction of the mere *rhetoric* of enterprise and the mere *trappings* of difference to the various players within the system. Their greater energy and cooperation is recruited (as compared with Fordism) to the degree that they are manipulated through the enjoyment of apparently greater scope for choice within an always severely restricted range of options which are more like "shopping selections" than genuine opportunities for creativity.

---

45. See Sen, *Idea of Justice*. In Sen's variant, in which moral relativism is elevated into a kind of High-Table Hindu indifferentism, a competitive logic within public institutions is balanced by a Statist concern to increase the ability of individuals to realize their "capacities" in both state and market sectors.

46. See Boltanski and Chiapello, *New Spirit of Capitalism*, 223.

In this way the "disorganization" of capitalism, by reducing the *esprit de corps* of the more organized firm of the past, decreases trust and security and reduces even productive decisions to simulacra of "consumer choices." In consequence, a capacity to innovate which *capitalism itself requires*, is in some measure compromised.

So the crucial irony here is that this sort of individualistic bias in both theory and practice is actually inimical to a genuinely free market. A culture of pervasive mistrust inevitably inhibits those qualities of initiative, risk, and creativity on which competitive enterprise depends. Moreover, one can argue that an overly "liquid" capital, which moves so fast that it can be increasingly indifferent to local limitations, is just as subject to the loss of "tacit knowledge" only available at the local level, as Hayek argued was the case for central state planning. If, for example, a speeded up economy requires that people frequently change jobs now become so automated (in every respect) that they are not difficult to move in and out of, it must still pay the dialectical price of losing that patient slowness which real creative innovation and prudential skill require, *even* with respect to the process of generating abstract wealth.

Hence the restoration of trust, the relocalization of the economy, and the use of "lighter" technology to empower individuals and small groups, rather than to render them evermore replaceable (a kind of *alternative* postmodern economy to that of post-Fordist disorganization), is actually *in line* with the logic of a free market, even though these things are also desirable in more properly social terms and it is impossible to gain the sheer economic benefit without *also* gaining (or regaining) the social benefit.[47] Therefore at a new dialectical limit the market economy requires some re-embedding for purely market economic reasons, *even though* this re-embedding will paradoxically tend to remove the very idea of such "purely economic" reasons, which belong to a disembedding that needs to be overcome. This phenomenon is akin to "the cultural contradictions of capitalism," except that the culture of trust is here more seen as *inherent* to economic contract itself. But the proviso must be added that nothing dictates that even good economic logic will be followed: the swiftness of late modern capitalism has an enormous mo-

---

47. See Blond, *Red Tory*, which is of general relevance for the theses of this chapter, although my own political allegiance is to Maurice Glasman's "Blue Labour"—a position theoretically anticipated by me as "Blue Socialism" in *The Radical Orthodoxy Reader*, 401.

mentum that establishes a habit which can often survive the evidence of its economic illogic. The United States well illustrates the inertia of an extreme capitalist system which survives and dominates despite the fact that it tends to quash local enterprise in favor of sluggish monopoly and engenders much material squalor and absence of real choice (over transport, food and clothing for example) even for the supposed possessors of moderate wealth.[48]

In the face of this *economic* incapacity of the neo-liberal model, we need to learn, as Bruni and Zamagni have suggested, from those traditions of Italian political economy stretching back to eighteenth-century Naples which have always stressed that social sympathy and reciprocity belong to economic contract itself, and not simply to the "compensatory" roles of civil society and governmental welfare as for the Scottish perspective, which was less authentically humanist.[49] Indeed, the more that contracts between people are based on trust, the more they are relatively informal, and the more that they embody a kind of gift-exchange, then the *less* you need the intervention of state control. The individualistic model of the market economy has (as Belloc correctly foresaw) paradoxically increased the power of the state, whose laws are required both to secure formal contract and to enforce marketization within the public sector, while also policing the resultant anarchy.

So a more moral market would also be a *more* genuinely free market: morality need not be just an external corrective to the economic sphere, as social democratic pathos tends to assume. Another aspect of this moralization of the market would be the genuine sharing of risk, which would remove the relative protection against risk currently enjoyed by the investor and money-lender as compared with both employees and consumers.

But if the economics of egoism do not work for the firm, then it turns out that they do not work at any level whatsoever. Here, as we have seen, anthropology refutes the third false assumption which derives from Adam Smith. We are *not* primarily a "trucking" animal seeking a good deal, but a gift-exchanging animal. For what human beings most desire is not material wealth, but rather social recognition. But this is always a mutual affair, and so we are rarely either purely interested or purely

48. Every observant European who has lived in the USA for a while will attest these surprising phenomena.

49. Bruni and Zamagni, *Civil Economy*, 45–75.

disinterested. Society is a spiral paradox of "non-compulsory compulsion," in which the giving of gifts (and every act and speech-act is a gift) half-expects but cannot compel a return gift. This is the very glue of all human society. It is at once a political and an economic glue, so that when we try to base our economy on desacralization and individualism, society is gradually abolished and humanity starts to contradict itself.[50]

If social recognition is fundamental also for the economy, then trust is basic for the economic firm. One could say (in line with the thinking of the seventeenth-century English Levellers)[51] that it should constitute a sort of benign semi-monopoly which prevents the emergence of malign monopoly. How so? Well on the basis of naked individualism, people strive for monopoly in order to produce the shoddiest possible products, buy the materials for those products as cheaply as possible and sell them as dearly as possible. In this way they undermine competitors and bad practice drives out good. But in the case of the firm that is a "civil enterprise" or partnership between owners, managers, workers, and consumers, good practice can drive out bad in a tendency that is actually more stable, as one can see for much of the history of a firm like the UK-based John Lewis Partnership. Such firms will tend to thrive in the long term, not by driving out *all* other competitors, but rather by forcing other firms to compete in terms of quality of produce, fairness of pricing and humane treatment of workers and customers. And a crucial aspect to "quality of produce" is the fact that *real* goods (including "relational goods" that we can only enjoy in common) are less subject to the law of diminishing returns. Habit dulls us to the appeal of the latest mutation of the chocolate bar from slender to chunky . . . But habituation only discovers ever *more* in the enjoyment of fine wines, beers, and ciders, and still more in the practice of fine cuisine and in all aesthetic and reciprocally enjoyed social goods in general.

It is perhaps at this point that ethical considerations about economics most pass over into metaphysical or religious ones. For much of human existence, it can seem as if bad habits are more powerful than good ones. But in the end, we discover that the reverse is true, and that otherwise we could not survive as social and linguistic animals.

---

50. See Godbout and Caillé, *World of the Gift*; Godbout, *Ce Qui Circule Entre Nous*.
51. See Black, *Guilds and Civil Society*, 126–27.

VIRTUE AND ECONOMY

Where might one locate such self-sustaining and intensifying good habits? One thing we ignore is that many elements of Catholic social teaching—opposition to usury, the just price, the just wage, guilds, corporations, distribution of assets, the primacy of land as sacred, solidarity, and subsidiarity—exist in certain degrees in many parts of the world where they have been tried and successfully tested (Germany, Austria, Italy, the Basque Country, for example). So they are not mere medieval survivals or nostalgic throwbacks, and, as Antony Black once argued, it is rather the case that both "liberal" freedom to choose (one's career, living place, and marriage partner in particular) and the principle of mutuality are *both* products of Christianity and *both* things which belong to "modernity" understood as the gradual emergence of a more economic and more urban society as opposed to a rural and military one from the twelfth century onwards.

As he also argued, while the seventeenth century and the Enlightenment saw the one-sided triumph of "liberalism," mutualism and the advocacy of the constitutive political role of the corporate guild and other intermediary bodies (held together in the end by reciprocal ties of friendship) persisted both in modern practice for a long time (for example in Germany and Italy) and in alternative but clearly modern theories like those of Althusius in the seventeenth century, Otto von Gierke in the nineteenth century and Emile Durkheim in the twentieth century.[52]

Let us consider briefly certain of these elements of Catholic social teaching and how they might be extended:

(A) Anti-usury legislation. We need to tie as much lending of money as possible to real investment and to make banks stakeholders and therefore risk-carriers in the enterprises which they fund. At every level we need to reconnect financial sign with material power in order to prevent the speculative and ecological threats of their disconnection.

(B) Just prices and just wages. At crucial defining limits as regards justice we cannot trust the market to deliver these and we need to make this matter something that comes first within the advisory power of "free

52. Black, *Guilds and Civil Society,* esp. 12–43 and 237–41. Black confusingly uses the term "civil society," following Hegel, to mean market liberalism. He does not discuss the Scottish use of the term, as in Adam Smith and Adam Ferguson which, as we have seen, referred to a realm which ambiguously replaced an older corporatism and yet also tried to compensate for its absence.

guilds" or corporate bodies concerning different regions of production and service which try to set standards for and offer advice to those firms which voluntarily belong to them. (See C, below.) But to safeguard the public interest in the last analysis, the adjudication of prices and wages is also something that should come increasingly within the purview of courts of law. At the same time, the achieving of justice in these areas should more usually and effectively be a matter of instilling a new sort of ethos in economic transactions, founded upon a new sense that a firm should not legitimately, as the Pope says, be pursuing profit alone, but ought to be pursuing some sort of publicly recognized social purpose. (Is not the opposite idea simply morally obscene?)

(C) Free Guilds. We need a general re-creation and reinvigoration of professional associations, guilds or "corporations," which still play a considerable role in Germany and Austria and which survive vestigially or exist in an over interest-protecting and giant form (like the Confederation of British Industry) in the United Kingdom. It is these institutions alone that can instill an inter-firm ethos based upon the idea that one achieves self-respect by making and trading something good and not by merely making money. Furthermore, it is the idea of the guild or corporation which truly resolves the *aporia* of monopoly whereby state anti-monopoly legislation is itself an unwarranted intrusion within market competition that can even help to further the rise of alternative monopolies. Here once more it is Polanyi who had the vital insight: monopolies tend to be generated by the most freebooting and egoistic participants in the market. Hence a guild-restriction of competition to those signed-up to guild-principles actually tends to ensure competition by slightly restricting competition. It thereby achieves what the Ordo-Liberals desired, but failed to see required a greater role for the corporatist dimension.

However, to avoid monopolistic corruption consequent upon guild-operation itself, as has undoubtedly occurred in the past, we need a new idea of *free* guilds which enjoy no legally established sole right to trade. Licensing by a guild-organization could then become economically advantageous in the way that a free trade label is today, because customers would receive thereby a certain guarantee of good quality of produce, fair treatment of all stakeholders in the enterprise, and of consumers themselves. This notion of a "free guild" also helps meet the objection that guilds cannot cope with *new* trades and industries which arise with ever increasing frequency. For the latter need not be inhibited by the vested interests of established "corporations" yet at the same time are provided by them with a model of the benefits of submission to guild standards which they can then imitate. At the same time, a certain subordination of technology to relatively stable human ends might be served by bringing new technologies within the scope of existing guilds: we could then more easily ask for example, *what* social purposes do the mobile phone and the computer precisely serve? This purposive conservatism of guilds could also have a radically protective function.

(D) The organization of welfare. As much of this as possible needs to be organized by state-aided voluntary bodies recognized as corporate economic actors in order to ensure that people understand that they are involved in a visible and comprehensible give-and-take and can themselves exercise a regular charity. Also pension provision needs on the whole to be organized within firms in order to ensure that the future needs of both employers and employees are as mutually bound-together and tied up with the destiny of the firm as possible. This might help to inhibit our current anti-virtuous volatility of employment.

(E) Wider distribution of assets. Everything possible should be done through local banks, credit unions, mutual manufacturing investment funds, co-operative housing associations, worker share-ownership, and so forth to ensure a general de-proletarianization and re-professionalization of the population. National and local Government should deliberately encourage the emergence of such institutions by offering tax advantages, privileged conditions of access to credit, and so forth. At the moment all is going in the reverse direction.

(F) A new political corporatism. If businesses and other corporate bodies (for example universities) are to be officially encouraged to take social responsibility, then reciprocally they should exercise a share in political governance. This is a left-wing theme all the way from Durkheim to Paul Hirst, as well as a right-wing one.[53] It has been perverted into totalitarianism when (a) it has altogether displaced representative government of individuals and localities and (b) it has been centrally directed and made compulsory and (c) has disguised a continued capitalist exaction of surplus-value from workers. Here the current Pope's support for stake-holding and share-distribution seems to indicate a break with the Germanic Catholic Ketteler legacy of reading "co-determination" as if

53. Hirst, *Associative Democracy*; Hirst and Bader, *Associative Democracy*.

capitalists were the authentic equivalents of feudal overlords rather than people whose wealth had mainly been acquired through unjust exploitation (since many historical processes are, indeed, "cynical"). One can add that these degenerations are discouraged if the churches and other religious bodies help to co-ordinate inter-corporate governance without this all this being rooted through the state. Christians should recommend that the House of Lords be reformed as a representative body of corporations, businesses, religions, universities, trade unions, etc. and not as a second House of Commons, which would dangerously dilute the latter's primary sovereignty.

(G) The primacy of land. As asserted by Vincent McNabb and H. F. Massingham in the middle of the last century,[54] Catholic Christians (Roman, Orthodox and Anglican) have always proclaimed that it is the countryside and the organic relation of the city to the countryside that most guarantees our animal rationality. The countryside is basic in terms of food provision, ecology, and our sense of beauty—which concerns supremely how we fit human with divine creative art: this is one crucial aspect of the Christians "pastoral."

Yet failure to comprehend the primacy of the land threatens the integrity of cities most of all, because a false primacy of the urban has encouraged over-concentration of population and the rise of the sprawling mega-city which inevitably destroys its real function as the fulcrum of trade, philosophical discussion, and craft and artistic flourishing, rather than as sites for debased modes of mass manufacture and monopolistic and self-serving financial services. We need to revisit attempts like that of Glasgow at the turn of the nineteenth-century to combine mass manufacturing with craft design, while at the same time grasping the ways in which new lighter and green technologies can permit once again a wider inhabitation of the surface of the globe. Rural and now remote areas can be brought to life once again, while cities can recover their functions as centers of human meeting, and concentrations of excellence and example.

Spiritual failure with respect to our understanding of our place within nature has also a physical equivalent. The more that land is enclosed, then the more also local ecologies are destroyed, until the earth depends increasingly upon one fragile global ecology. But in the end, of course, the global ecology of *gaia* depends itself upon the various local ecologies and with their increasingly reduced functioning would eventually collapse.

54. McNabb, *Church and the Land*; Massingham, *Tree of Life*.

It is arguable that the Latin Christian Middle Ages were unique, in contrast both to what went before and what came after, in shaping a civilization more on the basis of the countryside and the small towns than on the larger cities.[55] Towns and cities served the rural economy rather than vice versa; aristocrats based themselves in the rural hinterlands while investing in the towns, and kings ruled through the balancing of rural interests, through endless travel and the exchange of gifts and favors, rather than through the imposition of a central bureaucracy. Yet far from this ruralization being a regressive development as compared to city-based antiquity, it was just this switch that allowed the so-called great infilling in the twelfth century, the almost continuous cultivation of land in many areas and the adoption of several crucial technological innovations. This was moreover rendered possible by the gradual freeing of men from first slavery and then serfdom, which increased the appeal of staying on the land and developing it and released a craft creativity.[56] Such a gradually wider distribution of property also permitted the existence of intensive small-scale farming requiring crop rotation, common grazing and many practices of mutual assistance. All in all this beneficial circulation allowed the emergence of a good natural and social ecology: a fine balance of interaction between person and person and between person and nature. It was within *this* cultural soil that later revolutionary Western advancements in technology and natural science were able to take root.

Of course the good medieval features were accompanied by many that were horrendous and have fortunately vanished (though we tend to underrate how far the work of emancipation from overweening land-based domination began within the Middle Ages themselves). Nor can we restore this degree of rural primacy. Yet it can be possible to restore it in the new sense of a primacy of nature as a whole, and of humanity taken as a part of nature, though as wisely governing over it in order to perfect it through further beautification and intensified flourishing. Such a primacy would uniquely guard against the siphoning-off of real benefits for overly abstract urban purposes with a consequent leaching away of the meaning of nature, which then remains as so much mere material terrain to be expropriated and exploited.

55. Again I have these ideas from my son Sebastian Milbank. One can note here that the Latin bias to the rural began with the Romans, for all their origin as a city-state.

56. See Belloc, *Essay on the Restoration of Property*.

CONCLUSION

In conclusion it can be asked, what does it portend when all the sea is an inland sea? Does this mean that we are doomed to the demonic middle of commercial, zero-sum trade now that there are no localities and no remote exotic places merely rumored? Now that the sea has totally invaded the land—and could eventually do so literally?

Up till now it would seem so. But there is another possibility. This is that transport and communications could have truly provided the preconditions for the emergence of a global village. Globalization mostly destroys locality, but also renders it more and more possible for one locality to communicate directly with another in a totally distant part of the world. In this way it just could once more come to seem "common sense" that all the economy should be subordinate to social reciprocity. As Paul Claudel suggested in his epic play Le Soulier de Satin, we must, as Catholic Christians, assume that the seas were not conquered by Western Christendom for the sake of the victory of chaos, but rather for the material baptism in loving justice of all of humanity.[57]

---

57. Claudel, Le Soulier de Satin.

2

A Tale of a Duck-Billed Platypus Called Benedict and His Gold and Red Crayons

Tracey Rowland

A Tale of Two Readings

CARITAS IN VERITATE IS the most recent in a long list of papal interventions in the territory of social justice, and for most commentators there was nothing surprising in the document apart from its extraordinary length and the way in which it sought to offer a comprehensive overview of the whole tradition rather than isolating a couple of issues and focusing upon them. It was as if Benedict XVI reviewed the tradition, made an executive summary of what he regards as its most significant elements, and gave his papal stamp of approval to them, at the same time as enriching them with his own theological reflections. *Caritas in Veritate* can thus be read as a masterful synthesis of late twentieth-century papal social justice theory, with a special emphasis on the

71

social implications of the Trinitarian anthropology of John Paul II. The core theological ideas were all present in the young Professor Ratzinger's essay on the treatment of human dignity in *Gaudium et spes*, as published in the commentaries on the documents of the Second Vatican Council, edited by Herbert Vorgrimler in 1969.

The intellectual center of the encyclical is that "a humanism which excludes God is an inhuman humanism." This was precisely the argument made by Pope Benedict's fellow Conciliar *peritus* and co-founder of the *Communio* journal, Henri de Lubac, in the work first published in 1944 as *Le drame de l'humanisme athée* which offered a survey of the humanisms of Feuerbach, Marx, Nietzsche, and Comte. This principle rests a notion of authentic human development upon the theological anthropology enshrined in paragraph 22 of the Conciliar document *Gaudium et spes*—the idea that the human person only has self-understanding to the extent that he or she knows Christ and participates in the Trinitarian communion of love. As Pope Benedict says, "Life in Christ is the first and principle factor of development," and as John Paul II wrote in the very first line of his first encyclical *Redemptor Hominis*, "Jesus Christ, the Redeemer of man, is the center and purpose of human history." The whole of *Caritas in Veritate* can therefore be read as a plea to understand the limitations of a secularist notion of development.

Not all commentators have however given the document such a reception. In "*Caritas in Veritate* in Gold and Red,"[1] the American neo-conservative political and ecclesial commentator George Weigel promotes the idea that while some sections of the document appeared to be of papal provenance (those one might underline with a gold marker), others had clearly been drafted by members of the Pontifical Council for Justice and Peace, a body which has a long history of tension in its relations with the U.S. neo-conservatives, and these he suggested could be underlined with a red marker. According to Weigel, the "red" sections of *Caritas in Veritate* are "payback" for those sections of *Centesimus Annus* (the third social encyclical of John Paul II), which was championed by the neo-conservatives as a papal endorsement of the U.S. economic order—although other commentators did not see it as being nearly so broad in its affirmation of the value of the market. There were thus two readings of *Centesimus Annus*, a U.S. neo-con reading, and a reading which read the affirmation of the market passage within the context of

1. Weigel, "*Caritas in Veritate* in Gold and Red."

the Church's social teaching as a whole, with all the caveats about the need to regulate markets with reference to the common good. With *Caritas in Veritate* however, Weigel has not attempted to spin the "red" sections of the document to make them friendly to the U.S. economic order. He has had the intellectual honesty to acknowledge that some sections of the document do not sit comfortably with the kinds of policies espoused by the neo-conservatives. He concludes that the encyclical has the form of a "duck-billed platypus"—an Australian monotreme which looks like a baby otter at one end and a duck at the other. While the metaphor is a little opaque, one gets the general impression that one section of the body of the platypus (encyclical) is vastly different in shape and material from the other.

Leaving aside the source criticism issues of which papal advisor contributed which lines, one can argue that there is nothing in the pre-papal works of Benedict XVI to suggest that he was ever likely to be sympathetic to the neo-conservative tradition, which is also described as the Whig tradition, or even by some commentators such as Michael Novak, its most well-known champion, as "Whig Thomism." One would not need to place Pope Benedict under political pressure to get him to endorse themes in *Populorum Progressio*—the encyclical of Paul VI most hostile to the Whigs—which Weigel described as the "odd duck" in the roll call of social encyclicals of the twentieth century. Ratzinger, like his papal predecessors going all the way back to Leo XIII, has been critical of both utopian socialist and *laissez-faire* liberal capitalist theory. In pre-papal essays he observed that while the lives of many people are completely controlled by the laws of the market so that they have few choices about their lifestyle, liberal theorists argue that the market is morally neutral and associated with the promotion of human freedom. He described as astounding this idea that the laws of the market are either neutral or in essence good.[2] He believes that pre-existing values are always determinants in making market decisions.

In the context of the problem of Third World poverty, he even referred to the "tragic legacy" and "cruelty of the liberal capitalist system."[3] In an interview with the Italian Catholic agency SIR given in 2004 he said that he believed that economic affairs are often driven by a form of liberalism which "specifically excludes the heart" and the "possibility of

2. Ratzinger, "Church and Economy," 199–204.
3. Ibid. and *On the Way to Jesus*, 121.

seeing God, of introducing the light of moral responsibility, love and justice into the worlds of work, of commerce and of politics."[4] He argued that "if globalization in technology is not accompanied by a new openness to an awareness of the God to whom we will all render an account, then it will end in catastrophe."[5] Although he was a staunch opponent of liberation theology, Ratzinger was never of the view that the economic order of the Latin American countries was unproblematic. He simply opposed solutions to their problems by reference to politics and economics alone, and in particular, he opposed Marxist solutions which gave greater weight to sociology than to revelation and turned Christ into a revolutionary social worker.

CATHOLICISM BEYOND WHIG LIBERALISM AND MARXIST LIBERATION

While the Catholic political arena is popularly perceived as a contest between romantics who have been fed on a diet of liberation theology mixed with movies about Gandhi, and pragmatic American Whigs blind to the fact that something which is good for middle-class America might have a harmful effect somewhere else in the world or on some other class within their own country, there is another position which is less well known, perhaps because many of those who occupy this position are professional academics, rather than journalists or politicians or political activists working for Catholic agencies. Their interventions are often highly academic and even incomprehensible to those unschooled in theology and social theory. Their position is one of critical opposition to both the Whig and Marxist traditions and one which offers a genealogy of the roots of contemporary social and economic problems which reaches all the way back to the sixteenth century or even earlier. The leading contemporary names here are Alasdair MacIntyre, David L. Schindler, and William T. Cavanaugh.

Each in his own way has been critical of what in Catholic social theory is described as "Americanism," the idea that the U.S. political and economic order is not only consistent with Catholic teaching, but should provide a model for Catholics across the globe. Throughout the 1990s

4. Ratzinger, "Interview."
5. Ibid.

the volumes of the English-language edition of *Communio: International Catholic Review* frequently featured debates between David L. Schindler and George Weigel about the culture of America, while the journal *First Things* under the editorial guidance of the late Richard John Neuhaus ran a pro-Americanist agenda. Both groups claimed loyalty to the papacy of John Paul II.

Alasdair MacIntyre is a central figure in the sub-discipline of Catholic social theory both because of his lifelong critique of the liberal tradition (he claims that he has been opposed to liberalism since he was seventeen), and because of his early immersion in the Marxist tradition which, although he was later to describe it as "wrong-headed," gave him an insider's perspective on the attraction of Marxist ideas to several generations of intellectuals in the twentieth century. Where the Marxist and Catholic traditions differ most fundamentally is at the level of philosophical anthropology. Marxist anthropology is a mixture of Enlightenment and Romantic elements—there is an Enlightenment concept of social progress and a Romantic belief in the perfectibility of human nature, and when the two are taken together the vision is one of the perfectibility of human nature through scientifically driven social progress.

This is in stark contrast to the Catholic perspective according to which perfection is the result of virtuous practices contending against the wounds of original sin. Political and economic institutions may in their structure and ethos either hinder or encourage virtuous practices, and thus there is a relationship between the nature of political institutions and the practice of virtue. The relationship operates both ways: virtuous practices encourage the establishment of healthy institutions and healthy institutions encourage virtuous practices, while pathological practices (those which undermine the integrity of the self) give rise to pathological institutions, and pathological institutions discourage virtuous practices. However the development of a virtuous disposition is fundamentally a matter of self-mastery in accord with the work of grace and can never be achieved, as Marx hoped, by a reordering of the political and economic orders alone. It is precisely for this reason that MacIntyre holds that the solution to the pathology of liberal modernity will not be found primarily in political action but rather in moral rejuvenation. The latter will, of course, have consequences for the former, but when it comes to the question of primacy, MacIntyre's position is that the moral takes precedence.

This understanding of the nexus between virtuous dispositions and practices (or their opposite) and the character of political institutions, can be construed as a particular example of the Platonic insight that there is a relationship between order and disorder within the souls of citizens, and order and disorder within the culture of their polity. In his inaugural lecture as a member of the *Académie française* in the section *Sciences Morales et Politiques*, Cardinal Joseph Ratzinger, as he was, summarized the Platonic understanding of this relationship thus:

> [Plato] speaks of three parts of the soul of man, but we can instead speak simply of three fundamental modes of man's integration or disintegration. The form of the state will depend on which of these three fundamental anthropological forms wins the upper hand. We have the reign of that which is lowest in man—the reign of lust, the lust for possession, for power, for pleasure. Reason and heart become instruments to serve what is lower; man sees in another only a rival or an instrument for the extension of his own ego. Market forces and public opinion dominate man and become a caricature of freedom. All that stands above lust in Plato's anthropological formula is the naked will, the audacity of daring and of undertaking; but this remains blind.[6]

In contradistinction to the Platonic and one might add Aristotelian and Thomist positions, the post-Rousseauian belief that a certain kind of civilization is the cause of individual imperfection and consequently that there is a political solution to the human predicament has been described by Leszek Kołakowski as the "idolatry of politics." Ratzinger's position when he was the Prefect of the Congregation for the Doctrine of the Faith was very much that the liberation theologians were guilty of such a form of idolatry. They skirted around the problem of original sin, allowed their Christology to be informed by their sociology, and looked to the political and economic disciplines for a kind of this-worldly salvation.

THE LEGACY OF FRANCISCO SUÁREZ

While various authors have located different historical moments at which the Platonic and Aristotelian political traditions were decisively challenged, Francisco Suárez would seem to win the prize for having most effectively set Catholic social theory on its liberal trajectory. In *Three Rival*

---

6. Ratzinger, *Turning Point for Europe*, 131.

Versions of Moral Enquiry, MacIntyre argued that Suárez was both in his preoccupations and his methods already a distinctively modern figure and is perhaps more authentically than Descartes the founder of modern philosophy. Indeed, he says that it was no accident that Descartes was taught by Jesuits influenced by Suárez. John Finnis, in *Natural Law and Natural Rights*, also identified Suárez as a pivotal figure in Catholic political theory. One of his many significant contributions was to foster the "two ends" theory of human nature by which the human being has a natural end separate from the supernatural end. Over time these two ends became equated with the secular and sacred orders, notwithstanding the fact that the notion of the *saeculum* was not initially spatialized at all—it was rather a reference to that period in history before the consummation of the world and the renewal of the cosmos. It initially referred to time, not to space. The notion that there exists a "pure nature" unrelated to grace linked to a purely secular (non-sacred) social space, became known as the extrinsicist account of the relationship between nature and grace with their respective secular and sacred orders.

In *Marxism: An Interpretation*, MacIntyre wrote:

> When the sacred and the secular are divided, then religion becomes one more department of human life, one activity among others . . . This has in fact happened to bourgeois religion . . . Only a religion which is a way of living in every sphere either deserves to or can hope to survive. For the task of religion is to help see the secular as the sacred, the world as under God. When the sacred and the secular are separated, then ritual becomes an end not to the hallowing of the world, but in itself. Likewise if our religion is fundamentally irrelevant to our politics, then we are recognizing the political as a realm outside the reign of God. To divide the sacred from the secular is to recognize God's action only within the narrowest of limits. A religion which recognizes such a division, as does our own, is one on the point of dying.[7]

The criticism of the extrinsicist account of nature and grace and its corresponding two ends theory of human nature was begun in the twentieth century in the work of Maurice Blondel and followed through in works of Henri de Lubac who described secularism as "simply a new name for a variety of atheistic humanism."[8] Peter Henrici has described the seminal influence of Blondel in the following terms:

7. MacIntyre, *Marxism*, 9.

8. de Lubac, *Eternal Feminine*, 180–81.

Maurice Blondel first rediscovered, on philosophical grounds, that human life is intrinsically oriented toward the longing for the supernatural gift, and that this longing constitutes its real and unique meaning. Stimulated by Blondel's impelling thought, Thomists then rediscovered St. Thomas's teaching that man's "natural desire for the vision of God" as the very constituent of our intellectual life (Pierre Rousselot, Joseph Maréchal) and from there they went on to a rediscovery of the true Augustinian theology of grace (Henri de Lubac).[9]

Louis Dupré has argued that the validation of an autonomous "secular" order in late scholasticism by scholars preparing commentaries on the work of St. Thomas was based on an unintentional failure to distinguish between "pure nature" as an object of philosophical speculation, and pure nature in the order of concrete reality. De Lubac argued that this failure opened the door to secularism within the theological tradition. As James V. Schall has written: "If we treat man as only natural, he will no doubt end up being less than natural . . . the principle is not, get man's natural end right and you will be happy, but get man's supernatural end right or you will not be able to get his natural or this worldly end right."[10]

As a theory, Suárez's "two ends" was to have particular appeal in the twentieth century to Catholic Americans in a predominately Protestant culture deeply imbued with liberal values. By keeping the secular and the sacred in separate compartments, Catholics who wanted to baptize the liberal tradition could seek agreement with non-Catholics about public goods on the basis of a shared notion of "pure nature." Matters pertaining to the sacred were to be privately added on to the philosophically discernible purely natural goods and ends. This became the basis of John Courtney Murray's defense of Americanism, to which the contemporary Whig Thomists are the intellectual heirs.

The difference this makes to the way that Catholics approach the realms of politics and economics is well presented in the works of David L. Schindler. In the following paragraphs, he juxtaposes the Murrayite approach with that of de Lubac:

According to Murray: faith and grace do not determine the structures and processes of civil society: these are determined by reason, in the light of the lessons of experience . . . [The Church]

9. Henrici, "Response to Louis Dupré," 76.
10. Schall, "Certain Fundamental Truths."

does not aim to alter the finality of the state, but to enable the state to achieve its own finality as determined by its own nature. Conversely, for de Lubac, the state occupies no special "secular" space beyond the operation of the law of the relations between nature and grace. It is from within that grace seizes nature . . . It is from within that faith transforms reason, that the Church influences the state. For Murray, grace's influence on nature takes the form of assisting nature to realize its own finality; the ends proper to grace and nature otherwise remain each in its own sphere. For de Lubac, on the contrary, grace's influence takes the form of directing nature from within to serve the end given in grace; the ends proper to grace and nature remain distinct, even as the natural end is placed within, internally subordinated to, the supernatural end. For Murray then, the result is an insistence on a dualism between citizen and believer, and on the sharpness of the distinction between eternal (ultimate) end and temporal (penultimate) ends. For de Lubac, on the contrary, the call to sanctity "comprehends" the call to citizenship and all the worldly tasks implied by citizenship. The eternal end "comprehends" the temporal ends.[11]

In his essay on human dignity in *Gaudium et spes*, Ratzinger was highly critical of extrinsicism. He explicitly rejected the idea that it is possible to construct "a rational philosophical picture of man intelligible to all and on which all men of goodwill can agree, to which can be added the Christian doctrines as a sort of crowning conclusion."[12] He described such a theory as a "fiction," while Karl Rahner described the extrinsicist account of nature and grace upon which it is based as the "original and mortal sin of Jesuit theology," brought into the repertoire of Catholic theology by Francisco Suárez.[13] In the same essay Ratzinger was also critical of the tendency to distinguish between the Church and the world as though the two occupied two distinct ontological spaces. Consistent with both the Augustinian and classical Thomist tradition, he regards the Church as simply that part of the world which has been reconciled to Christ. As I. T. Eschmann noted, "however independent Church and State are [in classical Thomism] they do not escape being parts of one *res publica hominum sub Deo, principe universitatis.*"[14]

11. Schindler, "Religious Freedom," 79.

12. Ratzinger, "Commentary on the Introduction and Chapter 1," 119.

13. Rahner, *Faith in a Wintry Season*, 49.

14. I. T. Eschmann, "St Thomas on the Two Powers," 180.

AGAINST EXTRINSICISM

A new generation of Catholic political philosophers and theologians is emerging who prefer the Augustinian concept of the two cities to the Suárezian concept of the two ends and classical Thomist political thought to its Suárezian mutation. As William T. Cavanaugh has expressed the idea:

> Augustine does not map the two cities out in space, but rather projects them across time. The reason that Augustine is compelled to speak of two cities is not because there are some human pursuits that are properly terrestrial, and others that pertain to God, but simply because God saves in time. Salvation has a history, where climax is in the advent of Jesus Christ, but whose definitive closure remains in the future. Christ has triumphed over the principalities and powers, but there remains resistance to Christ's saving action. The two cities are not the sacred and profane sphere of life. The two cities are the already and the not yet of the Kingdom of God.[15]

According to Cavanaugh's reading of the intellectual and social history, the modern state arose not by secularizing politics but by supplanting the imagination of the body of Christ with a heretical theology of salvation through the state.[16] While modernity represents salvation through the state, postmodernity is coming to represent salvation through globalization. Cavanaugh has described the Murrayite project as "the self-disciplining of the Church's ability to make theological claims in public." The effect of Murray's extrinsicism is that "Christian symbols must be run through the sausage-grinder of social ethics before coming out on the other end as publicly digestible policy."[17]

Pope Benedict is thus critical of the various attempts to carve out of the world a space that is impervious to the sovereignty of Christ and of the various projects to link human development to economics and politics without reference to the human person's eternal destiny. To use the phrase of Robert Spaemann, he is not prepared for Christianity to become a "mere booth in the fairground of postmodernity." He believes that the Incarnation is an event that really did occur in human history

15. Cavanaugh, "From One City to Two."
16. Cavanaugh, *Theopolitical Imagination*, 5.
17. Ibid., 81.

and that it brought with it new prospects for human nature and society. It is not some Feuerbachian myth. In the collection of essays published in 1988 under the title *The Church, Ecumenism and Politics*, he noted with approval that the early Christians would not allow Christ to be included in the pantheon alongside the pagan gods.[18] This is not to be taken as the suggestion that Pope Benedict believes that the Catholic hierarchy should exercise any kind of juridical authority over the work of governments and their agencies, but it is to say that he believes that the sovereignty of Christ, in particular, the gifts of His grace, are not limited to certain domains of private social life or certain private institutions.

Another relationship which has been the subject of extrinsicist constructions that foster secularism is that of faith and reason. In this context in paragraph 30 of *Caritas in Veritate*, Pope Benedict makes the claim that "knowledge is never purely the work of the intellect." While "it can certainly be reduced to calculation and experiment," if it "aspires to be wisdom capable of directing man in the light of his first beginnings and his final ends, it must be 'seasoned' with the 'salt' of charity." Moreover, he emphasizes that Charity is not an added extra, like an appendix to work already concluded in each of the various disciplines: it engages them in dialogue from the very beginning. In effect "this means that moral evaluation and scientific research must go hand in hand, and that charity must animate them in a harmonious interdisciplinary whole, marked by unity and distinction."

The work of the intellect is thus assisted by faith and love, and also by the theological virtue of hope. In paragraph 34 of the encyclical, Pope Benedict wrote:

> Hope encourages reason and gives it the strength to direct the will. It is already present in faith, indeed it is called forth by faith. Charity in truth feeds on hope and, at the same time, manifests it. As the absolutely gratuitous gift of God, hope bursts into our lives as something not due to us, something that transcends every law of justice. Gift by its nature goes beyond merit, its rule is that of superabundance. It takes first place in our souls as a sign of God's presence in us, a sign of what he expects from us. Truth—which is itself gift, in the same way as charity—is greater than we are, as Saint Augustine teaches. Likewise the truth of ourselves, of our personal conscience, is first of all *given* to us. In every cognitive process, truth is not something that we produce, it is always

18. Ratzinger, *Church, Ecumenism and Politics*, 213–14.

found, or better, received. Truth, like love, "is neither planned nor willed, but somehow imposes itself upon human beings."

In this context Scot Armstrong has drawn attention to the significance of footnote 88 of *Caritas in Veritate* which expands on the above reference to St. Augustine. In this footnote Pope Benedict wrote:

> Saint Augustine expounds this teaching in detail in his dialogue on free will (*De libero arbitrio*, II, 3, 8ff.). He indicates the existence within the human soul of an "internal sense." This sense consists in an act that is fulfilled outside the normal functions of reason, an act that is not the result of reflection, but is almost instinctive, through which reason, realizing its transient and fallible nature, admits the existence of something eternal, higher than itself, something absolutely true and certain. The name that Saint Augustine gives to this interior truth is at times the name of God (*Confessions* X, 24, 35; XII, 25, 35; *De libero arbitrio* II, 3, 8), more often that of Christ (*De magistro* 11:38; *Confessions* VII, 18, 24; XI, 2, 4).

Armstrong observes that in *De libero arbitrio*, Augustine seems to go so far as to say that the "sense" actually identifies with the inner presence of the *Logos*! He concludes that "this would mean that the *Logos*/'Light which enlightens every man' (Jn1) is not just a capacity, but an initial presence destined to find its fullness in the *Logos/Sarx*"; and he further notes that this confirms not only the Nature-Grace position of Blondel and de Lubac, but provides an *etsi Deus daretur* approach to reason which would inevitably lead to the Reason in the light of which every reason operates. Such a *Logos* is *already* a *personal* presence, albeit radically in need of the fullness possible only through grace.[19]

Armstrong's reading of these references of Benedict XVI to Augustine is also consistent with the lecture Ratzinger delivered to the Bishops of Mexico in 1996 in which he explicitly rejected the Kantian idea of "pure reason" and with his commentary on *Gaudium et spes* in which he wrote that Augustine was well aware that the organ by which God can be seen cannot be a non-historical *ratio naturalis* which just does not exist, "but only the *ratio pura*, i.e. *purificata* [purified reason] or, as Augustine expresses it echoing the Gospel, the *cor purum* [the pure heart]."[20]

19. Armstrong, "Truth and Freedom."
20. Ratzinger, "Commentary on the Introduction and Chapter 1," 155.

Thus those who wish to argue that the Catholic tradition can be synthesized with the liberal are right to find this encyclical problematic. If liberal means resting on a Kantian epistemology, or a Suárezian construction of the orders of nature and grace, or an affirmation of the idea that the market is morally neutral, then *Caritas in Veritate* offers another point of view. As stated above, this other perspective rests on the explicitly Trinitarian anthropology of *Gaudium et spes* 22, with all the anti-extrinsicist orientations embedded within it.

CONCLUSION

In conclusion, within the academic discipline of Catholic social theory one can identify at least three, possibly four, groups. They might be broadly described as: (i) the liberation theologians or those strongly influenced by liberation theology even if they do not buy the whole package; (ii) the American Whigs; (iii) the *Communio* types, and then within the *Communio* camp there are subtle distinctions between those who arrive at their positions with egalitarian pre-dispositions and those of a more aristocratic orientation. The latter (one thinks of Aidan Nichols) combine the Tory sense of *noblesse oblige* with a reverence for the order of nature as a divine gift.

This notion of the beauty of the gift of creation and our responsibilities toward it is represented in the Catholic social justice tradition by the concept of the "stewardship of nature." A sensitivity to this is strong in the Franciscan and Dominican Orders. It is also strong in Anglo-Catholic spirituality with Prince Charles being an exemplary figure in this context. Indeed many of the Catholics who fit into this category are also strong monarchists since they appreciate the role of a royal family and an aristocracy which has the social strength to cut through the layers of middle-class pragmatism and reach the poor and those who are otherwise socially marginalized. In other words, the role of a Christian aristocracy such as it developed within Europe is primarily one of protecting and taking personal responsibility for the weak from a position of social privilege. Historically the middle classes have been too self-interested to do this and the "nanny state" tries to do it on behalf of the middle classes by fleecing them of ever increasing amounts of their income through the system of taxation. This system is notoriously impersonal and ineffectual.

Thus, there are those who might be described as "Turquoise Tories" (to borrow a term associated with Roger Scruton) who support institutions like the monarchy and aristocracy and combine this with a strong concern for the environment and a heavy personal involvement in charitable organizations, and there are those who are approaching social justice from a non-aristocratic position but who nonetheless reach very similar conclusions to the "Turquoise Tories" about the inadequacies of both the *laissez-faire* liberal and liberation theology alternatives. These two types have both published under the *Communio* banner. Regardless of where they stand on issues like the monarchy and the social value of a fully functional Christian aristocracy (which has its analogue in the American polity in groups such as the Knights of Columbus), they are in agreement that secularism arose from within the tradition of Christian theology itself, and that secularist approaches to welfare and social justice are ultimately inadequate and even sometimes inhumane.

It is precisely this last point that is so central to *Caritas in Veritate* and also the second half of *Deus Caritas Est*. Benedict XVI is trying to fight secularism in all of its various manifestations including that of secularist conceptions of social welfare and to emphasize the important personalist dimensions of economic exchange. This personalist dimension was strongly emphasized in the pre-papal writing of Karol Wojtyła and in his first social encyclical, *Laborem Exercens*.

The task of translating such high-minded visions of human labor and social development into really existing social practices remains a challenge for the currently emerging post-Conciliar generations. It will require the courage to look for a better way from the practices that got the United States and the Western world in general into its current economic crisis. Some people in the world of Catholic social welfare agencies will need to surrender their attachment to secular sociological theory, or at least enrich it with some theological anthropology; while others will need to learn that to take a critical look at the culture of America and its ideologies of development is not to be unpatriotic or impious. Some really great Americans have already had the courage to do this, including James Cardinal Stafford and Francis Cardinal George. While it is true that the Petrine office carries with it no particular expertise in the field of economics and the enterprise of making money, *Caritas in Veritate* was largely an attempt to set the Catholic endeavors in this field upon solid non-secularist anthropological foundations and to affirm the personalism of John Paul II in its application to the field of social welfare and human development.

The culture of America has been a liberal enterprise since its inception, and one might sympathize with some elements of it, such as the opposition to a tax on tea, but as Frederick Wilhelmsen wrote in *Christianity and Political Philosophy*: "There is another tradition (from the Whig) which runs back, like a narrow and straight road, through Chesterton and Belloc to the Tory-Radicalism of William Cobbett and beyond to the Cavaliers and to the King who died for England: there the road broadens into a great highway filled with the yeomen who rose in the Pilgrimage of Grace."[21] In addition to the gold and red crayons, one might also want to add a turquoise crayon. The platypus called Benedict is famously adept at creating his own works of art by reference to the best that the various traditions have on offer. *Caritas in Veritate* is such a synthetic work.

21. Wilhelmsen, *Christianity and Political Philosophy*, 99.

PART II

Christianity
and Socialism

3

"We Communists of the Old School"

Benedict's Encyclical and the Future of Christian Socialism

Eugene McCarraher

I know no previous instance in history of a nation's establishing a systematic disobedience to the first principles of its professed religion.

—John Ruksin, *Unto This Last* (1862)

ON "CHRISTIAN COMMUNISM" AND "CHRAPITALISM"

THOMAS CARLYLE ONCE FAMOUSLY dubbed economics "the dismal science," but Ruskin went his friend one better by denying that economics is a science at all. (That whatever it is, is still dismal, went without saying.) With a fine contempt that we've lost in our deference to the clerisy of the business schools, Ruskin declared his utter indifference to the banalities of the dismal science. "As in the case of alchemy,

89

astrology, witchcraft, and other such popular creeds," Ruskin mused in *Unto This Last*, "political economy has a plausible idea at the root of it": that human beings are motivated by self-interest. True, he conceded, but also trite and misleading, for men and women were more than the sums of jostling, acquisitive appetites. A human being, Ruskin reminded his readers, was "an engine whose motive power is a Soul"; and "the force of this very peculiar agent . . . enters into all the political economist's equations . . . and falsifies every one of their results." Because the humanism of "political economy" was so narrow and impoverished, Ruskin dismissed the discipline's claims to moral and intellectual authority. "I neither impugn nor doubt the conclusions of the science if its assumptions are accepted. I am simply uninterested in them, as I should be in those of a science of gymnastics which assumed that men had no skeletons."[1]

Restoring the soul to its rightful place at the heart of human identity, Ruskin envisioned a legitimate study of production, exchange, and consumption. Rooted in a genuine humanism, "the real science of political economy" instructs us to "desire and labor for the things that lead to life" and to "scorn and destroy the things that lead to destruction." Political economy was first and foremost an education in desire, for, in Ruskin's lovely and compelling phrase, "the desire of the heart is the light of the eyes." With transformed desires and pellucid eyes, we could discern the difference between "wealth"—"the possession of the valuable by the valiant"—and what Ruskin called "illth," that which wreaks "devastation and trouble in all directions." Just as Carlyle had once rued the "Enchantments" of the "Gospel of Mammonism," Ruskin aligned the deceptions of illth with the servility of "mammon service," the "accurate and irreconcilable opposite of God's service." Ruskin's renowned dictum that "THERE IS NO WEALTH BUT LIFE" drew its force from this moral and ontological distinction. Wealth partook of a sacramental realism in which everything "reaches into the infinite"; and as illth was,

---

1. Portions of this essay first appeared in a slightly different form in *Commonweal*, August 14, 2009. I have also included remarks from "Small Is Not Enough: A Critique of 'Sustainability,'" a talk given at Dominican University in Chicago in October 2008, and from the manuscript of a book I am completing, *The Enchantments of Mammon*. Thanks also to David Bentley Hart for recommending me as a contributor to this volume, and to Adrian Pabst for wisely taking his advice. For reading and commenting on drafts, I'd like to thank Matt Boudway, Paul Baumann, and Anthony Godzieba.

The opening epigram is from Ruskin, *Unto This Last*, 203. Ruskin, *Unto This Last*, 167–68, 170.

by implication, the possession of the worthless by the fearful, then it represented "ruin in the Economy of Heaven."[2]

A decade later, in open letters to industrial workers, Ruskin made unashamedly clear that this "Economy of Heaven" was communist. Calling himself "a Communist of the old school," Ruskin took a courageous stand on the roiling "social question" and rejected the "new school" communism of Marx, Engels, and other secular revolutionaries. Alluding to the Paris Commune, Ruskin feared that because the new school communists were too concerned with acquisition, their social order would degenerate into confusion and terror. Their attempt to create a "Common-Wealth" would become a "Common-Illth." Like the first Christians depicted in the book of Acts, "we Communists of the old school think that our property belongs to everybody, and everybody's property belongs to us." For the old school, charity as the form of the virtues coincided with gratuity as the form of economic life. Old-school communists thought of property in terms of self-expenditure, not accumulation. "We dark-red Communists exist only in giving."[3] For Ruskin, the real science of political economy was Christian communism.

Communism has almost certainly been relegated to the dustbin of political vocabulary. And it certainly seems that Ruskin lost the battle to discredit the dismal science. As one of our culture's "popular creeds," economics comes close to being our most rigid and uncontested form of orthodoxy. Indeed, with the apparent success of the cult of economics over the last generation, Ruskin's allusion to the spiritual arts seemed especially apt and portentous. During the *belle époque* of neo-liberalism that began in 1989, the *sacra doctrina* of the "Washington Consensus"— privatization, fiscal austerity, and de-regulation of business—beguiled not only politicians but the Western intelligentsia. For the last thirty years—until the latest systemic crisis began in the fall of 2008—corporate business almost utterly monopolized the symbolic universe of life in the West, as the iconography of capital achieved an unprecedented level of omnipresence. In advertising, marketing, and public relations; in management-speak and financial journalism; in the stream of stock prices that seemed to frame every image on cable news propaganda— business inscribed its commands and desires in the firmament of popular culture. The Market ascended into the ontological sublime; business

2. Ruskin, *Unto This Last*, 203, 209, 211, 222, 226; Carlyle, *Past and Present*, 144.

3. Ruskin, *Fors Clavigera*, "Letter Seven: Charitas," in *Unto This Last*, 294, 298, 301.

leaders rose into the pantheon of divinity; economists came into their own as the clerisy of a pecuniary civilization. With stock prices up and portfolios burgeoning, economics came into its own as the ethics and cosmology of a new world order.[4]

The market in cultural hegemony handled a brisk and voluminous trade, while the stalls abounded with entrepreneurs in the fashions of ideology, all hawking their wares in the rhetorical helium generated by the consciousness industries. Their business model was simple: fearlessly defend the rich and powerful as tribunes of the people; portray themselves and their clients as mavericks beleaguered by tree-hugging leftist throwbacks; pander to the info-glutted consumer of news and digitalized gadgetry. Dismissing opposition to business imperatives as the bray of losers or the economically illiterate, they celebrated corporate globalism as the hippest imperium in history. What millennium has ever been so cool? It was "the end of history," we were assured by the upscale merchants in millennial futures.[5] Bliss was it in that dawn to be start-up, and to go public was very heaven!

One might have thought that Christians would refrain from joining this mercenary jubilee. But the reigning attitude, among American believers, was militant, euphoric boosterism. From megachurches, think tanks, and foundations funded by pious employers of the minimum-waged, evangelical Protestants and Catholic conservatives rejoiced at the historic merger: "Chrapitalism," one could felicitously call it, the amalgamation of the Gospel of Christ with the Gospel of Mammonism. Under the sacred canopy of the "prosperity gospel" or a "theology of democratic capitalism," God and Mammon composed their differences and negotiated a lucrative partnership. Name it, claim it, God wants you to be rich! All those warnings about riches applied to the time *before we knew how to get wealthy.* (After all, He said poor *in spirit,* right? Wretched of the earth, I *feel* your pain.)[6]

---

4. Coming right in the middle of the latest Gilded Age, the finest account of these times is Frank, *One Market Under God.*

5. For examples, see Friedman, *Lexus and the Olive Tree*; Florida, *Rise of the Creative Class*; and anything by Malcolm Gladwell. The "end of history" was famously (mis)reported by Fukuyama, *End of History.*

6. On evangelical capitalism, see Connolly, *Capitalism and Christianity*; on the "theology of democratic capitalism," the classic statement is Novak, *Spirit of Democratic Capitalism*, 333–60.

Fearless defenders of the rich, well-armed, and incorporated *status quo*, the Chrapitalist clerics were an ecumenical lot—Richard John Neuhaus, Ted Haggard, Pat Robertson, and a host of lesser shills. At the Acton Institute, where neo-classical economics and scholastic philosophy enjoyed a closely chaperoned dalliance, Fr. Robert Sirico baptized the love child of Ayn Rand and St. Thomas Aquinas. (Now *there's* an ugly baby.) The most prolific cleric was Michael Novak, corporate theologian doing penance for his prodigal journey with the '60s left. The corporation, Novak informed us, is a "metaphor for the ecclesial community" and the "best secular analogue to the church." As a knock off of the Body of Christ that's buffeted by a resentful Cultural Elite, the corporation is a "Suffering Servant"—a poor oppressed creature who carries its cross all the way up the hill to the bank. And if you can't think of stocking Wal-Mart shelves as an *imitatio Christi*, you're a snooty egghead disdainful of Real People with degrees from the School of Hard Knocks.[7]

Now that the "best secular analogue to the church" is laying off parishioners, and now that Novak's and other brands of capitalist apologia stand revealed as faith-based buncombe, Pope Benedict XVI issues his encyclical *Caritas in Veritate*. Coming at a moment when neo-liberal ideology is more vulnerable than ever, Benedict's letter provides an opportunity to reissue Ruskin's challenge. It has all the perennial problems of the "social encyclical" tradition: a penchant for rhetorical obscurity that's rooted in political timidity; an apolitical and ahistorical approach to economics and technology; a reluctance to acknowledge the necessity of class conflict which issues in half-measures and compromises. But there's more in the document than moralizing twaddle about the latest ruling-class crime wave. At its best, *Caritas in Veritate* is a patristic text for a political economy of life. Against the mangy orthodoxies of scarcity and competition—"eternally, and in all things, the laws of death," in Ruskin's view—Benedict hints at abundance and friendship as the foundations of "the real science of political economy."[8]

While many commentators have compared the letter to earlier "social encyclicals"—and especially to *Populorum progressio* (1967)—I want to suggest that if *Caritas in Veritate* is to have any lasting impact, it will be as a catalyst for a Christian socialist economics. If that economic theology depends on a new ontology and humanism, we can do no better than

7. Novak, *Toward a Theology of the Corporation*, 29, 39.

8. Ruskin, *Unto This Last*, 202.

to examine the work of E. F. Schumacher and Father Herbert McCabe. Inhabiting different precincts of the intellectual world, the renegade economist and the socialist Dominican were not as far apart as their milieux may seem.

"Quotas of Gratuitousness and Communion": The Ontology of Scarcity, Competitive Humanism, and the Blunted Challenges of Benedict's Encyclical

The Realism of Charity of Truth

The title of Benedict's encyclical is simple but significant. The virtue of charity, Benedict argues, is inseparable from an account of the real world, without which it becomes "a pool of good sentiments": pleasant to wade in for a little while, but still shallow and ultimately stagnant. If love is a mere sentiment in a hardscrabble world of privation, then it's easily dismissed as a virtue of the callow, of those saintly few who've never contended with payrolls, schedules, and cost-cutting measures. But a charity that dwells in truth is a formidable realism. And the truth, Benedict maintains, is that love leavens the very architecture of creation; that creation is a realm of abundance; and that humanity is the image and likeness of a triune and infinitely loving God.[9]

By this standard of *realism*, "economics" stands exposed, not only as a dismal science, but as an insidious illusion, resting on a mangled metaphysics of scarcity and a humanism of belligerence. "Scarcity" is, of course, the ontological bedrock of conventional economics, and what a hard, implacable foundation it is. It's on page one of every textbook, day one of any introductory course. It's Genesis without the creation story— beginning in chapter three with the Fall—and it serves an invaluable disciplinary function in the moral imagination of capitalism. According to the dogma of scarcity, the world is a parched abode of stinginess and infinite want, and that harshness compels incessant labor that ceases only with death, retirement, or a killing in the market.

Scarcity has always been considered a curse of the human condition, but it didn't become an axiom of economic thinking until the eighteenth century, when its stony face appeared in the patristic texts of classical economics. In his *Essay on the Principle of Population* (1798),

---

9. See Benedict's *Deus Caritas Est* for his reflections on the theology of charity.

Rev. Thomas Malthus deemed material scarcity one of God's more in-
genious devices. Surveying the privation and struggle of the poor from
the comfort of his vicarage, Malthus had received one of history's nasti-
est epiphanies: "moral evil is absolutely necessary to the production of
good."[10] Starvation, drought, and other natural calamities are "instruments employed by the Deity" to promote hard work and ingenuity—
especially among the poor, whose taste for sexual delights struck the
reverend as the source of their misery. The reckless and improvident
rabble produced too many children for the world to feed, Malthus
reasoned; and since charity would sap initiative, and redistribution of
property would disturb God's wise arrangements of estate, the well-to-
do should resign themselves to the suffering of the lower orders. But
what about those starving children, especially the helpless infants? "The
infant is, comparatively speaking, of little value to society, as others will
immediately supply its place." (As Auden's Herod puts it, "really, the
world is admirably arranged.")

Malthus' near-contemporary, the economist Nassau Senior, insisted with even greater vehemence on the providential necessity of evil.
Scourge of trade unions, opponent of child labor laws, and defender of
the hungry from all misguided humanitarian measures, Senior lectured
the bleeding hearts of his day with the eloquence of an executioner.
"Nature has decreed that the road to good shall be through evil—that no
improvement shall take place in which the general good shall not be accompanied by partial suffering." As Boyd Hilton has documented, such
hosannahs to scarcity had an enormous impact, not only on the nascent
discipline of economics, but on the British evangelical social thought
that shaped government policy toward the Irish famine of the 1840s.

As one might expect, Americans put a more positive spin on the
dogma of scarcity. In *The Spirit of Democratic Capitalism* (1982)—one
of the *ur*-texts of contemporary Chrapitalism—Novak transforms the
skinflint vision of life into a romantic religious quest. The passage is
worth quoting at length, as it captures the cruel and clueless nihilism at
the core of establishment economics:

> The "wasteland" at the heart of capitalism is a field of battle, on
> which individuals wander alone, in some confusion, amid many

10. In this and the following paragraph, the quotes from Malthus and Senior can be
found in McNally, *Against the Market*, 80–81, 85. On the Irish Famine, see Hilton, *Age
of Atonement*, esp. 108–14, 248–50.

> casualties . . . like the dark night of the soul in the inner journey
> of the mystics, the desert has an indispensable purpose . . . [it is]
> the sphere of the transcendent, to which the individual has access
> through the self, beyond the mediations of social institutions.

This is Thomas Hobbes decked out as St. John of the Cross. It couldn't be more apparent that capitalism rests on an ontology of violence, anomie, and death. As Kelly Johnson sharply observes, capitalism is a "just-war theory of economics": every man and woman is a mercenary, a soldier of fortune hardened to the inexorable misery of collateral damage.[11]

Benedict implies that the dogma of scarcity is a calumny against creation. "Nature," he writes in *Caritas in Veritate*, "speaks to us of the Creator and his love of humanity." God is a spendthrift, supremely indifferent to our fearful property lines. "Earth, water, and air [are] gifts of creation that belong to everyone." This metaphysics of gift underlies Benedict's endorsement of "economic activity marked by quotas of gratuitousness and communion." No business school homilies about scarcity there, no Malthusian theodicy for a stingy world and its mean-spirited Deity. Since capitalist humanism is rooted in "scarcity," it's equally sinister and illusory. It's the laborious cant of the Work Ethic, the sado-moralism of management writers like Steven Covey and of preachers like Rick Warren, aiming to turn us into "effective people" with "purpose-driven lives." In its anthropology of competition, economics enshrines Augustine's restless heart as an ideal, not a malady; as an engine of labor and accumulation, not a longing for contemplative peace. Benedict implicitly rejects this competitive humanism as a desecration of the human person. "The human creature is defined through interpersonal relations," he writes in *Caritas in Veritate*—not in the arena of clashing autonomies that requires a "just-war theory of economics." Against individualism—against what Charles Mathewes has called society "as a collection of solitudes"[12]—Benedict poses "a metaphysical interpretation of the '*humanum*' in which relationality is an essential element." To put it (I hope) more elegantly, the ever-flowing love that enlivens the Trinity is the model of human life. No Trinitarian theology speaks of competition among the Persons—does the Spirit compete with the Father and Son to "improve" the "performance" of all three? Does each Person calculate the marginal utility of each procession in the divine economy? Here we

11. Novak, *Spirit of Democratic Capitalism*, 348; Johnson, *Fear of Beggars*, 215.

12. Mathewes, *Theology of Public Life*, 120; Ratzinger, *Introduction to Christianity*.

should recall, not only *Deus caritas est*, but *Introduction to Christianity* (1968), in which then-Father Ratzinger wrote that "only the lover can understand the folly of a love to which prodigality is a law and excess alone is sufficient."

The triune God is not a miser, or a manager obsessed with efficiency. Like an artist or a lover, God creates out of sheer delight, lavishing abundance without regard for measure or repayment. God is not only profligate, but utterly indifferent to the equivalences demanded by bourgeois economic justice: return love for hatred, blessings for curses, prayers for indignity and mistreatment. Most left-wing Christians will rightly welcome this riposte to competitive humanism, but it also contains a challenge to one of the most precious progressive shibboleths: "if you want peace, work for justice." That's a comforting cliché among the middlebrow left, easily attachable to a bumper sticker in the interest of self-righteous display. But if love is the form of the virtues, and if love is nothing if not unmeasured, then that tiresome twaddle gets things exactly backwards. If you want justice, work for peace; or better, if you want peace and justice, love your neighbors.

Benedict's peaceful ontology and humanism pervades the trenchant sections on the environment and technology. In Benedict's view, charity must define the necessarily but not exclusively technological relationship between humanity and the rest of the natural world. Recalling the biblical charge given to humans to replenish the earth and subdue it, Benedict notes that technology cannot be a mere instrument of power. As an indispensable form of human action, technology should "enforce the covenant between human beings and the environment," Benedict intones, but he reminds us that this covenant "should mirror God's creative love." If designed and employed in charity, technology will afford, not only survival, comfort, and beauty, but also "an encounter with being and truth." There can be, this implies, a sacramental technology, one that transforms labor into liturgy by enhancing knowledge, skill, and sensibility in the use of creation. Benedict's remarks represent a welcome advance, I think, over John Paul II's *Laborem exercens* (1987), in which nature is too often cast as humanity's splendiferous workbench.

Though Lynn White's notorious thesis about the Christian origins of ecological destruction is now considered overwrought, its power and persistence owe much to the fact that "subduing the earth" has been one of the most aggressively misunderstood phrases in Genesis. Taken as a license to plunder the planet—especially by evangelical Protestants fond of the Work Ethic and dubious about global warming—the charge to "subdue" has become a warrant for the most reckless and willfully ignorant sanctimony.[13]

That shouldn't surprise anyone, given that, as Benedict observes, "the way humanity treats the environment influences the way it treats itself, and vice versa." As our current and impending ecological turbulence demonstrates, the nature of our technological mastery will always mirror the human condition, loving or exploitative. Echoing Marx's reflections on work, nature, and objectification in the "economic and philosophic manuscripts," Benedict writes that "man recognizes himself and forges his own humanity" in part by technical means. If so, then what he recognizes in the mirror may well frighten him. Wherever technology embodies a sheer will to power—as it does, in Benedict's opinion, in the realm of bio-technology—it will "flounder in an illusion of its own omnipotence."

The Shortcomings of Benedict's Social Encyclical

As suggestive as *Caritas in Veritate* can be of a new, non-capitalist economics, it falls short on several counts. Of course, papal encyclicals are not manifestos, and the Vicar of Christ is not God's Policy Wonk. Still, like his predecessors in the social encyclical tradition, Benedict engages in too much euphemism and circumlocution. For one thing, such mealy-mouthedness lays open Benedict to the charge, leveled by Slavoj Žižek, that the letter is "a disgusting spectacle of cheap moralization." That's overwrought but not entirely off-base, as it points to the murkiness of passages in which, for instance, the Pope muses that "the market can be a negative force, not because it is so by nature, but because a certain ideology can make it so."

"Market" is one of those words that always requires an adjective in front of it, as Benedict seems to recognize when he adds "certain ideology." Why not just say *capitalist*? Clearly, the specter of Marxism still haunts the papal imagination. That's understandable, I suppose, but it's also unfortunate, because the only way to dispel a specter is to bring it into the light of day. Despite all the controversies over "liberation theology" since the 1960s—controversies which, truth be told, the current Pope

---

13. White, "Historical Roots of Our Ecologic Crisis."

did his utmost to quash and not to resolve—Christian theology has yet to really confront and assimilate the Marxist tradition. Theologians and popes should take it as a sign of strength when Marxists such as Žižek, Alain Badiou, and Terry Eagleton are busy drawing upon theology.[14]

Benedict's reluctance to call capitalism by its name is also evident in his call for a "new way of understanding business enterprise" that balances capital accumulation with "social responsibility." This is the palaver of Starbucks, NGOs, and Muhammed Yunus. It's the bray of the Servant Leader, shepherding his Soulful Corporation into the valley of morally uncontaminated profits. At the risk of saying I Wish He'd Consulted Me About This, I could only say to Benedict that, as a historian, I've seen this movie before, and I know how it ends. In the 1920s, it was "Service"; in the 1950s, it was "Social Responsibility"; now, it's still "Social Responsibility," aided by discursive attendants such as "Diversity," "Sustainability," or some future buzzword *du jour*.[15] In one brand or other, "social responsibility" has always been the highest form of professional and managerial ideology, the *noblesse oblige* of the corporate elite, the opium of the bourgeoisie. Highlighting the *policies* of corporations rather than their *governance* and *political structures*, "social responsibility" distracts attention from class relations and property forms. And because it leaves unaddressed what used to be called "the social question," it obscures the object of "social responsibility" itself. Responsible, we should ask, to what kind of society? Benedict's imaginative parsimony is even more painful when he hedges about gratuity. What's that again about quotas of gratuitousness and communion? That's the one hand keeping constant surveillance on what the other is doing. When Benedict asserts that "the principle of gratuitousness and the logic of gift" must "find their place within normal economic activity," that "normal" signals a capitulation to the logic of incessant accumulation. Why not call for gift exchange as the new normal economic activity?

A similar shortcoming appears in the much-ballyhooed section on technology. Benedict's salutary warning about the promethean temptations of technological ingenuity can degenerate into a determinist form of obscurantism. "When technology is allowed to take over," he

14. Žižek, *Puppet and the Dwarf*; Žižek and Milbank, *Monstrosity of Christ*, 24–109; Badiou, *Saint Paul*; Eagleton, *Reason, Faith, and Revolution*.

15. I trace the evolution of what I call "corporate humanism" in my forthcoming *The Enchantments of Mammon*.

writes, "the result is confusion between means and ends, such that the sole criterion for action in business is thought to be the maximization of profit." The "confusion" there is, I think, in Benedict's mind, and it's a confusion that's been endemic to critics of technology from Martin Heidegger and Jacques Ellul to deep ecologists and eco-feminists. As Lewis Mumford, Harry Braverman, David Dickson, David F. Noble, or many other scholars could point out, "technology" is never "allowed" to "take over": rather, human beings use technology to further interests, and they can use it in such overweening and disastrous ways that the technology, and not the human interests, becomes the object of fear and obloquy.[16] Moreover, profit maximization is not "thought" to be the "sole criterion for action in business": under capitalism, it *is* the sole criterion, a fact underlined by the statutory mandate in U.S. law that *requires* corporations to consider shareholder equity the only legitimate standard of business conduct. And to bring these objections together, the design and use of technology in capitalist settings is always for the purposes of profit maximization. *Technology* has never taken over; rather, capital has taken over the planning and implementation of technological development. Automation has been enforced, not by an army of wild machines, but by the echelons of corporate managers and professionals charged with expanding the accumulation of capital. It's true, as many technophobic critics opine, that technology is "never neutral"; but to stop there is to abort the indispensable task of investigating *whose* interests it serves. Those who blame "technology" for many of our woes only distract, albeit unwittingly, from the necessary *political* struggles over the ends and means of production, communication, and science.

But it's painfully clear that this Pope, like his predecessors, rues the prospect of social and political conflict, and this reluctance to acknowledge the necessity of struggle lames the impact of *Caritas in Veritate*. It's not that Benedict doesn't see the reality of antagonism, or that he wants the capitalists to win. He's not the cheerfully odious Warren Buffett, who once observed when the economic crisis began, "Of course there's a class struggle, and my side is winning."[17] Like earlier pontiffs, he insists on the need for labor unions to protect the rights of workers. He enjoins labor

---

16. Heidegger, "Question Concerning Technology," 307–42; Ellul, *Technological Society*; Braverman, *Labor and Monopoly Capital*; Dickson, *Politics of Alternative Technology*; Noble, *Progress Without People*.

17. Warren Buffett quoted in Stein, "Class Warfare."

unions to be bastions of solidarity, and even implies that they should enlarge their ambitions beyond wages and benefits: unions, he writes, should address "wider concerns than the specific category of labor for which they were formed." Protecting rights, fostering solidarity, and addressing "wider concerns" are inescapably matters of class conflict under capitalism; but like so many Catholic natural lawyers, Benedict is so committed to an ontology of harmony that he has a hard time taking history seriously. One of the persistent features of the social encyclical tradition has been blindness to the fact that class conflict is *endemic* to capitalism, or to any other class society, for that matter. Class struggle is not a product of envy, or a moral lapse, or a Big Misunderstanding; it's the inexorable result of a society in which the means of production are owned and controlled by a few. Because it's an indelible element of the system, class conflict can't be resolved by prayer, or homilies, or sympathetic understanding. With capitalism—as with feudalism and all previous class societies—class conflict will end only with the abolition of the system that makes such struggle inevitable.

Here again, the inability to confront the Marxist specter leads to a lack of political seriousness. Aside from Marxist atheism, the prospect of violent revolution and repression has bedeviled the papal economists. For all the indisputable historical reasons, this is not an irrational fear. But with the demise of Marxism, must the "utopian" imagination be suppressed? Do Christians in particular have nothing to offer but a holier resignation? Is not a theory of peaceful revolution one of the urgent political assignments of our age? As rich as they are, neither Benedict's letter nor the other papal epistles can deliver such a vision. For that, we must look elsewhere, to the more diffuse and motley lineage of Christian socialism.

"THE ULTIMATE REVOLUTION": THE ONTOLOGY OF ABUNDANCE, THE HUMANISM OF FRIENDSHIP, AND THE PROMISE OF CHRISTIAN SOCIALISM

The Long Tradition of Christian Socialism

While most commentators have compared Benedict's letter to earlier "social encyclicals," it should also be read in the light of a wider tradition in Christian economic thought. As John Milbank has demonstrated, *socialism*—Ruskin's communism of the old school—began as a Christian attempt to blend industrial modernity and workers' democracy with the bonding element of *agape*. Far from being what Marx and Engels vilified as "the heartburn of the aristocrat," what later had to be specified as *Christian* socialism emerged from among threatened artisans, industrial workers, and dissident clergy, intellectuals, and professionals, many of whom looked to medieval guilds as models for a beloved community of production. Often derided as tepid and reformist, Christian socialists were among the more visionary and thoroughgoing radicals of the left, advocating direct worker control over production and technology; a recasting of unions as updated versions of medieval guilds; the decentralization of state power; a more harmonious and ecologically sensible relationship between countryside and city; and an alignment of moral and aesthetic criteria for the just evaluation of goods and their distribution ("the possession of the valuable by the valiant").[18]

As yet, no historian has attempted to rewrite the history of socialism in the light of this Christian origin. Milbank's historical account of Christian socialism ends in the mid-nineteenth century with Ruskin, though he seems to want to include the "distributist" lineage of G. K. Chesterton, Hilaire Belloc, and Eric Gill, among others. Yet the Christian socialist tradition extends right down through the twentieth century, and calls for its "renewal" must rest on a retrieval of that historical memory. There are threads that tie together, for instance, the distributist "religion of small property," preached not only by the Chesterbelloc but by Dorothy Day's Catholic Worker movement; R. H. Tawney's Anglican socialism; Simone Weil's "eucharistic" anarcho-syndicalism; and E. F. Schumacher's "Buddhist economics," which was always (and not so covertly) Catholic. Schumacher's work, especially, represents both a milestone in the history of Christian socialist thought and an invaluable complement to *Caritas in Veritate*. The most important of all their affinities were an ontology of peace and a humanism of friendship that rejected the dogmas of capitalist economics.

Today, cultural conservatives lay claim to the distributist estate, often affirming its support for patriarchy, tradition, and a "romance of orthodoxy." Together with paeans to C. S. Lewis and J. R. R. Tolkein, homage to the Chesterbelloc forms a repertoire of anti-modernism. When neo-liberals such as Novak invoke the distributists, they invariably laud

18. Milbank, "Were the 'Christian Socialists' Socialists?" 63–74.

the movement's aversion to the "servile"—read welfare—"state." What's lost in both of these readings (especially the latter) is the distributist opposition to capitalism, an inconvenient truth airbrushed out of history as effectively as Trotsky from old Bolshevik photographs. For one thing, as even a cursory reading of Belloc or Chesterton reveals, the "servile state" referred, not just to "big government," but to the entire corporate order of proletarianized labor, centralized production, and merely stockholder property. But more significant for our purposes is that what Chesterton anointed as "the religion of small property" rested on a sacramental theology of economics that exposed the ontology of capitalism as fundamentally false and empty. Chesterton saw the illusory metaphysics of capitalism exemplified in the stockbroker. "A very poetical figure," the broker composes his ethereal verse in the rhetoric and meter of money, which never quite sates the fleshly desire for the prosaic delights of matter. Reduced to ciphers in the poetry of avarice, material objects pass before brokers like "mere scrolls of symbols." Matter does not matter for these rarefied bards, so inaptly condemned as materialists. Turning things into airy and profitable phantoms, stockbrokers were masters in the pecuniary transubstantiation of matter. Against these bards and wizards of Mammon, Chesterton defended the material world as a realm of sacramental goodness. Needing "something that is always on the spot," they require, Chesterton wrote in sacramental fashion, "a real presence." People who truly cherish the world revere it as a realm of "holy things," in Eric Gill's words, "things in which and by which God is manifest." Thus, "to labor is to pray," Gill thought; labor is a "training of persons for the end envisaged by religion . . . to see all things in God."[19]

The English distributist religion of small property had American missionaries among the Catholic Workers. Led by Dorothy Day and Peter Maurin, the Catholic Workers appeared in the depths of the Depression, and still serve as holy fools of poverty and peace for an American Church now largely corrupted by middle-class nationalism. Aiming in part to undercut support for Communists among the urban working class, the Workers melded Catholic theology and anarcho-syndicalist demands for direct worker control of production and the eradication of wage labor. As Day, Maurin, and countless other writers maintained

19. On the "servile state" as the corporate order, see Belloc, *Servile State*, 81–101; on the "religion of small property," see Chesterton, *Outline of Sanity*, 184–93, esp. 188–90; Gill, *Sacred and Secular*, 39.

in the movement's periodical, the *Catholic Worker*, the restoration of a sacramental quality to work and technology was a religious as well as a political enterprise. "Using mind and brain to work on beautiful objects," Day wrote, the artisan or farmer especially cultivated "a sense of the sacramentality of things, the holiness, the symbolism of things." The craftsman's loving proximity to matter fostered a deeper intimacy with the divine that partook of "God's creative activity."[20]

Unfortunately, the craft and farming communities that the Workers set up to live out their sacramentalist vision failed abysmally—mainly, I think, because of larger systemic forces that will overwhelm any localized attempt to escape the logic of the capitalist market. Still, their critique of secular radicalism and their decentralist alternative remain indispensable to any renovation of economics. Because, in the Workers' view, Marxists accepted proletarianization as a painful but necessary stage in the historical trajectory toward communism, they practiced an "idolatry of the machine" which only further entrenched the alienation that paralyzed radical political action. Since they based their own opposition to industrial capitalism on a conception of the person as a "Temple of the Holy Ghost," it was "on these grounds," Day explained, that personalists recoiled from the separation of mental and manual labor and called for a genuinely revolutionary transformation of the system. Indeed, the Workers' sacramental theology of economics sanctioned and even mandated a democratic transfiguration of production more thoroughgoing than Marxists could allow, given their commitment to the "inexorable" logic of capitalist development. The Workers allowed for a variety of property forms; as Day summarized their program—a bricolage of distributist proprietorship and anarcho-syndicalist communism—the Workers advocated "ownership by the workers of the means of production, the abolition of the assembly line, decentralized factories, the restoration of crafts, and ownership of property."[21]

Although he placed more faith in conventional politics than the Chesterbelloc or the Catholic Workers, Tawney—a revered stalwart of the Labour Party—adhered to a similar theology of economics. Like the secular G. D. H. Cole, Tawney recoiled from the state centralization favored by Sidney and Beatrice Webb and others in the Fabian Society. Also like Cole, Tawney acknowledged debts to Ruskin; to the medieval-

20. Day, *Long Loneliness*, 191.
21. Ibid., 225.

ism of William Morris; to the Christian Socialist League, the Guild of St. Matthew, and other Anglicans on the pre-World War I left; and to the guild movement led by G. R. S. Taylor, Arthur Penty, and the *New Age* circle. A product of the Balliol-Toynbee Hall nexus that gave Britain many of its Christian socialists, Tawney maintained that the point of socialism was, in Ruskin's terms, valiance in wealth, not wallowing in illth. His deepest fear was that, bereft of a religious spirit, socialism would end up being little more than the equitable distribution of illth. "As long as the working classes believe, and believe rightly, that their mentors rob them," he wrote just after an upsurge of industrial unrest in 1912, "so long will they look on the restoration of the booty as *the* great reform, and will impatiently waive aside more fundamental issues."[22]

Later, in his trilogy of Christian socialism—*The Acquisitive Society* (1920), *Religion and the Rise of Capitalism* (1926), and *Equality* (1931) —Tawney made the case for a socialist democracy in which charity and justice were the leaven of industry. Like Gill, Tawney lauded the medieval economic imagination, in which work and goods were judged in the light of the beatific vision. Surveying the wisdom of scholastic philosophers and canon lawyers, Tawney reclaimed their conviction that "the ideal— if only man's nature could rise to it—is communism," since sharing in communion was the order of heaven. Seen in this light, corporate capitalist property and production were grotesque distortions of the divine economy. Against the corporate order which protected stockholders and other parasitic classes who merely *owned* and lived off the labor of others, modern Christian socialism would, Tawney hoped, revive an older conception of property as "an aid to creative work, not an alternative to it." Artfully made and justly distributed, material goods could be tokens of beatitude, "aids to blessedness," as Tawney put it.[23]

22. Tawney, *R. H. Tawney's Commonplace Book*, 61. Tawney kept this journal from the spring of 1912 until shortly after Christmas 1914. While Ross Terrill suggested in his biography of Tawney that the historian's Anglicanism was earnest but intellectually undeveloped, the *Commonplace Book* suggests theological acuity and depth.

23. Tawney, *Religion and the Rise of Capitalism*, 35; *Acquisitive Society*, 52–83 (59). Often admired but now rarely consulted, Tawney's work deserves a spirited revival. His historical account of religion and capitalism is richer and more astute than Max Weber's, and his socialist vision is far more than the moralistic palaver that Raymond Williams and the young Alasdair MacIntyre thought it was. Williams judged Tawney venerable but analytically unsatisfying in *Culture and Society 1780–1950*, 216–26. In his youthful Marxist phase, Alasdair MacIntyre dismissed Tawney in *Against the Self-Images of the Age*, 38–42. "Goodness is not enough," MacIntyre concluded —a point that Tawney would have gladly affirmed.

Tawney's affirmation of the beatific ideal was echoed by Simone Weil, the anarcho-syndicalist and spiritual nomad whose fascination never ceases to wane. Always a contrarian on the French left, Weil was a brilliant and vociferous critic of Marxist progressivism and scientism, preferring a position on what Lenin had once denounced as the "infantile left" of anarchists and syndicalists. In the mid-1930s, Weil spent time working in the Paris Renault plant, where she encountered both the degradations of Fordist labor and the possibilities of working-class solidarity. Over the course of the 1930s and 1940s, she turned from secular radicalism to a theology of labor and technology, contending that, along with art and science, work and technics were sacramental points of "contact with the divine order of the universe." When thought and action were united in the workplace, laborers touched "the reality, truth, and beauty of the universe and the eternal wisdom which is the order in it." When skilled workers assembled to complete a task, it was "a fine sight," she marveled, to see them assess the problem, make individual suggestions, and then "apply unanimously the method conceived by one of them, who may or may not have any official authority over the rest." In such free association, where mental and manual labor were wedded and no distinct managerial cadre reigned, a type of person emerged who could "see in every work-fellow another self occupying another post, and would love him in the way that the Gospel maxim enjoins." While certain passages on agrarian life in *The Need for Roots* (1943) would seem to align Weil with the distributists, she never believed that a sacramental humanism mandated any primacy of the rural. "A plant or factory could fill the soul through a powerful awareness of collective life."

Like the Chesterbelloc and the Catholic Workers, Weil exhibited a profoundly sacramental understanding of human labor, so deep that she compared its management and automation to the most horrific act of blasphemy. "It is a sacrilege to degrade labor," she wrote, "in exactly the same sense as it is sacrilege to trample upon the Eucharist."[24]

Because of her unchurched Christianity, and thanks to the aura of her personal austerity, Weil gradually became an iconic spiritual figure among the Western literati after her death in 1943—"our kind of saint," as the literary critic Leslie Fiedler dubbed her in 1952—and her social thought went into abeyance. Yet her thinking on work and technology,

24. Weil, *Oppression and Liberty*, 101, 168; "Factory Work," 369; "Human Personality," in *Selected Essays*, 185.

while obscured, was not entirely forgotten, and in conjunction with Day's Catholic Workerism, it galvanized the postwar stage of religious personalism. Meanwhile, Weil also appealed to New Left students disenchanted by the embrace of unbounded industrial development by Marxists and social democrats. The English translation and publication in the early 1970s of Weil's Depression-era writings was part of a wave of discontent with the social and ecological consequences of scientific and technological hubris. Many critics of industrial modernity who were popular at the time—Paul Goodman, Ivan Illich, Lewis Mumford, and Theodore Roszak, to name just a few—were also critics of the secular, technocratic, and managerial consciousness sponsored quite literally by corporate capitalism.[25]

The Meta-Economic Revolution of E. F. Schumacher

This movement helped to clear a path for the British economist E. F. Schumacher. Often dismissed as a guru for the Birkenstock-and-granola set, Schumacher was, for much of his life, an impeccably Establishment figure. Born in Germany, he studied economics at Berlin, Oxford, and Columbia. He was a protégé of John Maynard Keynes, who drew on Schumacher's ideas for his own recommendations to the 1944 Bretton Woods financial summit. After working on the British Control Commission which guided German economic recovery, Schumacher became chief economist for the National Coal Board, a post he held until 1970.[26]

During his tenure at the Coal Board, Schumacher grew increasingly disillusioned with conventional economic policy. While travelling to Burma and India several times during the 1950s and 1960s, Schumacher decided that Western-style "modernization" projects in "underdeveloped" countries were socially and ecologically destructive. In his view, enormous investments in advanced industrial technology not only perpetuated dependence on capitalist nations but also ruined the soil and desecrated the skills and dignity of ordinary people. At the same time, Schumacher came to see that Western nations themselves were reaping the harvest of their own industrialization: urban congestion,

25. Fiedler, *Waiting for God*, ix; Goodman and Goodman, *Communitas*; Illich, *Tools for Conviviality*; Mumford, *Myth of the Machine: Vol. I* and *The Myth of the Machine, Vol. II*; Rozsak, *Where the Wasteland Ends*.

26. Wood, *E. F. Schumacher: His Life and Thought*, 1–104. Wood's biography of her father is invaluable but, for obvious reasons, also largely uncritical.

suburban ugliness, pollution, technological glut, anomie in the midst of consumer abundance. Although Schumacher had long been associated with the Labour Party, he recoiled from the technophilia of Harold Wilson's government. Increasingly convinced that Wilson's "white heat of technology" was melting down everything lovely and valuable in human life, Schumacher embarked on a new career as activist and seer. In 1966, together with other disgruntled economists, technical specialists, and politicians, he founded the Intermediate Technology Development Group (ITDG, now Practical Action), dedicated to moving both underdeveloped and eventually over-developed nations away from capital-intensive, large-scale technologies toward smaller, human-scale technics. After leaving the Coal Board, he joined and later assumed the presidency of the Soil Association, the respected advocacy group for local organic farming. And he became a trustee of the Scott Bader Commonwealth, a cooperative enterprise set up on Quaker principles of equality and pacifism. Established in 1921, the Commonwealth instituted employer-employee common ownership and control; controlled the conditions of its own expansion; and prohibited the making or sale of any of its products for purposes of war.[27]

While Schumacher was pursuing this alternative path, he was reading widely in Hindu, Buddhist, and Roman Catholic literature: Gandhi, Ananda Coomaraswamy, J. C. Kumarappa (a philosopher and economist), St. Teresa of Avila, and Thomas Merton, as well as Chesterton, Belloc, and McNabb. Shortly before he brought together the reflections of a lifetime in his classic *Small Is Beautiful* in 1973, Schumacher converted to Catholicism. This little-known piece of intellectual history puts the "Buddhist economics" for which he's known in an entirely different light. First, it shows that Schumacher's spiritual pilgrimage was inseparable from his infidelity to the canons of his discipline. When Schumacher blasphemed what he called "the religion of economics," he was not engaging in mere rhetorical flourish. But his conversion also suggests that a genuine albeit underdeveloped Catholic theology propelled Schumacher's quest, cut short by his sudden death in 1977, for a new ontology and humanism of economics. The term "Buddhist economics" obscured Schumacher's numerous references to the Beatitudes, the Epistles, scholastic philosophers, and papal encyclicals. Schumacher himself conceded that he'd misrepresented his position, telling an interviewer shortly after

27. Ibid., 120–35, 228–39.

the book's publication that "I might have called it 'Christian Economics,' but then no one would have read it."[28] Given the historical conflation of Christianity and capitalism, as well as the interest among youth in Asian religions as an alternative, that was a clever but too effective ruse. But with the passage of almost forty years, it's arguably well past time for us to highlight and learn from Schumacher's Christian socialism.

Schumacher's work was enlisted so quickly in debates about energy and ecology that its assault on *economics* was easily overlooked. To be sure, Schumacher did urge developed nations to drastically curtail their dependence on oil; he did campaign against nuclear power and other grandiose technologies; and he did advocate a "non-violent" approach to nature that echoed the rising "green" movements in the North Atlantic. On all of these issues, Schumacher proved prophetic, and the veracity of his foresight makes reclaiming his wisdom all the more urgent in the face of a discredited but still arrogant neo-liberalism. But if we do, it will be essential to recall that Schumacher's concerns about fossil fuels and natural despoliation provoked him to denounce and reconstruct his discipline. More than any other danger facing humanity, environmental devastation called "the entire outlook and methodology of economics into question," he asserted. The "narrow and fragmentary" approach to reality inscribed in economics would prove catastrophic, Schumacher warned, unless it was "completed by a study of meta-economics."[29]

Though Schumacher never defined this term with any precision, "meta-economics" appeared to provide a sketch of the larger ontological and ethical framework within which an economics proper would make sense. As things currently stood, Schumacher explained, the "sort of meaning the method of economics actually produces" was wholly pecuniary: "something is uneconomic if it fails to earn an adequate profit in terms of money." Really existing economics treats goods "in accordance with their market value and not in accordance with what they really are." Yet what goods "really are" was determined by whether they are "man-made or God-given . . . freely reproducible or not." The capitalist market must disregard *these* meta-economic distinctions as irrelevant and even

28. Fager, "Small Is Beautiful, and So Is Rome," 325; on "Buddhist economics," see Schumacher, *Small is Beautiful*, 50–58. Schumacher himself told readers that "the choice of Buddhism for this purpose is purely incidental: the teachings of Christianity, Islam, or Judaism could have been used just as well" (49).

29. Schumacher, *Small Is Beautiful*, 40, 49.

as potential sources of inefficiency, as they might hinder the creation of exchange value essential to capital accumulation. Schumacher had no doubt that capitalist economics had its own brand of meta-economics: "Western materialism," as he dubbed it, the reduction of everything to manipulable, vendable matter. As Chesterton, Gill, or Day might object, a sacramental theology of economics should dispute the "materialism" of this so-called materialism. Still, this fundamentally "metaphysical position" provided the criterion for economic conduct, and determined that the natural world is nothing else but a "quarry for exploitation." Thus, Schumacher traced the ecological and economic crises of our time to metaphysical ignorance. The West's "absence of metaphysical aware-ness"—its blindness to the fundamental realities of the world—enabled it to pursue unlimited economic growth at the literal expense of hu-man and non-human nature. "We are suffering from a metaphysical disease," Schumacher rued, and "the cure must therefore be metaphysi-cal." Without forsaking the indispensable projects of social and politi-cal transformation, restive youth must undertake an even grander and deeper revolution. "The task of our generation," Schumacher declared, "is one of metaphysical reconstruction."[30]

Sadly, Schumacher himself never completed this assignment, and we can only infer the import of his own attempts at the "metaphysical reconstruction" of economics. In my view, Schumacher was beckoning toward an economics based on an ontology of gift, peace, and abun-dance and on a humanism of friendship and charity. The world itself was "God-given," and one of the first lessons we had to relearn was that we are infinite debtors: "we are poor, not demi-gods." Bestowed on us by a loving God, nature, rather than being a quarry, was a nurturing and salu-brious home, pervaded by the presence of divinity. In *Small is Beautiful*, for instance, Schumacher alluded to Paul's eschatological remarks about nature in Romans when he observed that "the living environment . . . aches and groans and gives signs of partial breakdown" under pressure from our technological rapacity. By contrast, Schumacher praised the ITDG and the Soil Association for promoting manufacturing and agri-cultural technologies that exhibited "non-violence and humility towards the infinitely subtle system of natural harmony." In *Good Work* (1979), a posthumously published collection of essays, Schumacher derided mechanized production for violating the transcendentals: mechanical

30. Ibid., 29, 40, 46–47, 50, 86, 93–94.

methods, he observed, bear "no element of Beauty, Truth, or Goodness." Perhaps the most provocative and seminal mite of wisdom came at the conclusion of *A Guide for the Perplexed* (1977), which Schumacher finished shortly before his death and which he considered his *magnum opus*. With its title borrowed from Maimonides's twelfth-century treatise on philosophy and theology, it's a wide-ranging and altogether magpie rumination, but it all converges in the end on a rejection of the onto-logical basis of economics. Indeed, Schumacher's declaration of apostasy from the "religion of economics" could not have been more lucid and forceful. "The generosity of the Earth allows us to feed all mankind," he wrote. "We know enough about ecology to keep the Earth a healthy place; there is enough room on the Earth, and there are enough materi-als, so that everybody can have adequate shelter; we are quite competent enough to produce sufficient supplies of necessities so that no one need live in misery . . . we know how to provide *enough* and do not require any violent, inhuman, aggressive technologies to do so." In fact, Schumacher stated boldly, "the economic problem has been solved already"; indeed, he added, *"there is no economic problem and, in a sense, there never has been"* (my italics).[31] If "the economic problem" has been identified in the capitalist tradition as *scarcity*, then Schumacher was calling for the end of economics as the dismal science.

Yet if there was no economic problem in the capitalist sense, there was, he continued, "a moral problem": the avarice and powerlust that drove humanity to create and prolong the economic problem. What Marx had called the rage to accumulate stemmed, Schumacher implied, from the fear of scarcity that itself arose from a lack of faith in God's bounty. By encouraging this distrust—especially by installing it at the concep-tual core of economics—capitalism herded men and women into what Schumacher called "the people of the forward stampede." Acquisitive, competitive, and convinced that every economic and ecological problem has a technological solution, the forward stampede destroys anything and anyone that stands in its way. If the advertising and technophilia of capitalism was relentlessly unctuous and optimistic, the humanism of the forward stampede was calculating, agonistic, and merciless. And as Schumacher summarized the political imagination of this more-or-less organized panic, "there is no alternative" to unfettered expansion—a

31. Ibid., 139, 148; Schumacher, *Good Work*, 27; Schumacher, *Guide for the Per-plexed*, 139–40.

chilling anticipation of the dismissive and ominous dictum of neo-liberalism.[32]

If Schumacher envisioned a metaphysics of gift and plentitude, he also gestured toward a recovery of Christian humanism—the other essential feature of a new meta-economics. Schumacher propounded his Christian humanism most vividly in *Small Is Beautiful*, particularly in the chapter, only slightly less famous than "Buddhist economics," on "technology with a human face." Echoing the lineage of Ruskin, Morris, Mumford, and Illich, Schumacher lamented the technics of the forward stampede, epitomized in mass production, as "inherently violent, ecologically damaging . . . and stultifying for the human person." Against this inhuman apparatus of illth, Schumacher called for a "gentle . . . non-violent approach" to tools, machines, and methods, embodied in what he dubbed, by turns, "intermediate technology," "self-help technology," or "democratic, people's technology"—"production by the masses" rather than "mass production." Unlike the massive, centralized production systems of industrial modernity, this non-violent technology would be small-scale and artisanal, fostering human skill rather than seeking to degrade it in the interest of reducing costs. Such forms of technology, he insisted, could arise only from people who had escaped or been exiled from the forward stampede: "home-comers," in his words, those who had, like prodigal children, returned to the estate after grabbing and wasting the wealth bestowed by their Father. Home-comers do not seek riches, or conquest, or promethean achievement; rather, they seek only, as Aquinas had advised, to "enjoy nothing more than to be creatively, usefully, productively engaged with hands and brains." Home-comers, Schumacher noted, "base themselves upon a different picture of man from that which motivates the people of the forward stampede":[33] as gifted (in all senses), loving, and peaceful. For home-comers, the laws of economics were a joyful science, eternally inscribed in the Beatitudes.

To allow space for this beatific humanism, Schumacher's joyful science sanctioned a variety of property and organizational forms, almost all of which he included under the rubric of "socialism." For all his concern with resource and ecological questions, Schumacher devoted a good quarter of *Small Is Beautiful* to issues of ownership and organization

32. Schumacher, *Guide for the Perplexed*, 140; Schumacher, *Small Is Beautiful*, 146–47.

33. Schumacher, *Small Is Beautiful*, 138–51.

which, in his view, had been poorly addressed in the mainstream socialist tradition. Schumacher's Christian socialism rejected Marxist and social-democratic orthodoxies about nationalization and centralized control. Most modern socialists, Schumacher thought, were themselves "devotees of the religion of economics": because they accepted the necessity for unlimited growth and large-scale technology, they differed little or not at all from the capitalists they hoped to dispossess. With his Coal Board experience no doubt in the background, Schumacher wondered if nationalization was still a worthwhile strategy for socialists. Echoing Cole and Tawney—especially the latter, whom he quoted extensively and venerated as "one of the greatest ethical thinkers of our time"—Schumacher distinguished between "property that is an aid to creative work and . . . property that is an alternative to it." The assignment of ownership hinged, he argued, on the delineation of "specific rights and responsibilities in the administration of assets." For this reason, Schumacher introduced "the principle of subsidiary function," the classic Catholic notion that large institutions should not, if possible, perform what smaller associations could do.[34] Thus, while subsidiarity served a crucial role in Schumacher's social thought, "small is beautiful" was bound up with a *socialist* conception of work and property.

Schumacher's moment in the 1970s was promising, but all too brief. For a few years after the appearance of *Small is Beautiful*, the quiet scholar became an unlikely celebrity, giving talks at universities, public meetings, academic conferences, and government agencies. (He even enjoyed a conversation with an admiring President Jimmy Carter.) Riding a wave of ecological concern among the North Atlantic middle classes, and calling for an end to reliance on oil as gasoline prices were rising dramatically, Schumacher assumed a role as prophet of the simpler life to the West. But even before his death in 1977, forces had been gathering on the political right that would end the springtime of prophecy. To Margaret Thatcher, Ronald Reagan, and other spearheads of neoliberalism, Schumacher's kind of infidelity to the religion of economics was intolerable. Condemning such lack of faith, the North Atlantic right summoned up the demons of venality, resentment, and credulity, and for the next thirty years the dreams of avarice overwhelmed the realities of economic and ecological crisis.

34. Ibid., 210–81 (230, 239, 247).

Although Schumacher's work has attracted a devoted following since the 1970s, its failure to make a deeper impact on the broader economic and ecological imagination stems in part, I think, from two significant drawbacks. Despite his insistence on the need for social and political change, and despite his adherence to socialism, Schumacher had little conception of class struggle. As perhaps befitted a self-proclaimed partisan of the "small" and local, Schumacher always appeared wary of large-scale projects of transformation. To the extent it can be discerned, Schumacher's transformative vision was piecemeal and cumulative: his essays abound with references to local experiments in intermediate technology, organic farming, alternative currencies, etc., the eventual tally of which, one infers, would amount to a new political economy. This politics of the local has clear affinities with the lineage of utopian—now called "intentional"—communities, and it dovetails with admonitions to "think globally, act locally." However clever a sound bite that is, it obscures the fact that many of the structures of exploitation must be confronted, at the very least, at levels beyond the local. At the same time, "acting locally" has been almost entirely construed in terms of *consumer* politics—buying from local farmers, *not* buying from adolescent-exploiting corporations like Nike, researching commodities for pesticides or genetic modification. Local action rarely involves *producer* politics— in other words, the politics of workplace democracy and corporate power that inevitably requires organization along the non-local lines of class. Striking directly at the managerial and professional prerogatives of corporate capital, "intermediate technology" and "production by the masses" entail the revitalization of the labor movement, but the necessity for class politics is virtually absent from Schumacher's work—just as it is virtually nowhere to be found in the papal social tradition. It should not surprise anyone that, lacking any anchorage in working-class concerns, Schumacher's kind of eco-economics could be assimilated by middle-class progressives to evoke a kinder, gentler capitalism—the politics of "bourgeois bohemians," as they're often called in America.[35]

The popularity of a tepid, localist eco-economics among the "enlightened" middle classes coincides with the growing appeal of New Age spirituality. Thus, we might want to revisit Schumacher's decision to write about "Buddhist economics," not as a necessary gambit in the cultural

35. For a stringent critique of localist anti-capitalism, see Henwood, *After the New Economy*, 159–86; on "bourgeois bohemians," see Brooks, *Bobos in Paradise*.

politics of the 1960s, but as a reinforcement of new brands of corporate cultural hegemony. As Žižek has forcefully and courageously written of "Western Buddhism"—the Buddhism of Alan Watts, D. T. Suzuki, and others, which would have been the Buddhism known to Schumacher's readers—it now represents, along with other New Age religions, one of the purest forms of capitalist ideology. A "pop-cultural phenomenon preaching inner distance and indifference toward the frantic pace of market competition," Western Buddhism offers middle-class professionals a way, Žižek argues, to "fully participate in capitalist dynamics" while maintaining a stance of condescending dismissal toward the tawdry spectacles of greed and consumerism. On the whole, Žižek contends, New Age enables well-educated and culturally liberal Western elites to maintain and embellish their moral authority.[36] Certainly, Schumacher cannot be blamed for New Age ideology or saddled with the crimes of Buddhists. But just as the absence of class presents an obstacle to the realization of Schumacher's political economy, the lack of an explicit theological underpinning for his joyful science is a problem.

The Legacy of Herbert McCabe

On both scores, we might require the intervention of Father Herbert McCabe, the British Dominican whose essays and sermons are now finding an enthusiastic audience in the United States. One of the finest Thomist philosophers and theologians of the twentieth century, McCabe was a friend of and/or mentor to Terry Eagleton, Alasdair MacIntyre, Denys Turner, Seamus Heaney, and Anthony Kenny, as well as to two generations of Dominicans at Blackfriars, Oxford, and elsewhere.[37] A moving homilist, a lucid scholar, and formidable and witty controversialist, McCabe was also a socialist, and his politics were rooted in and shaped by his fundamental fidelity to Christ. Though a bit too indulgent toward revolutionary rhetoric, McCabe was a more subtle and generous thinker than many a tenured guerilla, and he offers theological and spiritual discipline for a revitalized Christian socialism.

36. Žižek, "Self-Deceptions." I plead agnosticism on the subject of whether or not Western Buddhism can be identified with Asian Buddhism. For his part, Žižek maintains that Zen monks and writers have had a long history of militarism and repression, citing Suzuki's support for Japanese imperialism in the 1930s.

37. McCabe, *Law, Love, and Language*; *God Matters*; *God Still Matters*; *God, Christ, and Us*; *Good Life*; *Faith Within Reason*; *On Aquinas*.

McCabe first addressed political issues in the late 1960s, when many of his students and friends—Eagleton, Turner, Father Laurence Bright, O.P., and others—were partisans of the British Catholic New Left. Although the *enrages* published their own journal, *Slant*, out of Cambridge, McCabe opened the pages of *New Blackfriars* to their political theology. With myriad disquisitions on revolution, socialism, the Eucharist, the priesthood, the Incarnation, and other issues, *Slant* and *New Blackfriars* contained some of the most incisive and effervescent theo-political writing of the Cold War era. Yet the Catholic New Left, like Schumacher's moment, faded in the late 1970s, and its adherents went their separate paths, into Marxism, Christianity, or some liberationist hybrid of the two.[38] Like Schumacher, McCabe never repudiated socialism; like Chesterton, Day, and Weil, he affirmed a sacramental imagination; but like Tawney and Ruskin, he did persist in thinking that class struggle was indispensable to social transformation.

Unlike Schumacher and Benedict, McCabe never recoiled from the reality of social conflict. "The class war is *intrinsic* to capitalism," he reminded readers of *God Matters* (1987); "it is not something we are in a position to *start*" and "it is not something we are in a position to refrain from."[39] "It is just there," McCabe asserted; "we are either on one side or the other." This kind of stark political realism isn't favored much anymore; it's either vilified as Marxist doctrinal vulgarity, or slighted as the piety of 1960s dinosaurs by the acolytes of Blair, Clinton, and Obama. Hoping earnestly for "change they can believe in," today's "progressives" are virtuosi of political bathos; McCabe's unsentimental sobriety is shared by confident combatants on the other side such as Warren Buffett. You know things are bad when we have to be reminded of class struggle by a billionaire.

By insisting on class struggle, McCabe opened himself to the criticism that he was sanctioning a hatred and bloodshed diametrically opposed to the Gospel. McCabe's reply to this objection was straightforward if not, I think, entirely convincing. "The Christian demand for love and peace is precisely what motivates us to take part in the class struggle," McCabe countered; if the struggle is already there, the questions are *how*

38. On the British Catholic New Left in the 1960s and 1970s, one could peruse almost any issue of *Slant* or *New Blackfriars*; see also Wicker, "Justice, Peace, and Dominicans, 1216–1999: Viii-*Slant*, Marxism, and the English Dominicans," 436–43.

39. McCabe, *God Matters*, 191–92.

and *for what* you end it, not whether or not you end it. Once we decide to join the struggle for the sake of love and peace, then "the Sermon on the Mount provides us with the appropriate revolutionary discipline for effective action." Extending the just war tradition to include revolutionary violence, McCabe argued that the love manifested in the Beatitudes could justify the shedding of blood. Violence was "admittedly not a perspicuous manifestation of love," McCabe conceded, but "that does not mean that it is a manifestation of a lack of love."[40] That's a lame argument, to say the least, and I can't help thinking that McCabe himself was slightly embarrassed by it. Truer to the spirit of the Beatitudes would be Schumacher's hero Gandhi: we must be the change we wish to see in the world. The whole point of the Sermon is that the *end* of the struggle against the powers of the age is contained in the *means* we employ—that the poor and the meek and the charitable are *already* "blessed," already residing in the kingdom of God.

McCabe himself offered reasons to forswear violence in the pursuit of socialism. Even in the heady days of 1960s revolutionary euphoria, McCabe admonished Christians that, however just and fraternal, socialism would *not* be the kingdom of God. The Christian "cannot *identify* his Christianity with participation in the revolution," he cautioned in 1968, because there is "a fundamental disagreement between Christian and Marxist . . . about the nature of revolution." While Marxist revolution sought to abolish the structures of injustice, what McCabe called "the Christian revolution" goes "to something deeper, to the ultimate alienation of man which is sin and the ultimate transformation which is death and resurrection." Even though McCabe urged Christians to join in radical political struggle, he issued a salutary warning that "Christian belief . . . cannot be adequately stated in today's political terms, for no revolutionary belief can be stated in the terms of the society it subverts *and Christianity preaches the ultimate revolution*" (my italics). The good news of redemption is "not a programme for political action," as McCabe explained in *God Still Matters* (2001); it is "a critique of action itself, a reminder that we must think on the end." This critical detachment partakes not of strategy but of eschatology; the "end" of political action was not only earthly justice but the kingdom of God. Because the Christian socialist trains her mind on ultimate things, she can be at once more impassioned and more detached—"more complex, more ironic"—than

40. Ibid., 195–96.

her secular comrades. Her eschatological conviction that history has already been made right enables her to be a different kind of revolutionary warrior. When defeated, she recalls that Christ himself "accepts his failure and refuses to compromise his mission by using the weapons of the world against the world." When granted any real but contingent success, she crowns it "not with triumphalism but with forgiveness and mercy, for only in this way can the victory won in the fight remain related to the kingdom of God."[41]

If the love of the kingdom could animate political commitment, then friendship could leaven economic life. As an exemplary Thomist-Aristotelian, McCabe held that "the good life for human animals is one in which friendship is fostered and preserved." Friendship or *philia* was political as well as personal, and it thrived where friends shared the common task of building and maintaining a *polis*. Drawing on Aquinas, McCabe contended that the highest end of humanity, blessedness or *beatitudo*, entailed political life. "The political virtues . . . take their place in . . . our vocation to the heavenly *polis*, the divine life." McCabe even identified *philia* with "*agape* or *caritas*, the friendship that God shares with us," and warned that fraternity cannot survive unless it is rooted in this rapturous, immeasurable Love. "There is no way to build a human society that is really human unless it is *more* than human." Like the triune God of loving processions, or like Christ whose cross "is the ultimate sign of God's love for us," human love is most itself when it is utterly open, unguarded, and vulnerable. "We are the kind of being that finds its fulfillment, happiness and flourishing only in giving itself up, in getting beyond itself." But giving ourselves up is exactly what we fear; the loss of self-mastery, especially in capitalist society, is considered a nightmare rather than a glory. And so we seek to secure our lives in the makeshift and inevitably malevolent apparatus of property: title deeds, security systems, police departments, military-industrial complexes. These were the trophies of our damnation. With so profoundly sad a vision of the Fall, and with so bounteous a vision of love, McCabe never ceased to be astonished and appalled at the celebration of antagonism in capitalist culture. Indeed, writing at the zenith of neo-liberal hegemony,

41. McCabe, *Law, Love, and Language*, 163, 166–67, 170, 172; *God Matters*, 99; *God Still Matters*, 90–91. If we follow McCabe, it would seem that Eagleton is not quite right to say, in his introduction to a recent edition of the Gospels, that Jesus was "both more and less" than a revolutionary: Eagleton, *Terry Eagleton Presents Jesus Christ and the Gospels*, xxx.

McCabe thought it utterly "bizarre" that the competitive market had become the paragon of human life. Not competition but "friendship is an illuminating image or metaphor for a human living which would be an imitation or reflection" of God.[42]

McCabe linked divine love and economics most clearly in one of his finest homilies, "Poverty and God," in which he brilliantly deconstructed the false opposition between abundance and poverty. Unlike the standard mythology of capitalist culture, "the success story for Christians is from riches to rags." Recalling the tale of Jesus and the rich young man, McCabe implied that most Christians walk off with the grieving playboy—while beating their breasts, of course. There's nothing wrong with being rich, they reassure themselves, as long as you have poverty *of spirit*. McCabe rejected this self-serving twaddle and insisted that the whole point of the story is that there is indeed "something wrong with being rich and something right with being poor." "There is something less than human about needing to live with riches," he asserted, and "there is something godlike about being able to live in poverty." God has and can have no possessions, McCabe explained; since possessions are things used for some benefit to the owner, and since nothing can benefit God, then God can't possibly own anything. Thus, God is poor "because he simply and literally has no possessions." But since God creates, He creates without owning; the only beneficiary of God's creation is creation itself. (As the unlikely theologian Henry Miller once remarked about creation, "God doesn't make a cent on the deal.") God creates for no reason other than sheer joy and delight; and as "God makes without becoming richer," then His poverty and abundance are one. Since, as creatures, we *must* act for *some* benefit to ourselves, *we* have need of possessions; but we can imitate God's poverty—and thus, help distribute His abundance—by living for others. Possessing as little as possible, we can nonetheless offer our talents to others in joyous self-expenditure. As McCabe put it, "the one who aims at poverty knows that we can only live by throwing ourselves away"—an echo of Ruskin's dark-red, old-school Communists who exist only in giving. "Human society flourishes, not to the extent that it possesses riches, but to the extent that we give life to each other, to the extent that we imitate the creativity of God."[43]

42. McCabe, *Good Life*, 52, 87–88; *God Matters*, 94, 98; *God, Christ, and Us*, 56–57.

43. McCabe, "Poverty and God," in *God, Christ, and Us*, 53–57; see also "Mammon and Thanksgiving," *God, Christ, and Us*, 133–37.

McCabe's wisdom of poverty as abundance should be the foundation of a joyful economics. Like Schumacher, McCabe declared "the economic problem" a false and sinister quandary; like Ruskin, he traced its origins to our sinful refusal of self-expenditure. And like both great "Communists of the old school," McCabe knew that charity is not some treacly ideal but the very nature of the universe. Against the acquisitive fantasies enabled by the lies of the dismal science, we will need that kind of sacramental realism in the turbulence of the twenty-first century. The real science of political economy provides an education in love, since its object is not accumulation but the holiest of dissipation. Out with widgets, units, and marginal utility; in with loaves and fishes, birds and lilies, wine at wedding feasts!

4

Beyond the Culture of Cutthroat Competition

The Pope Takes the World by Surprise

Mark and Louise Zwick

INTRODUCTION

POPE BENEDICT XVI's SOCIAL encyclical, *Caritas in Veritate*, took the economic world by surprise.[1] While readers on both the right and the left were waiting for more statements about capitalism and socialism, they found instead a challenge to Catholics and other people of good will toward a profoundly new way of understanding business enterprise. The Pope did not approve the status quo, but in what he called the social *magisterium*, addressed the global dimension of the social question in the midst of a very serious economic crisis, displaying a surprising

1. All references to *Caritas in Veritate* will be given parenthetically in the text.

understanding of what has been happening in the contemporary international economic scene.

Benedict recognizes the disconnect between the Word of the Gospel and the current economic culture. Jesus told us his Gospel is not about building bigger barns (or bigger banks). It is about giving rather than receiving. Speaking at the Synod of the Word in the fall of 2008 as he was preparing the encyclical, the Pope reminded us that the Word of God is the true reality and that the disappearance of hope along with the money in the crash of 2008–2009 was the result of building our lives on sand.

The economy that collapsed was based on "barn-building," on individual and corporate self-interest. Its marks included a scandalous divide between salaries of CEOs and workers in their companies. Deregulation and privatization around the world left the market and human services to wolves. Hedge funds and other oddly named financial institutions speculated in complex derivatives that not even the regulators who remained could understand. Banks pursued reckless policies and were saved by massive government bailouts. People were owned by their credit cards, by debt at exorbitant interest rates. Environmental concerns were sacrificed. Thousands of people lost homes and jobs in the United States and the situation of people to the South became desperate. The media, which might have informed the citizenry, were a part of the conglomerates. The wild credit card spending and shopping sprees among consumers led one commentator to say that men over fifty would never need to buy anything again except for fruits and vegetables, pasta and olive oil, underwear and socks.

The government's response to the financial crisis, at least initially, was to enrich the very people and institutions that caused the problem in the first place and to continue the same approach: "What is needed is more of the same, more free market, more free trade, more credit for lending at interest." Not even mentioned was all the extra assistance to multinational corporations that they take for granted—more subsidized agriculture, more freedom and power for lobbyists to the U.S. Congress for corporate interests which often hurt the poor. It is hard to believe that, even today, politicians can get away with denigrating any reference to a better approach by crying, "Socialism! Communism!"

For believers, our economics has been upside down. More of the same is not the answer. According to the encyclical, we actually have to expect the businessperson, as well as the politician who must provide a strong juridical framework for finance and economics, to live according to the Gospel. It may be very difficult for the Catholic business man or woman who is accustomed to business as usual, where profit is king, to embrace the papal plan, but Benedict XVI insists that our vocation as persons even on a practical level is a transcendent one. In *Caritas in Veritate,* he reminds us that there is a link between the wild spending of some while others do not have enough. Quoting John Paul II in *Centesimus Annus,* he asks us again to change our lifestyles: "What is needed is an effective shift in mentality which can lead to the adoption of new life-styles in which the quest for truth, beauty, goodness and communion with others for the sake of common growth are the factors which determine consumer choices, savings and investments."

THE RECEPTION OF *CARITAS IN VERITATE*

As Catholic Workers in Houston we are sharply aware of international economics as we receive in hospitality the immigrants and refugees whom business rejects, those who have been uprooted from their homes by the extremes of the global market and the military defense of it. In addition to receiving the immigrants who leave their countries because they cannot find work to sustain their families, we care for and help support many people injured on the job, some completely paralyzed from falling from scaffolds, some in wheelchairs but with the use of their arms, some able to walk again but not able to work. At Casa Juan Diego we experience what the poor experience, as we feed the hungry, clothe the naked, give hospitality to the stranger, and care for the sick and injured in our two clinics with volunteer doctors. Our perspective on economics and politics is interwoven with the life and suffering of the migrant.

God brought Dorothy Day and Peter Maurin together to form the Catholic Worker movement at a time when the world was facing an economic crash similar to today's. As they received in hospitality and in soup kitchens the refugees from the economic system during the 1930s, in their newspaper they critiqued robber barons, banks, the financial system, the free-market ideology known in their time as *laissez-faire* capitalism, and the state of constant preparation for war to protect the economic gains. Dorothy Day criticized the appeal to acquisitiveness that dominates advertisement. Dorothy and Peter endorsed subsidiarity and quoted the papal encyclicals to do so. Peter Maurin tried to convince readers of *The Catholic Worker* that it is more important for a person to become better than to become "better off." At a time when Communists were trying very hard to recruit all the workers to their cause, Dorothy and Peter presented their newspaper and their vision of the movement as an alternative to both capitalism and Communism, one based on the Gospel, on Catholic social teaching, and the lives of the saints.

Unlike Dorothy and Peter, who understood very well exactly what was going on in economics, some Christians have sadly been patriots-in-arms in promoting the machinations of the worst of the "marketeers" in recent times, attempting to equate Catholic ethics with no-limits capitalism. It was really quite bold, fearless actually, of the Pope to speak so strongly against the powers that be, with so many Catholics involved in the market—what had become a greed operation. It will take courage and good research for those who will try to implement the ideas in *Caritas in Veritate,* as they face the monopoly of multinationals around the world. Some of these same patriots-in-arms for unfettered markets have come out strongly against *Caritas in Veritate.* They continued a tradition of a handful of prominent Catholic writers who have refused to accept Catholic social teaching. William Buckley made the first famous public refusal with his "Mater, si, Magistra, no," response to John XXIII's *Mater et Magistra,* thus establishing the tradition of cafeteria Catholicism.

Some years ago Michael Novak, video-recorded on C-Span television, remarked that those who objected to the enormous salaries of CEOs while the masses of workers in their companies received a pittance should remember that the sin of envy was condemned in the book of Deuteronomy. Given that perspective, it is perhaps not surprising that Novak undermined *Caritas in Veritate* as soon as it came out in *First Things Online.* He rather amazingly said that the encyclical lacked a description of capitalism's "tangible benefits to the poor" and that therefore the work of the staff supporting the Pope was poor and inadequate. It has always been difficult to see any tangible benefits for the poor following the theory of the economy of wealth raising all boats, as the rich got richer and more boats sank, but with the devastating effect of the financial crisis around the world it is hard to fathom that anyone would want to enter the fray with the same failed system.

Those who endorse what is known around the world as neo-liberalism promote an economic ideology which advocates greed and crushing others, all the while presenting that system as helping others.

Chesterton once noted that it may be very difficult for modern people to imagine a world in which men are not generally admired for covetousness and crushing their neighbors, but he assured them that such strange patches of an earthly paradise do really remain on earth.

George Weigel claimed that half of the *Caritas in Veritate* was written by someone else—he described the parts he did not like as out of tune like the warbling of an untuned piccolo. This was an especially offensive reference when describing the writing of an accomplished musician like Benedict. Perhaps Weigel's contention that the bad half of the encyclical must have been written by the staffers at the Pontifical Council for Justice and Peace was related to statements from that Council in response to the financial crisis. Not long before the encyclical was published, Cardinal Renato Martino, president of that Pontifical Council was quoted as saying: "The logic of the market up to now has been that of maximum earnings, of making investments to obtain the greatest possible profit. And this, according to the social teaching of the Church, is immoral." The Holy Father himself wrote: "Once profit becomes the exclusive goal, if it is produced by improper means and without the common good as its ultimate end, it risks destroying wealth and creating poverty" (*Caritas*, 21).

Another group, rather than confront the papacy, simply declares that the Pope agrees with them, that he loves unfettered finance, that even St. Thomas Aquinas loved and promoted their type of economics. Writing in the *Wall Street Journal*, Fr. Robert Sirico of the Acton Institute libertarian/Calvinist think tank attempted in this way to appropriate the Pope's writing in *Caritas in Veritate* by claiming that it stood squarely in the "classical liberal tradition"—in other words along Sirico's libertarian lines. He went so far as to insist that the Pope's writing was similar even to the secular (neo-liberal/libertarian) F. A. Hayek of the Austrian school of economics. Sirico does not mention the Chicago School, perhaps because their professors and students, while promoting free capitalism, free markets, etc., endorsed regulation and pointed out before the current crisis that it was lacking. (We have always been aware of the Chicago School of economics because Mark attended classes in a building next to where Milton Friedman was teaching when he studied at the University of Chicago for his master's degree in social work.)

Neo-conservative refusers complained that Benedict didn't say enough about the importance of wealth creation. Those critics neglected to mention section 60 of the encyclical where he does speak of wealth creation, but a wealth creation which would help the poor, not just the rich: "In the search for solutions to the current economic crisis, development aid for poor countries must be considered a valid means of creating wealth for all." They didn't, perhaps, understand or accept his words: "Without the perspective of eternal life, human progress in this world . . . runs the risk of being reduced to the mere accumulation of wealth." He said the market is not, and must not become, the place where the strong subdue the weak and that the economy must not be seen as just an engine for wealth creation but be directed toward the common good.

Upon reflection, one can understand why the "marketeers" are so much in opposition to the Pope, because their ideological approach to economics and politics is so different from that of Church leadership and teaching. These men had been at the forefront of expanding and exporting an economics which sought ever more profit through lower wages, privatization of services, and lack of support for the local communities, all controlled by the corporations who fund their work in "think tanks."

With this encyclical, it becomes clear that the work in economics and politics of the refusers of Catholic social teaching was simply a part of the corporate culture. Their chant that it is not necessary to listen to the Pope on questions of economics and war because they are covered under prudential judgment rather than faith and morals emphasizes the split between modern culture and the Gospel. The publication in *First Things*, of all places, of the ringing endorsement by 68 evangelicals of *Caritas in Veritate* gives hope that some Protestant economists, university presidents, and professors at least will enthusiastically study and implement the social teaching of this outstanding encyclical.

What Do Gratuitousness, Gift, and Reciprocity Have to Do with Economics?

Benedict XVI endorses creative, alternative enterprises that have emerged in recent years beyond, as he says, the for-profit and non-profit methods that have been in existence, indicating that they can "no longer do full justice to reality or offer practical direction for the future." He mentions a number of types of enterprises as examples in a "broad new composite reality embracing the private and public spheres, one which does not exclude profit, but instead considers it a means for achieving human and social ends." He presents the idea that ideas like gift and reciprocity can be included within businesses.

Writing in the *National Review*, Weigel questioned the Pope's proposal that such kind words as "gift" might be included in any discussion of economics, suggesting that the language in those sections of *Caritas in Veritate* is so "clotted and muddled" as to suggest a confused sentimentality of precisely the sort the encyclical deplores among those who detach charity from truth. It would appear from this comment that this group of refusers is so out of tune with Catholic social teaching that talk of social responsibility, of gift, of gratuitousness, of reciprocity, of communion in business and economics is incomprehensible.

Weigel's response to *Caritas in Veritate* reminds us of an experience we had when we were giving a talk on Catholic social teaching to a study group at one of the parishes in Houston. Before the meeting started, we spoke to the leader about some options for people to live out their faith in areas regarding economics—ways to implement the preferential option for the poor. Presented with the option to buy a half-a-million-dollar house or a one-million-dollar one (theirs is a rich parish!), we said, why couldn't the Catholic believer stay in his quarter-of-a-million-dollar house and use the extra money to buy houses for the poor in a low-income neighborhood? Or why couldn't other Catholic believers purchase a fifteen-thousand or twenty-thousand-dollar car instead of buying a thirty-, forty- or fifty-thousand-dollar car?

The leader, while sympathetic, felt he had to explain. "Mark, you don't understand! You don't understand! They see this as virtue. These people have worked hard and prayed hard and lived right all their lives. They have a right to enjoy the fruit of their efforts. God is rewarding them for faithfulness and hard work." As for those who do not have the half-a-million-dollar choice in this scenario the clear implication is that there is something wrong. Why don't they have the same blessings? What did they do wrong? Why are their lives filled with failures and poverty? This Calvinistic thinking, combined with that of Adam Smith and his contemporary disciples, is very influential among Catholics today. Cardinal Francis George of Chicago pointed out that, although we may not be aware of it, all of us in the United States (and perhaps a few other countries as well) are Calvinists, including Catholics.

The approach of *Caritas in Veritate* is very different from an economy run on rugged individualism, cutthroat competition, self-interest, and consumers who feel they must at all costs purchase the latest fashion and style. Perhaps that is why George Weigel found it so difficult to be in tune with the encyclical. Since it is so difficult for you to imagine the use of the words *gift, gratuitousness*, and *reciprocity* in the area of economics, Professor Weigel, let us explain what Pope Benedict is saying in one example he gives. When he says that the Church's social doctrine holds that authentically human social relationships of friendship, solidarity, and reciprocity can also be conducted within economic activity, when he speaks of gratuitousness, of "gift," he mentions a specific economic model. That practical example, developed in the Focolare Movement throughout the world, is the Economy of Communion, which was launched in 1991 when Focolare founder Chiara Lubich visited Focolare communities in Brazil. During that visit Chiara was disturbed to find a whole ring of shantytowns in a circle surrounding the city, the *favelas* where people lived in abject poverty, "a crown of thorns" around the city. Those involved with the Focolare in Brazil included not only professionals and the middle class but many of these poor. After that visit, in order to help meet the material needs of that local community, Chiara Lubich proposed a new economic model in which for-profit businesses could generate additional jobs and voluntarily share profits in three ways. One third of the profits would go to those in need, one third to build up the civilization of love, and one third into the business for continued development.

The EoC spread throughout the globe through the Focolare Movement. The EoC has brought together 754 companies worldwide that are committed to pursuing higher goals than just profit. The authors came to know the Focolare Movement in Texas and have interviewed people involved in Economy of Communion businesses. They are an inspiration. Presently there are businesses in various production and service sectors on every continent following this model, most of them small and medium sized, but some with more than one hundred employees.

EoC businesses commit themselves to building sound relationships with employees, customers, regulatory agencies, the general public, and the environment. These new relationships include those who receive aid, who are truly active participants in the project. Sharing one's needs with dignity and sincerity is appreciated as a contribution to increase the life of communion, and many renounce the help just as soon as they reach a bare minimum of economic independence. The Economy of Communion is seen as an economic expression of the spirituality of communion of the Focolare Movement. The Economy of Communion represents a very different model and a very different concept from what is commonly referred to as "business ethics."

NOT JUST ANY ETHICS WHATSOEVER

When a local Catholic university invited one of the Catholic patriots-in-arms of *laissez-faire* capitalism to speak at the opening of their business ethics center some years ago, we felt we had to speak. We could not stand by when the speaker represented the refusers or re-writers of Catholic social teaching. We wrote in the *Houston Catholic Worker* that inviting Michael Novak to speak on business ethics was like asking Hugh Hefner to speak in defense of marriage. Various professors at the university were quite surprised, but came to dialogue with us.

The refusers have a number of think tanks that supposedly address "business ethics." Weigel went so far as to call his corporation "The Ethics and Public Policy Center." That center, the American Enterprise Institute that employs Michael Novak, and Fr. Sirico's Acton Institute have organized seminars and "retreats" to present policies that favor large corporations and the wealthier few as "ethics." These men's public identification as Catholics has led some to believe that their ideology represented the teaching of the Church. Nothing could be further from the truth.

The Pope indicates that he is aware of much talk about ethics, that various centers for ethics and business, ethics and the economy, have been developed, but that the term *ethics* in some of these ventures has lost its meaning, or could mean almost anything—even decisions and choices contrary to justice and authentic human welfare. He insists that the economy needs ethics in order to function correctly—not, however, any ethics whatsoever, but rather an ethics that is "people-centered."

In the majority of university economics classes, where what Pope Pius XII called the "superstition" of the invisible hand of the market has reigned, monopolistic business practices have not been challenged. Too often the invisible hand of the market has had a knife in it for the poor. The knife, wielded around the world, is invisible until researchers expose corporations' practices.

Benedict XVI teaches that much in an authentic ethics depends on the underlying system of morality and that it is here that the Church's social doctrine can make a specific contribution in economics. The two pillars of this teaching, he says in *Caritas in Veritate*, are the inviolability of the human person and the transcendent value of natural moral norms. He immediately and daringly applies these principles to business practices:

> When business ethics prescinds from these two pillars, it inevitably risks losing its distinctive nature and it falls prey to forms of exploitation; more specifically, it risks becoming subservient to existing economic and financial systems rather than correcting the dysfunctional aspects. Among other things, it risks being used to justify the financing of projects that are in reality unethical. (*Caritas*, 45)

Benedict places the whole human project in the perspective of a pilgrim of the absolute living in this world working for justice and the development of peoples without becoming ensnared by the fashions of the moment.

THE STAKEHOLDERS, NOT JUST STOCKHOLDERS

One of the "new" proposals in *Caritas in Veritate* would be a major change for firms on Wall Street. Businesses have a responsibility, says the Pope, to all the stakeholders who contribute to the life of the business, not simply to shareholders (those who buy stocks). The stakeholders are the workers, the suppliers, the consumers, the natural environment, and the community of reference. In Western culture, the concept is strong that people who have done well and helped build our churches have a right to what they have earned or to their tremendous income from the stock market. The idea of sharing with the other stakeholders is foreign to the way our business climate is oriented.

The practice of basing all decisions on what will please the stockholders has caused immeasurable harm to stakeholders in various types of business and industries. Using only stock market indicators to run businesses that affect the lives of human persons directly is, as the Pope said, unethical. Measuring everything by a related ambiguous figure called the Gross Domestic Product and "growth" is not a human measure at all.

An outrageous example in recent decades of disregarding stakeholders as the global market has expanded has been the massive development of *maquiladoras* or outsourcing by multinational companies for cheap labor with no provision for helping the local community. Strict enforcement against labor organizing, what the Pope calls the deregulation of the labor market, has created miserable working conditions and under-subsistence pay for poor workers in many countries. At the Houston Catholic Worker, speaking with the immigrants and refugees who come to our doors, we have been aware since the 1980s of the practices of the *maquiladoras*, where companies have ignored most of the stakeholders where the work is performed, with negative impacts not only on the workers, but on the local communities. The workers, whose salaries did not provide enough to support their families, often have been forced to migrate, while the multinationals that operated the factories and their stockholders made unusually high profits.

During the 1990s, for example, immigrants from Honduras who came to take refuge at Casa Juan Diego told us that they made $14.00 a week in a *maquiladora*. They could not pay the rent and feed their families on that income. (One said that his father, in an older, more established job, made $28.00 a week and he could survive.) Some workers who came to the United States could not believe the high prices here for the products they had sewn or assembled for a pittance. Less publicized than bank and business failures in the current crisis has been the human suffering that has come from turning everything into a for-profit business, from the field of medicine to privatized prisons, as stakeholders are disregarded.

Health care has been a scandalous example of this practice in the past decades as medicine has been transformed from a profession into a big business. Hospitals, health insurance companies, and pharmaceutical companies depend on the stock market. The decisions based on their rating each day in the market—will people buy their stocks or dump them that day in favor of a more profitable venture?—determine the practical life-and-death outcome for patients. When the encyclical especially mentions the rigid assertion of the right to intellectual property in the field of health care, one immediately thinks of the pharmaceutical companies with their patented expensive medicines unavailable to the poor of the world. In the United States, however, it seems that even to mention that the development of medicines needed by everyone should not even be on the stock market would lead to accusations of "Socialism! Communism!" and even political instability.

The complaints and debates around health care reform regarding rationing health care often have neglected to point out that it is already rationed by insurance companies, hospitals, and pharmaceutical companies. The key stakeholders, the patients, seem to be the last to be considered. This is especially true of the uninsured and the poor. Examples of suffering and human tragedy in the "business" of health care are everywhere. Houston, Texas, is home to one of the greatest medical centers in the world. One of the wealthiest hospitals with several major branches in Houston sends poor people to Casa Juan Diego, the Houston Catholic Worker, to have their prescriptions filled. When people go to the emergency room, all hospitals are required by law to treat them for their illness. The hospital staff examines them and makes a diagnosis, but apparently do not provide medicine for those who do not have insurance. Even though in its original foundation this large hospital system is designated as a charity hospital, people frequently arrive at our door to bring us prescriptions from that hospital, begging for help with their medicine. This is certainly one way for this major hospital to score well on the stock market. Can you imagine Casa Juan Diego, funded solely by donations, where we have to decide each day what help we can offer the poor vs. massive hospital systems? We are fortunate in Houston, however, to also have a somewhat unique county health system that serves the poor, including immigrants. While it is often difficult for people to navigate the paper work and documents proving their living situation and income, at least the possibility of care exists.

One of the worst examples of the direct harmful effect on people of running businesses on the basis of the stockholders without reference to the stakeholders is the for-profit prison business. Here one finds the very opposite of everything Benedict recommends in his encyclical, but especially the violation of the dignity of the human person. More and more prisons across the United States are being run by private companies for profit, on the stock market. They provide a commercial motive for imprisoning more and more people. This booming business has been a windfall for the stockholders, at the expense of poor people caught in this trap. The huge expense for taxpayers of building prisons and keeping people in jail for extended periods of time has somehow turned into profit for stockholders, and their income on the stock market is counted as a part of the "growth" or GDP of the United States.

The private prison business includes detention centers for immigrants, who are no longer jailed for a few days until they can be deported, but rather for months and years. When the custom of releasing Central American immigrants on their own recognizance was ended in 2005, the massive building program for prisons to detain them began. As prisons for immigrants grew rapidly, stockholders for detention centers were enriched greatly, and they became richer as more immigrants were arrested and jailed. The more arrests, the richer stockholders became. Those who are held because of not having proper documentation have broken the civil law, not the criminal law, but they are held in a punitive situation together with robbers and murderers, with windfall profits on the stock market.

Former Vice President of the United States Dick Cheney was actually indicted by a grand jury in South Texas for conflict of interest in having many millions invested in these prisons at the same time as he was pushing legislation for imprisoning more immigrants. These detention centers are promoted by Congressional representatives as sure money makers for local communities. Congress approved a budget for the 2008 fiscal year, providing funding for a 4,500-bed increase in the immigration detention beds to 32,000 beds from the prior year's 27,500. Private corporations, including the Corrections Corporation of America and the Geo Group, bid against each other to win contracts to operate new prisons.

The same companies run the prisons and the detention centers. They have their own lobbyists to increase profits and to ensure that the commercial prison system continues. The Associated Press reported in 2007 that the Corrections Corporation of America spent 2.5 million dollars lobbying the federal government. CCA's lobbying of the government that year focused on three major areas: 1) lobbying to privatize the Bureau of Indian Affairs prison system, 2) lobbying against the Public Safety Act that would outlaw private prisons, and 3) lobbying against the Private Prison Information Act that would give the public the same access to private prison information as public prisons. Some even speak of kickbacks to judges who imprison more and more people to fill the privatized jails.

BENEDICT XVI AND THE CONCEPT OF REDISTRIBUTION
OF WEALTH AND USURY

Some readers of *Caritas in Veritate* were startled, if not enraged, to find that Benedict had gone so far in defending stakeholders that he recommended a large-scale redistribution of wealth on a worldwide scale. Some feared that he would take what they had and give it to the poor. What the Pope has done is to make respectable the sharing of wealth, when in the past, attempts to do so were shouted down as Communism.

As the Holy Father speaks of redistribution of wealth, as he notes the grave imbalances in wealth and poverty around the world, however, he makes what seems at first to be a strange request. Instead of sounding like a modern-day radical Robin Hood ready to swoop down on the rich, rob their wealth, and give it to the poor, he cautions us to be careful that the very important redistribution does not hurt the poor or redistribute poverty. He is aware that in the past several decades instead of following the recommendations of Pope Paul VI in *Populorum Progressio* to which this encyclical relates, the economic powers found a way to transfer the wealth of the southern hemisphere to the countries in the North.

Much of this transfer of wealth from the developing South to the richer North was accomplished through the loans given by the World Bank and the International Monetary Fund to the countries emerging from colonialism, supposedly to assist them. The countries were required by the international financial institutions to change the ways their economies were run in order to receive continuing assistance. When he asked in 2007 that the process of debt cancellation and reduction for the poorest countries be continued and accelerated, Pope Benedict XVI insisted that these processes must not be made conditional upon structural adjustments that are detrimental to the most vulnerable populations. Many asked in response, what are structural adjustments?

Almost forty nations were coerced into participating in what were called Structural Adjustment Programs in order to reschedule payments on loans taken out more than three decades ago from the International Monetary Fund and the World Bank. The focus was on debt reduction and repayment. Priority was given to exporting the products that brought in the most cash, even if it included paying slave wages, using environmentally destructive methods of production, exporting the best and most nutritious food, and devaluations, announcing that the value of local money was not what it used to be. These pressures encouraged politicians to favor giant commercial farms and the takeover of local business by multinational corporations. Financial dealings such as these hurt people on a massive scale.

In negotiating Structural Adjustment Programs since the 1980s, the IMF and/or the World Bank typically dictated privatization of basic services previously provided by the government and cuts in government services, along with currency devaluation. This insistence on the privatization of government services to put them in the hands of multinationals on the stock market is another example of stockholders vs. stakeholders. It is hard to imagine that the concerns and needs of the people were considered in the imposition of these harsh programs.

Pressure to privatize has included the sale of the most basic resources necessary to human existence—such as the sale of water distribution centers of various countries to corporations seeking profits. A prime example was the sale of much of the water supply of Argentina to Enron, and the giant Monsanto expressed great interest in obtaining water resources in various countries.

Caritas in Veritate relates the powerless of citizens in many countries to exactly those "budgetary policies, with cuts in social spending often made under pressure from international financial institutions." As he notes that such "powerlessness is increased by the lack of effective protection on the part of workers' associations," Benedict XVI encourages labor organizing,

Friends from Latin America have told us how they begged some of the refusers of Catholic social teaching who were influential at the World Bank at the time, not to give usurious loans to their country when it was being run by repressive military dictators propped up by the United States, by those whose economic policies made the poor much poorer. During this period the World Bank and the International Monetary Fund were making huge loans to Latin American and African "leaders" who obviously did not have the welfare of the people of their country at heart. Our friends knew, as the financiers who lent the money had to also know, that the money would not be used to help the people, but for the enrichment of national leaders in whose name the loans were made. Our friends' pleas were not heard, their country became more and more indebted and more obligated to follow an economics that devastated their land while transferring their money to the North by demands for always larger interest payments. The country has become one of the Latin American countries that is hostile not only to the countries of the North, but is in conflict with the Church.

The IMF and World Bank gave huge amounts of money to repressive military dictators in Latin America that were supported by the United States in the name of stopping Communism. As they have emerged from horrifying times with death squads and the disappearance of many citizens, the people are now expected to repay the loans the dictators arranged. Eduardo Galeano recently asked the question: How can they expect us to pay back the money given to these cruel dictators?

The film *Life or Debt*, which was shown in Museums of Fine Arts across the United States, has been frequently used in university class-rooms to explain what happened to the countries coming out of colo-nialism. It dramatically illustrates the destruction caused in one country, Jamaica, by these policies which have created what Pope John Paul II called a new colonialism, a new serfdom. Usury is at the heart of these injustices. As the banks continued to increase the interest rates on loans already given, the countries were told that all that they had repaid had been applied only to the interest and that the whole loan was still owed. This is the scandal and immorality of usury. Cardinal Bertone, Secretary of State of the Vatican called it by its name: "I've repeated many times the judgment of experts and entire bodies of bishops: the international loans made by the World Bank and the International Monetary Fund, as well as bilateral loans, are by now a form of usury and should be declared ille-gal." Usury is blamed by reasonable people for the 2008–2010 worldwide financial crisis. Although for many centuries usury was condemned by the Church, with the advent of capitalism, being against usury was con-sidered unacceptable, even rather odd. What was considered extremist is now the diagnosis of the problem.

Peter Maurin, who so often spoke of living according to Gospel simplicity, also spoke of a philosophy of work, one opposed to usury and speculation: "Man should earn his living by the sweat of his brow, and a gentleman, truly speaking, is one who does not live on the sweat of someone else's brow."

Speaking of usury, not many have mentioned how the religious communities in the United States have been hurt by the financial crisis, but even worse, how religious in developing countries were sometimes devastated when their investments turned out to be worth little. Some missionaries who do most to help the poor lost much. While Pope Benedict XVI did not mention this tragedy in his encyclical, it would be a welcome change in canon law to not require religious to invest in the most lucrative, and therefore risky, sections of the stock market. In addition to the devastating usurious loans to developing countries that have resulted in transfers of large amounts of money to the North, international trade agreements have benefitted the North, increased poverty in countries to the South and pushed people to migrate.

AGRIBUSINESS CORPORATIONS—AGAINST THE PEOPLE AND THE POPE?

The effect of NAFTA (North American Free Trade Agreement) was to destroy the farms of the people of Mexico in favor of huge agribusinesses. Mexican farmers were not able to compete with the lower prices of subsidized grains flooding their market from the United States. It is extensively documented that between 1.2 million and 2 million Mexican farmers lost their farms in the wake of NAFTA. In a move echoing the enclosure of the commons in England centuries ago, the traditional *ejido* lands which had belonged to the people in Mexico through the indigenous tradition and later blessed by Mexican law were broken up through NAFTA. Many of the landless people are now forced by necessity to work for the new agribusiness owners of their lands or to work as migrant farmworkers in the United States.

In El Salvador, the equitable land reform recommended in *Caritas in Veritate* has caused violent struggles for many years, even centuries. There, as in so many other countries, the land is owned by the few. The authors lived in El Salvador at the beginning of the civil war in the late 1970s. As Archbishop Oscar Romero said there in regard to agrarian reform, you can speak about anything in Latin America, propose all means of solutions in the fight for social justice, "but when you touch the land, it calls forth its martyrs." Land reform will be even more complicated as multinational corporations have begun to purchase the arable land in the Global South.

The growth and processing of corn had traditionally been at the heart of local Mexican agriculture, and the government, through Conasupo, was the purchaser of last resort for those who might be unable to sell their crop. With the unbalanced provisions of NAFTA in agriculture, the United States could continue subsidies to American farmers and agribusiness, but the Mexican government could not subsidize farmers. Companies like ADM and Cargill took control of the whole corn market in Mexico. These very large companies could set prices at will and they could hoard grains for price advantage and speculation. Costs of transportation of grains for processing to a central location in Mexico and for staff from the United States were figured into the costs. The price of staple foods in Mexico like tortillas rose astronomically.

Small businesses were also destroyed throughout Mexico, as Wal-Mart moved in after the NAFTA agreements with hundreds of stores, often using different names locally for their stores, using the old-fashioned method in the tradition of the robber barons. Wal-Mart was successful because they could undersell for a period of time until the local businesses had folded, and then become the local price-fixer, as they have done in small towns throughout the United States. We have received migrants uprooted by NAFTA in our Houses of Hospitality in Houston, including those who told us they used to have a small business, but were unable to compete when the multinationals came in.

The Center for International Policy's Americas Program described the effect of this economic upheaval: "Since NAFTA, the Mexican economy rests on four pillars: the informal economy, non-renewable resources (oil and gas), remittances from migrants in the United States, and drug trafficking." To call that a shaky foundation, they said, would be an understatement. The expansion of free trade agreements to other countries has had to be imposed by force, for example, in Central America. In Guatemala protesters against CAFTA were shot and killed.

What has been happening in agriculture in the decades since the publication of Paul VI's encyclical *Populorum Progressio* is at the heart of a new colonialism. In agriculture many of the stakeholders around the world are having their resources redistributed to the big agribusiness corporations, and as a result, food insecurity grows. Family farms have almost gone out of existence in the U.S. as agribusiness has taken over, but the problem has reached massive proportions in the Global South, where for many centuries, thousands of years, small farmers produced the food needed for their families without making payments to multinational corporations. Enter the "experts" of agribusiness with their claims of creating more food through chemicals, fertilizers, herbicides, pesticides, and, of all things, seeds stolen and patented in the United States as their own. In what was perhaps mistakenly called a Green Revolution, farmers have been told that the only way to avoid famine and starvation is to use chemicals and to buy all seeds from agribusiness companies. The emphasis was on rice and soya beans and perhaps wheat, not representing the diversity of crops raised, for example, in India, where the majority eat a vegetarian diet that includes lentils and a variety of oils, traditionally grown by their farmers. Later, farmers from the South were told to plant cash crops rather than food for their families, which would give them money to buy things. They could then import their food, which turned out to be more expensive.

Pope Benedict, following *Populorum Progressio*, makes important recommendations for agricultural development in poorer countries and for eliminating the structural causes that give rise to the problem of food insecurity. This can be done, he says, "by investing in rural infrastructures, irrigation systems, transport, organization of markets, and in the development and dissemination of agricultural technology that can make the best use of the human, natural and socio-economic resources *that are more readily available at the local level*, while guaranteeing their sustainability over the long term as well" (*Caritas*, 27; emphasis added).

Local peoples may rejoice that while advocating the above, he tells the powerful: "All this needs to be accomplished with the involvement of local communities in choices and decisions that affect the use of agricultural land." This is a radical and fearless stance in favor of local communities and local agriculture in the face of the growing stranglehold of multinational agribusinesses on international agriculture: Most are not aware that the majority of the world's farmers are women, often single women supporting their children through subsistence farming. In the field of agriculture Benedict turns out to be a champion for women and human rights.

The Pope's recommendations on ethics as applied to agriculture and subsidiarity, on traditional as well as innovative farming techniques and on local community choices are undermined by the power of multinational companies involved in agribusiness and the practice in recent decades of patenting life forms. A decision of the U.S. Supreme Court laid the groundwork for multinational companies to copyright in the U.S. patent office plants and seeds which have been developed by farmers in developing countries for thousands of years—essentially robbing the intellectual property rights of farmers around the world. This decision began the dominance of patents within the food chain by companies that seek ever greater profit. This concept of patenting life, which is sacred, is absurd. What will be on the selling block next?

Almost ten years ago Catholic Workers from Houston protested in Alvin, Texas, with scientist and environmentalist Vandana Shiva from India against biopiracy. The Rice-Tec company in Alvin had attempted to copyright basmati rice, developed over thousands of years by farmers in India. The protests helped to at least limit the extent of their copyrights. One of the companies that controls much of worldwide agriculture is Monsanto, notably the most powerful in thwarting local development, the subsidiarity in agriculture that the Pope recommends. Monsanto not only markets chemicals and discourages traditional agricultural methods, but entices people everywhere to use their genetically modified, patented seeds. At first they often give the seeds at no cost. In order to use Monsanto's seeds, however, farmers must sign a contract not to save any seeds for the next year, but to always buy new seeds and herbicides from Monsanto. Local courts and even the World Trade Organization have upheld Monsanto's right to prosecute any farmers who saved a few seeds for the following year. These prosecutions have included quite a number of those who did not sign a contract with the company, but whose fields were contaminated by genetically modified seeds blown over from neighboring fields by the wind.

Investigative reporter Marie-Monique Robin, brought to public notice in her book *The World According to Monsanto*, observes that Monsanto now owns 90 percent of genetically modified food grown worldwide (mainly soy, corn, cotton, and canola). In an interview published on the Irish Seed Saver Association Web site, she describes the extent of Monsanto's control of seeds and plants from the countries of the South: "Between 1983 and 2005 Monsanto alone obtained 647 patents for plants, almost all originally from the Global South," also purchasing more than fifty seed companies in various countries.

It is difficult, if not impossible, for the small farmer to compete against a company with a $10 million budget and many investigators checking the fields. The concern over Monsanto's policies and policing and the toxicity of their pesticides is so great that organic farmers in the United States organized a campaign called "Millions Against Monsanto" in order to slow down the spread of toxic products through this company. They were successful in obtaining the support of major food distributors and school districts in refusing to carry milk containing hormones and antibiotics. The organic farmers remind all that Monsanto is the company that sold Agent Orange during the Vietnam War and continues to deny that it caused any problems.

Attempts to blunt Vatican criticism and guidance in economics have often included lobbying in and conferences at universities in Rome by the refusers of Catholic social teaching. Not to be outdone, the supporters of monopoly in agriculture have been holding such conferences where the influence of powerful companies like Monsanto can be felt. Two of these conferences, held in 2009, apparently were meant to influence the Synod of Bishops for Africa, whose working document contained critical language on corporate-controlled genetically modified crops. Press reports indicated that the Synod's document asserted that imposition of GMO (genetically modified organisms) risks "ruining small landholders, abolishing traditional methods of seeding, and making farmers dependent on production companies."

Many who work in the Global South were discouraged to learn of the conferences in Rome, at which basically all the papers presented Monsanto's view that biotechnology is essential in order to have enough food in the world. *The National Catholic Reporter's* John Allen wrote about the spring 2009 conference: "in one sign of concern about the appearance of corporate influence, sources told *NCR* that plans for the study week originally called for a couple of Monsanto employees to discuss public/private partnerships in the delivery of GMO technology. Roughly a month ago, however, the Monsanto officials were quietly advised not to attend."

Catholic News Service reported that Cardinal Renato Martino, the head of the Pontifical Council for Justice and Peace, addressing the scandal of hunger in the world, declared that the responsibility for the food crisis "is in the hands of unscrupulous people who focus only on profit and certainly not on the well-being of all people. A more just system of distribution and not the manufacturing of genetically modified foods is the key to addressing the problem," he said, adding that "if one wants to pursue GMOs one can freely do so, but without hiding that it's a way to make more profits."

Some who commented on *Caritas in Veritate* within a few days of its publication posited the idea that some well-known philanthropic foundations would have to be congratulated because they appeared to be doing what the Pope recommended. They may not have had time to read the encyclical carefully or to analyze the multinational links that such foundations have in biotech areas such as large grants to Monsanto in Africa as well as aggressive population control programs in developing countries, before rushing to judgment.

The implementation of the Pope's recommendations in agriculture and economics will be enormously difficult because of the corporate political power and propaganda of the agri-industry and biotech industries, and the "free trade" agreements set up to protect their monopolistic practices and the profits they bring to their countries. Perhaps that is why he asks for a reform of the United Nations Organization, as well as reforming economic institutions and international finance (e.g., World Bank, IMF, WTO), so that the concept of the family of nations "can acquire real teeth." The catch-22 here, of course, is that the WTO incorporates some of the worst legislation affecting the developing nations, and the WTO regulations take precedence over some national laws.

Much could be done, however, with the common good of all in the global economy in mind. The Supreme Court of the U.S., which can choose which cases to hear, and sometimes does choose cases that may affect or change decisions made in previous decades, could change the decision approving patenting life forms developed in other countries. Local initiatives in states and counties against the authoritarian absolute control of one company may bring such cases to the court. A more nuanced approach—such as traditional laws in Canada where higher life forms, including plants, could not be patented unless Parliament mandates it—would be a major improvement. With the unprecedented situation of six Catholics Justices sitting on the U.S. Supreme Court, there is a special opportunity to revisit this decision that has done much to promote a new colonialism. If those Catholic Justices as well as others of good will would carefully read *Caritas in Veritate* and apply its teaching, much could be done in the way of economic reform.

The Pope's recommendations for subsidiarity and support for local agriculture support the concept of distributism, championed by Chesterton and Belloc and the Catholic Worker Movement. Distributism supports the idea of private property, but insists on private property for everyone, not just the wealthy few. These recommendations also support those from the Global South who advocate small, independent farms with biologically diverse crops that would be more resistant to drought, disease, and flood.

MIGRATION IN EPOCHAL PROPORTIONS

The redistribution of wealth from the South to the North has pushed people to attempt to migrate to where their resources have been transferred, to a place where they could find work for their families. People become desperate when they simply cannot compete on a local level with the products sold by the agro-industrial monopolies. A scene in the film *Wetback: The Undocumented Documentary* brings to life the problem for the small grain processor. In the film, a Nicaraguan who prepares to migrate to the United States explains that his little business is no longer viable because he cannot compete with the product from Mexico called *Maseca*, the already prepared *masa* for tortillas. While the film does not mention it, a little research quickly shows the connection of *Maseca* with ADM, which (after NAFTA) developed an enormous processing plant in Mexico. The Nicaraguan whose attempt to migrate is unsuccessful may not have known that *Maseca* is from a multinational that controls the market, but he did know that it put him out of business.

The Merida Initiative, also known as Plan Merida, in 2008 began to provide millions of U.S. dollars to Mexico to militarize their southern border purportedly to control the importation of drugs. Like the militarization of the U.S.-Mexico border, however, the result is the massive deportation of migrants attempting to cross Mexico. This plan continues and escalates payments of the United States to Mexico for capturing and deporting Central Americans who attempt to migrate. Even in the 1980s we were told by immigration agents in Mexico that their department was given between $50 and $100 per head to deport Central Americans before they got as far as the United States.

Immigrants have made a tremendous contribution to the U.S. economy over many years. They built the houses, cut down trees, cut people's lawns, and cared for many of the children of Houston as live-in nannies. As the economy in the United States worsened in recent years, however, the migrants who had often been taken advantage of by businesses (sometimes not paid at all) were convenient scapegoats for economic problems in the North. We wrote in the *Houston Catholic Worker* in 2007: "The animosity and hostility towards immigrants in today's world is very hard to fathom, especially as U.S. foreign and economic policy forces immigration." It is as if the Ku Klux Klan is in charge of Public Relations, spitting out untruths and half-truths about immigrants, as they did in 1927 ridiculing Slovaks, Italians, Catholics, Jews, and Chinese people, and insisting on legislation to limit immigration to Northern Europeans. We remember as yesterday our mother telling stories of the Klan warning our father against being Catholic at that time. It would have been better if he was not Catholic.

The same negative campaign is being built up today against immigrants. One hears a barrage of comments scapegoating them for whatever difficulties the citizen writer or caller encounters. Economic woes are frequently laid at the feet of immigrants, accusing them of eating up all of our tax money with nothing left for citizens. No, it is the other way around. Money made from the undocumented immigrants' cheap labor means more profits, which go to CEOs and stockholders, not to immigrants. A fact often forgotten is that immigrants are taxpayers in every sense of the word. If they use a false social security number, the owner of the number reaps the benefits upon retirement. They pay sales tax; they contribute to property tax when they rent. They are eliminated, however, from receiving benefits from the taxes—a pretty good investment for everyone else.

It is no wonder that those who call in to talk shows are upset. The prevailing economics does not help the average citizen or poor person. CEOs and some stockholders do very well, but the so-called gains of the trickle-down theory have never trickled down. This is not the fault of the immigrant workers, but of an economics that is unjust. What trickles down is not benefits for the worker, but rather drops of blood. It is the height of duplicity to reject the immigrants after they have made a major contribution to our economy. To be in any way truthful, one simply cannot hire the undocumented at cheaper wages, longer hours, and harder work and then accuse them of being lawbreakers and potential terrorists, not to mention arresting them and deporting them or putting them in prison and breaking up their families. It almost appears that attacks on immigrants are promoted to make the immigrant more vulnerable and thus willing to work for less. They are treated as a disposable people—like disposable diapers.

SCAFFOLDING PHOBIA

Every time we see new construction going up in our neighborhood with scaffolding arranged in front of the building, we suffer anxiety attacks because we have seen what happens to construction workers who have fallen off these scaffolds and ended up with broken backs in three places, not able to move a limb. They can receive nothing from the community. There is no disability or compensation for their work. This is true of all the men and women injured or incapacitated for any reason. They are left to their own resources, which often do not exist. Harris County in Texas has the unusual possibility for them to receive eligibility for a short time for medical services, but strict rules for application or re-application may eliminate large numbers. There is no disability to assist with living, however, and no one to help with expenses for so many medical supplies needed.

The volunteer doctors of Casa Juan Diego assist when possible, although it is impossible to address the numbers who are in need. One of the very important services of the Casa Juan Diego and Casa Maria clinics is to help diabetic immigrants who otherwise become blind or lose a limb. Some find us too late, when their sight is almost gone or they no longer have feeling in their feet. Casa Juan Diego assists badly wounded people when we can with diapers, supplies to care for tracheotomies, and catheters. So often people need wheelchairs; when wheelchairs are donated, we pass them along to those in need. Imagine the government money saved by the refusal to aid the sick and injured immigrant. It would be in the billions—what a contribution to the economy! Hospital social workers call and ask for help because the person has no family here. If the person is alone here, the only real possibility is to make arrangements with a personal care home, a small business operated for the purpose of receiving ill people. In many cases, however, there is family, and the family struggles with what to do in a terrible crisis.

One of the saddest moments at Casa Juan Diego occurs when a family arrives saying that the private or public hospital had sent them to us to help them survive with a seriously injured family member. The hospital has no resources for follow-up after the emergency room. The ritual begins with tears in Casa Juan Diego's library where the family members narrate the awful accident or illness that has left a family member in serious physical condition and totally handicapped. Some have been sent home in a coma for the family to care for. The whole family is in crisis, and the employer of the paralyzed person will not help. The government will not help. The driver who injured the person in an accident ran away and cannot be found. The thief who shot the person cannot be found or has no resources to help. Someone supports the family, but another family member cannot work because someone must be available to take care of a very sick person, not to mention caring for their children. The ambience of a morgue lightens when we mention that Casa Juan Diego can help with some of the expenses. We can testify that the attacks in recent years blaming immigrants for our economic problems not only were untrue, but outright calumny. The raids on businesses, the imprisonment of immigrants, and the cruel, hurtful laws against them passed in many states have destroyed lives and families, not helped the economy.

Caritas in Veritate addresses the migration question directly, describing it as a striking phenomenon of epoch-making proportions because of the sheer numbers of people involved, the social, economic, political, cultural, and religious problems it raises, and the dramatic challenges it poses to nations and the international community. Benedict recommends bold, forward-looking policies of international cooperation to handle migration, policies that would safeguard the needs and rights of individual migrants and their families, and at the same time, those of the countries to which they go seeking work:

> The phenomenon, as everyone knows, is difficult to manage; but there is no doubt that foreign workers, despite any difficulties concerning integration, make a significant contribution to the economic development of the host country through their labor, besides that which they make to their country of origin through the money they send home. Obviously, these laborers cannot be considered as a commodity or a mere workforce. They must not, therefore, be treated like any other factor of production. Every migrant is a human person who, as such, possesses fundamental, inalienable rights that must be respected by everyone and in every circumstance. (*Caritas*, 62)

CONSISTENT ETHIC OF LIFE

A major theme of *Caritas in Veritate* is the unity of social justice, development of peoples, and respect for life. Those who denigrate the idea of a consistent ethic of life will not find support in this document where Benedict XVI states:

> The Church forcefully maintains this link between life ethics and social ethics, fully aware that a society lacks solid foundations when, on the one hand, it asserts values such as the dignity of the

person, justice and peace, but then, on the other hand, radically
acts to the contrary by allowing or tolerating a variety of ways in
which human life is devalued and violated, especially where it is
weak or marginalized. (*Caritas*, 15)

Rugged individualism does not find support here. The Pope specifically repudiates the claim of some that they owe nothing to anyone,
except to themselves. When he speaks of rights, he reminds us that
rights presuppose duties and responsibilities to and solidarity with others, and that elementary and basic rights remain unacknowledged and
are violated in much of the world. The Holy Father puts together the
right to life, the right to food, the right to water, the necessity to protect
the environment, and the development of peoples. A special concern
is infant mortality indicating that concern for life includes concern for
small babies.

Benedict XVI emphasizes the importance of the family and speaks
of responsible procreation as making a positive contribution to integral
human development, as opposed to state-mandated "family planning"
and forced sterilizations in which poor women may not even be informed of what is happening to them. He also points out the difficulties
countries are having where birth rates are very low.

While Natural Family Planning (NFP) is not mentioned in the encyclical, it is a practical response to the idea of responsible procreation.
The secular world is generally unaware of NFP, sometimes equating it
with the old rhythm method that did not work. Critics of the Church
might take note of the Pope's commitment to life here in his words of
responsible procreation. He is not suggesting that everyone have twelve
children, but to be open to life and to caring for young children.

Some years ago it was widely reported that a third of the women of
Brazil had been sterilized so that their factory work would not be interrupted. Because of our work with immigrants, we have been aware of the
demands of corporations, especially foreign or multinational corporations, on women in developing countries regarding pregnancies. Many
maquiladoras (outsourced factories) require proof that women are not
pregnant and not likely to become pregnant in order to be given or to
continue employment. Foundations and NGOs whose role is ostensibly
to help people often insist on contraception and sterilization, and governments in developing countries are pressured to mandate "family planning," at times a euphemism for forced procedures. Women sometimes

come to our clinics, for example, to have intrauterine devices removed. They had been under extreme pressure to accept their placement in their bodies, but they had found no clinic willing to remove them.

An important part of our work in Houston is receiving pregnant immigrant women who may have no one to help them, giving them hospitality during their pregnancy and afterward to help them get started again with their lives. We also receive pregnant women who are being asked to leave their homes by family members if they refuse to have an abortion. Generally, immigrant women are seeking not abortions but help during these few months and to get on their feet after the child's birth. Discussions of life issues in the United States are controversial. It is not always recognized that the decision a woman makes to have an abortion may not be unrelated to economics and the pressures of a consumer culture that countenances every form of self-indulgence. In that environment it is harder to expect average people to practice heroic virtue in carrying a child through a difficult pregnancy, or a pregnancy that will affect a family's lifestyle or a woman's work in a profession.

When everything is based on profit, the protection of life, food, and water that the Holy Father advocates is obviously not the priority. He asks for solidarity, sharing, in the protection of the environment and the conservation and development of energy resources, so that all might live:

> The technologically advanced societies can and must lower their domestic energy consumption, either through an evolution in manufacturing methods or through greater ecological sensitivity among their citizens. It should be added that at present it is possible to achieve improved energy efficiency while at the same time encouraging research into alternative forms of energy. What is also needed, though, is a worldwide redistribution of energy resources, so that countries lacking those resources can have access to them. *The fate of those countries cannot be left in the hands of whoever is first to claim the spoils, or whoever is able to prevail over the rest.* (Caritas, 49; emphasis added)

CONCLUSION

It is unusual to begin a study of economics, as Benedict XVI has done, with an insistence on truth in addition to the standard elements of Catholic social teaching such as solidarity, subsidiarity, and respect for workers. A closer look reveals that truth is often exactly what has been missing in discussions of business and economics, whether within a company, in reports to regulatory agencies, in advertising and public relations, or in presentations to stockholders or stakeholders. It is somewhat like the recent invention of government, what they call "truthiness," which may be only distantly related to the truth. The words used by economists sometimes seem to convey the opposite of their true meaning. This is especially noticeable in words related to freedom—for example, free trade, or free market, which is only free for huge monopolistic corporations or governments of wealthy nations. Statistics are used to disguise harsh realities in glowing terms. It is also true of the word "gift," as used by U.S. foundations linked with multinational corporations. The "gift" often has so many strings attached to it in relation to seeking future markets for the companies that it could hardly be called a gift in the true sense of the word.

We have wondered for years and written in the *Houston Catholic Worker* about why it might be that the economics and business departments of most Catholic colleges have adopted the same economics as their secular counterparts, seemingly without reference to what is taught in theology departments. In *Caritas in Veritate* Benedict XVI attributes many of the problems that limit success in the development of peoples to the rejection of metaphysics by the human sciences, what he calls the excessive segmentation and fragmentation of knowledge. This echoes Peter Maurin's writing about responses in his time to the encyclicals of Pius XI, who asked Catholics to transform the social order. Peter went to Catholic universities to ask Catholic professors what they were going to do about the social order. Their excuse for not addressing the question was the fragmentation of knowledge: "That's not my field!" *Caritas in Veritate* teaches that philosophy, theology, and socio-economic concerns cannot be separated, that "the broadening of our concept of reason and its application is indispensable if we are to succeed in adequately weighing all the elements involved in the question of development and in the solution of socio-economic problems" (*Caritas*, 31). Benedict insists that we must apply reason and a person-centered ethics to the powerful new forces of globalization, "animating them within the perspective of that 'civilization of love' whose seed God has planted in every people, in every culture" (*Caritas*, 33).

When we examine what Benedict means by integral human development in charity in truth and compare it with global realities of power, dominance, materialism, and cutthroat competition, the task of changing the economic system seems an enormous, almost impossible task. The Pope frames his argument, however, full of hope and trust that a new way is possible, if approached through truth and charity and joy:

> Only if we are aware of our calling, as individuals and as a community, to be part of God's family as his sons and daughters, will we be able to generate a new vision and muster new energy in the service of a truly integral humanism. The greatest service to development, then, is a Christian humanism that enkindles charity and takes its lead from truth, accepting both as a lasting gift from God. Openness to God makes us open towards our brothers and sisters and towards an understanding of life as a joyful task to be accomplished in a spirit of solidarity. (*Caritas*, 78)

Benedict also refuses to separate social ethics from spirituality. "Development requires attention to the spiritual life, a serious consideration of the experiences of trust in God, spiritual fellowship in Christ, reliance upon God's providence and mercy, love and forgiveness, self-denial, acceptance of others, justice and peace" (*Caritas*, 79). All this is essential, he says, if hearts of stone are to be transformed into hearts of flesh.

When Dorothy Day's cause for sainthood was introduced in Rome by Cardinal John O'Connor of New York, he said that "much of what she spoke of in terms of social justice anticipated the thought of John Paul II"—and that is true of Benedict XVI as well. Dorothy spoke about the need for a revolution—a revolution of the heart—to break away from the grip of materialism that tries to replace our values and take possession of our souls. Dorothy and Peter Maurin not only endorsed and taught Catholic social teaching as presented in the papal encyclicals and the practical implications of it, but also lived it, caring for those who were refugees from the economic system. Their views on economics and on the social order flowed from Church teaching on the common good, the universal destination of goods, the dignity of the human person, and the responsibility for God's creation held in trust for future generations. The very name Catholic Worker reflected their understanding that the concept of the common good must include the good of the masses who worked. Were Dorothy to be canonized, the reception and implementation of Catholic social teaching and specifically this encyclical would be encouraged.

Caritas in Veritate says: "God gives us the strength to fight and to suffer for love of the common good, because he is our All, our greatest hope." Given the machinations of the marketeers supported by theories taught in most universities and the suffering of the people around the world because of it, we will need all that strength to fight and suffer for the common good in our time and for an economics of communion and a civilization of love.

PART III

Civil and Political Economy

5

Fraternity, Gift, and Reciprocity in *Caritas in Veritate*

Stefano Zamagni

INTRODUCTION

O NE OF THE MARKS of our time is a constant call for ethics, which
has progressively replaced, over the past quarter of a century, the
persistent call for politics typical of the 1960s, when it was imagined that
"everything was politics." But this agreement on the primacy of ethics
ceases when it comes to tangible moral issues. As Alasdair McIntyre observed in *After Virtue*, the apodictic use of moral principles serves only
to put an end to the ethical dialogue itself. In other words, the broad
convergence on ethics in public debate almost never translates into ethical consensus.

The teaching of Pope John Paul II insisted constantly on this aspect. In his speech to the United Nations on October 5, 1995, the pontiff
stressed that it is possible to reach an agreement on social and political
issues on a shared common basis since "the universal moral law written

in the heart of man is a sort of 'grammar' which helps the world face the debate over its future."[1] In February 2004, in his address to the members of the Congregation for the Doctrine of the Faith, John Paul II—after recalling that the natural moral law can be a dialogical tool for everyone—said that the main obstacle to this was "the diffusion among faithful of an ethics based on fideism," hence the lack of "an objective benchmark for laws, which are often based on social consensus alone." This line of thought—embraced, even more strongly, also by Benedict XVI—has in *Caritas in Veritate* its first complete theorization. For that matter, before becoming Pope, Cardinal Ratzinger wrote the following: "Natural law reveals to us that even nature contains a moral message. The spiritual content of creation is not only mechanical or mathematical . . . There is a surplus of spirit, of 'natural laws' in the universe, which is imprinted with and which reveals to us an inner order."[2]

That said, in this essay I will discuss the manifestation of the principle of fraternity in economics. More specifically, I will try to answer this question: What does it mean and what does it imply, in today's economic systems, to embrace the fraternal principle, that is to say, the principle of reciprocity, as interpreted in Chapter 3 of *Caritas in Veritate*? But first it is necessary to explain properly what the principle of reciprocity is. The simplest way to do that is to compare the principle of exchange of equivalent values with that of reciprocity. The former states that whatever A does or gives to B, with whom he freely chose to start a relationship of exchange, must be counterbalanced by B doing or giving something of equal value to A. This "*something*," in our market economies, is nothing but the market price.

This principle is subject to two main qualifications. First of all, establishing the market price logically precedes the transfer of property right from A to B. (If A wants to sell his/her house to B, they must first of all reach an agreement on the price, and only afterwards can they go on to transfer the property right). Secondly, the transfer from B to A is not a free one; on the contrary, it depends on the transfer from A to B. In fact if B refused to fulfill the agreement, he/she would be compelled to do so by law. This means that in the exchange of equivalent values there is freedom *ex ante*, since the parties to the agreement are not forced to negotiate among themselves, but there is no freedom *ex post*.

1. John Paull II, *Teachings of John Paul II*, 732.
2. Ratzinger, *God and the World*, 142.

In reciprocity, by contrast, neither of these two features exists: A acts freely to help B in some way based on the *expectation* that B will do the same, eventually, for him/her or, even better, for C. In reciprocity there is no previous agreement on price, nor is B obliged to repay A. A simply forms an expectation, and if that expectation is disappointed, what happens is that A puts an end to (or changes) the relationship with B. This is why reciprocity is a fragile interpersonal relationship. The person who initiates the relationship always runs the risk of running into some opportunist fellow who only takes and never gives.

The two principles also differ in two other respects. First, the value of what B will give to (or do for) A or C need not be equivalent to what A gave to B. Reciprocity, in fact, is based on proportionality, not equivalence, as Aristotle understood perfectly: each gives according to his/her real possibilities. Second, while the *primum movens* of the exchange of equivalent values is to pursue a (legitimate) interest, reciprocity always starts as a free gift: A approaches B with the attitude of someone who wants to make a gift, not to make a deal.

TRANSCENDING OLD, OUTDATED DICHOTOMIES

The first important message we find in the encyclical *Caritas in Veritate* is the call to overcome the now outdated dichotomy between the economic and the social sphere. Modernity left us as a legacy the idea that setting profit as one's main goal and being moved by self-interest alone is a prerequisite to access the economy's club; which is the same as saying that one cannot be a true entrepreneur if one does not pursue profit maximization. Otherwise, one should be satisfied with belonging to the social sphere. This absurd idea—deriving from the theoretical error which confuses the market economy, a *genus*, with one of its particular *species*, namely capitalism—led us to identify the economy as the place where wealth (or income) is produced and whose basic principle is efficiency, and the social sphere as the place where wealth is distributed and solidarity is put into practice.

The encyclical, on the contrary, tells us that it is possible to do business even while pursuing socially useful goals and acting for pro-social reasons. This is one of the possible tangible ways to bridge the gap between the economic and the social sphere—a gap which is all the more dangerous considering that while it is true that an economy that simply leaves out the social dimension is not morally acceptable, it is also true that a social sphere consisting solely in redistribution, completely ignoring the resource constraint, would not be sustainable in the long run: one can only distribute what has been already produced.

In his document, the pontiff challenges the well-rooted commonplace that economic activity is too serious and difficult an activity to allow it not to be influenced by the four cardinal principles of the social teaching of the Church, namely: the centrality of the human person; solidarity; subsidiarity; and the common good. From this same commonplace comes the practical implication that the values of the social teaching only apply to works of a social nature, since the task of leading the economy must be left to those who are capable to guarantee the pursuit of efficiency.

Yet, contrary to what people commonly think, the *fundamentum divisionis* for telling what is an enterprise and what is not is not efficiency, for the simple reason that efficiency belongs to the order of means and not of ends. Indeed, one must be efficient in order to attain in the best possible way the end that one has freely chosen. However, the choice of ends has nothing to do with efficiency *per se*. Only after the end has been chosen can the entrepreneur act efficiently. Efficiency as an end to itself would become an ideology (the "efficiency ethos"), which today is one of the most frequent causes of the destruction of wealth, as the current economic-financial crisis sadly confirms.

Generalizing a moment the argument, it is certainly true that the market economy presupposes competition, since there cannot be a market where there is no competition (although the opposite is not true). And no one can ignore that the fruitfulness of competition lies in its implying a tension, which presupposes the presence of a third party and the relationship with a third party. Without tension there is no movement, although such movement—and this is the point—can also be lethal, it can cause death. This form of competition is called positional. It is a relatively new form of competition, rare in the past, and particularly dangerous, for it tends to destroy the bond with others. In positional competition, economic activity does not strive towards a common goal—as should be clear from the etymology, competition deriving from the Latin *cumpetere*—but follows Hobbes's "*mors tua, vita mea.*" And it is precisely here that we see the foolishness of positional competition, which selects the best, giving victory to those who arrive first, but eliminates or neutralizes those who come in "second," the losers. Under positional competition, the social bond turns into a mere trade relationship and economic action tends to become inhuman, therefore inefficient.

Now, the advantage—and not a minor one—that *Caritas in Veritate* offers us is to stand for a concept of market, typical of the tradition of the school of thought of civil economy, according to which one can live the experience of human sociality inside a regular economic life, and not outside or beside it, as the dichotomous model of society suggests. This point of view is an alternative both to the idea of the market as the locus of exploitation, domination of the strong over the weak and to the anarcho-liberal idea of the market as the place where all the problems of society can be solved by using its proper mechanisms.

Civil economy becomes an alternative to the tradition descending from Adam Smith, which seems to see the market as the only institution that democracy and freedom really need. The Church's social teaching, instead, reminds us that of course a good society is the fruit of the market and of freedom, but also that there are needs, which can be reduced to the fraternity principle, that cannot be ignored, nor left to the private sphere or to philanthropy. At the same time, Catholic social teaching does not side with those who fight against the markets and who see economic action as in endemic and natural conflict with the good life, who cry out for less growth and for the retreat of the economy from life in common. Rather, what the encyclical proposes is a multi-faceted humanism where the market is neither resisted nor "controlled," but considered as an important moment for the public sphere—much broader than the sphere of the State—which, when conceived and experienced as a place open also to the reciprocity principle and to gift, can build the "city"—the *civitas*.

FROM FRATERNITY, THE COMMON GOOD

The key word expressing this need better than any other, today, is "fraternity," a word enshrined also in the motto of the French Revolution but that was then dropped by the post-revolutionary order—for well known reasons—and eventually cancelled from the political and economic lexicon. It was the Franciscan school of thought that attributed to the word *fraternity* the meaning it has kept over time. An important point should be stressed right away: not to confuse solidarity with fraternity.

For as solidarity is the principle of social organization that enables un-equals to become equals, fraternity is the principle that allows equals to be diverse. Fraternity allows people who are equal in dignity and in their fundamental rights to make different life plans, or to express their charisma in different ways. The centuries we have left behind, the nine-teenth and even more the twentieth century, were characterized by huge battles, both cultural and political, in the name of solidarity, and this was certainly positive; just think of the history of labor unions or the struggle for civil rights. The point is that the good society in which to live cannot be satisfied with the perspective of solidarity alone, because a society based only on solidarity and not on fraternity would be a society that everyone would try to get away from. The truth is that while a fraternal society is also one where solidarity is put into practice, the reverse is not necessarily true.

Having forgotten that a society of human beings without frater-nity—where everything comes down to improving transactions based on the exchange of equivalent values on the one hand, and to increas-ing transfer from public welfare structure on the other hand—cannot be sustainable explains why, despite the quality of intellectual resources deployed, we have not yet found a credible solution to the famous trade-off between efficiency and equity. A society from which the principle of fraternity has faded is not capable of generating a future; a society where there exists only the idea of "giving to get" or else "giving out of duty" is not capable of progress. This is why neither the liberal and individualist idea of the world, where nearly everything is exchange, nor the state-centered idea of society, where nearly everything is due is a safe path out of the shallows in which our modern societies are mired.

The question is as follows: why is it that over the past quarter of a century the perspective of the discourse on the common good, following the definition of the social teaching of the Church—after at least two centuries in which it had left the scene—is now coming to the surface again, like a subterranean river? Why is the shift from national to inter-national markets over the last twenty-five years now lending new life to the discourse on the common good? At a glance I can observe that what is happening is part of a broader movement of ideas in economics, a school of thought focusing on the relationship between religion and economic performance. Starting with the idea that religious beliefs play a fundamental role in shaping the cognitive maps of individuals and in molding the rules of social behavior, this school wants to study to what extent the predominance in a given country (or area) of a particular religion influences the emergence of categories of economic thought, welfare programs, educational policy, and so on. After a protracted period when it had seemed that secularization had settled the religious question once and for all, at least in the economic sphere, what we are experiencing is truly paradoxical.

It is not too hard, actually, to find a reason for the resurgence of the standpoint of the common good, the distinctive feature of the Catholic ethic in social and economic issues, in the contemporary cultural discussion. As John Paul II clearly pointed out on several occasions, the social teaching of the Church is not to be interpreted as one more ethical theory in addition to the many already available in the literature, but as a "common grammar" for them, for it is based on a specific idea, the idea of caring for the human good. Indeed, while the various ethical theories have their foundations in the search for rules (as is the case of positivist natural law doctrine, under which ethics derives from law) or in men's actions (as with Rawlsian neo-contractualism or neo-utilitarianism), the fulcrum of the social teaching of the Church is "being together." The meaning of the ethics of the common good is that "[i]n order to be able to grasp the object of an act which specifies that act morally, it is . . . necessary to place oneself 'in the perspective of the acting person'"[3]—and not that of a third party (as in natural law) or (as Adam Smith suggested) a neutral spectator. As a matter of fact, as the moral good is a practical thing, it is known mainly not by those who theorize about it but by those who practice it: these are the people who can spot it and therefore choose it with certainty any time the moral good is under discussion.

The Principle of Gift in the Economy

What does embracing gratuitousness in economic action practically entail? I would like here to briefly discuss two of the many consequences. The first concerns the way we look at the relation between economic growth and welfare programs. Which comes first, economic growth or welfare? In other words, is welfare expenditure to be considered social consumption or social investment? The thesis sustained in *Caritas in*

---

3. *Veritatis Splendor*, 78.

Veritate is that, in the current historical situation, it is far more credible and justifiable to see welfare as a factor of economic growth, rather than seeing growth as the cause generating welfare.

It is well known that in the second half of the twentieth century the Welfare State had two main goals: reducing poverty and social exclusion by redistributing, through taxes, income and wealth (the "Robin Hood" function) and providing social insurance services to foster efficient resource allocation over time (the "piggy-bank" function). The *ad hoc* strategy adopted was, basically, the following: governments should use the dividend of the economic growth to improve the *relative* position of the worst-off without worsening the *absolute* position of the better-off. But a series of circumstances—globalization and the new technologies—caused, in Western developed countries starting from the 1980s, a slowdown in potential growth. This eventually fueled the idea, in the last decade, that the cause of the slowdown was taxation and social insurance redistribution, which were consequently blamed for a scarcity of resources for government social action.

Where this way of interpreting welfare has led is now clear to all. Not only is the old Welfare State today incapable of dealing with the new poverty; but it is also helpless in front of rapidly worsening social inequalities in Europe. For instance, over the last quarter-century in Italy the profit share of GDP has risen from 23 to 30 percent, while that of labor has fallen from 77 to 70 percent. As the last CENSIS survey shows, Italy is by now a country with "narrow gauge mobility:" people on the bottom of the social ladder *today* find it more difficult than in the past to move up to higher rungs. This is eloquent evidence that there are real poverty traps: once you fall in, you cannot find the way out. Today, the inefficient person is cut off from full citizenship, because no one recognizes the proportionality of resources. In other words, the inefficient people (or those less efficient than average) don't qualify to take part in the production process; they are inexorably excluded because *decent* work is only for the efficient guys. For the others there is indecent work or public (or private) compassion.

What is to be done, then, if one takes seriously the message of the *Caritas in Veritate*? The first step is to transcend the outdated concepts of equality of *outcomes* (cherished by the social-democratic political position) and equality of *starting* positions (the approach favored by the liberal line of thought). Rather, we should conjugate the concept of equality of capabilities (in Amartya Sen's sense) by interventions to distribute resources (monetary and other) to people so that they can improve the quality of their life. Sen's approach to well-being suggests shifting our focus from the goods and services we intend to make available to people in need to these people's actual ability to function thanks to those goods and services. This is why the new welfare must overcome the self-referential distortion of the old welfare. When health services, public assistance, education and so on, even if of high quality technically, do not enhance their beneficiaries' capability to function, they reveal themselves to be ineffective, or even harmful, because certainly they do not foster development. In practice, this means that we must quickly abandon the mistaken idea that individual human rights (life, liberty, property) and social citizenship rights (dealt with by the Welfare State) are mutually incompatible and that one can only protect social rights at the expense of individual rights. As we are well aware, in Europe this idea was at the origin of pointless ideological battles and significant waste of productive resources.

There is also a second step to be taken. The new welfare must be subsidiary, that is to say, it must use public resources coming mainly from general taxation not to finance—as is currently the case—the supply side, but the demand side of the welfare system. This is because when the State directly funds the various supply agencies, it alters the nature of the services they provide and makes their costs rise. Not only that, but funding the needy increases their responsibility and self-reliance and mobilizes organized civil society to take action. Let us not forget that direct funding of supply tends to alter the nature of the identity of the entities within civil society through red tape that tends to cancel the peculiarities of each one—the very peculiarities on which the creation of social capital depends.

My conclusion is that the arguments for the trade-off between social security and economic growth are far less plausible than those against it. It is simply not true that strengthening social security condemns us to lower growth, making it unsustainable. On the contrary, a post-Hobbesian welfare system, mainly based on policies promoting individual capabilities, in the current post-industrial era—marked by the emergence of new social risks—is the most effective antidote against possible antidemocratic temptations and therefore the decisive factor for economic progress.

The second consequence of assigning the principle of gratuitousness a key role in the economy has to do with the diffusion of the culture and the practice of reciprocity. Reciprocity, together with democracy, is one of the founding values of our society. Indeed, it is precisely in reciprocity, one could say, that democracy finds its ultimate meaning.

In what "places" does reciprocity reside; where, that is, is it practiced and nourished? The first such place is the family: just think of the relationship between parents and children, brothers and sisters. Then there come cooperatives, social enterprises and the many forms of association. Is it not true that the relationships between the members of a family or between the members of a cooperative are relationships of reciprocity? Now we know that the civil and economic development of a country basically depends on how widespread the practice of reciprocity is among its citizens. Without mutual acknowledgement of a common belonging, no efficiency, no economic growth can survive. Today, there is a desperate need for cooperation: this is why we must develop new forms of gratuitousness and strengthen the existing ones. Those societies that uproot the tree of reciprocity are doomed to decline, as history has taught us over the centuries.

What is the function of the gift? It is to make people understand that besides the goods of justice, there are also gratuitous goods, and therefore that a society which is satisfied with only the goods of justice is not genuinely human. What is the difference? Justice goods are those originating in a duty; gratuitousness goods are those arising out of an *obligatio*. In other words these goods derive from the realization that one is tied to someone else and that, in a certain sense, this someone else is a part of me. This is why the logic of gratuitousness cannot be simplistically reduced to a purely ethical dimension; gratuitousness is not a moral virtue. Justice, as Plato once taught us, is a moral virtue, and we all agree on the importance of justice, but gratuitousness rather deals with the supra-ethical dimension of human actions since its logic is superabundance, while the logic of justice is equivalence. *Caritas in Veritate* tells us that in order for a society to function and progress, its economic activity needs to involve people who understand what the goods of gratuitousness are; in other words, that it is clear to all that we need to bring the gratuitousness principle back into our society.

Benedict XVI encourages us to accept the challenge and fight to restore the gift principle to the *public sphere*. Genuine gift, by establishing the primacy of the relationship over its exemption, of personal identity over profit, must find a way to express itself everywhere, in whatever field of human action, economy included. The message of the encyclical is to think of gratuitousness, and consequently of fraternity, as a mark of the human condition, thus looking at gift as the necessary prerequisite for the State and the market to function for the common good. Of course there can be an efficient market and an authoritative State (even a just State) even without gift, but people will not be helped to attain *joie de vivre*. In fact efficiency and justice, even together, are not enough to ensure people's happiness.

ON THE REMOTE CAUSES OF THE FINANCIAL CRISIS

Caritas in Veritate does not fail—how could it?—to "read" the current economic and financial crisis. It does so by dwelling on the remote (and not the proximate) causes of the crisis. The encyclical points out three main factors of the crisis that it analyzes in depth. The first cause concerns the radical change in the relationship between finance and the production of goods and services that has taken place over the last thirty years. Starting in the mid-1970s most Western countries linked their retirement commitments to investments that depended on the sustainable profitability of new financial instruments. At the same time, the creation of these new instruments has progressively exposed the real economy to the caprices of finance, therefore necessitating the allocation of an ever-growing share of value added to the remuneration of the savings thus invested. Pressure on businesses from the stock exchange market and from private equity funds translated into even greater pressures elsewhere: on managers, who are obsessively driven to continuously enhance their performance in order to profit by their stock options; on consumers to persuade them, through sophisticated marketing strategies, to buy more and more even when they have no purchasing power; on businesses in the real economy to persuade them to increase shareholder value. And so it happened that the persistent demand for ever more brilliant financial results started to have an impact, with a typical trickle-down mechanism, on the economy as a whole, until it became an authentic cultural model. In pursuit of an ever more radiant future, we forgot about the present.

The second major cause of the crisis is the diffusion at the level of popular culture of the efficiency ethos as ultimate yardstick and justification of the economy. On the one hand, this ultimately legitimated greed—the best-known and most widespread form of avarice—as some sort of civic virtue: the *greed market* that supplants the *free market*. "Greed is good, greed is right," said Gordon Gekko, the hero of the movie *Wall Street* (1987). On the other hand, the ethos of efficiency is what caused the now systematic alternation between greed and panic. It is not true, as more than once commentators tried to explain, that panic is the consequence of irrational behavior by market agents. That is, panic is nothing but euphoria with the minus sign in front of it, and since euphoria is irrational, according to the dominant theory, so is panic.

Finally, *Caritas in Veritate* addresses the cause of the causes of the crisis: the specific cultural matrix that was consolidated over the past decades on the wave of globalization on the one side and of the third industrial revolution on the other. It is worth analyzing one particular aspect of this cultural phenomenon: namely, the more and more common dissatisfaction with the way the principle of freedom is interpreted. As we know, freedom is made up of three constituent aspects: autonomy, immunity, empowerment. Autonomy is about freedom of choice: you are only free if you can choose, i.e., if you enjoy positive freedom in Isaiah Berlin's sense. Immunity rather concerns the absence of coercion by external subjects. In other words, it is basically negative freedom (that is to say, "freedom from"). Finally, empowerment means the capacity to choose, to attain the objectives that the individual sets himself, at least to some extent. We are not free if we never realize our life plan, at least in part.

It is a fact that while the anarcho-liberal approach ensures the first and second of these dimensions of freedom at the expense of the third, the State-centered approach, whether in the mixed economy version or in the social democratic version, tends to give the second and third precedence over the first. The free-market approach can indeed serve as the motor of change, but it is not equally capable of managing the negative consequences, due to the substantial temporal asymmetry between the distribution of the costs of change and the sharing of its benefits. The costs are immediate and tend to be levied on the weakest members of the population. The benefits arrive with time and tend to go to the most talented. Yet the social market economy—in all its versions—

while proposing the State as the subject in charge of coping with this asynchrony, does not weaken the logic of the Darwinian market; it only narrows the area of its operation and impact. The challenge that *Caritas in Veritate* invites to meet is to keep—at least ideally—all three dimensions of freedom together.

We can see, in the light of the foregoing, why the financial crisis cannot be called either unexpected or inexplicable. This is why, taking nothing away from all the fundamental regulatory actions and the necessary new forms of control, we will not be able to prevent other similar events from happening in the future unless we attack the root of the evil, unless we intervene on the cultural background underpinning the economy. This crisis sends a double message to the government authorities. First of all, it says that in no way can the more-than-justified critique of the "interventionist State" delegitimize the central role of the "regulatory State." Secondly, it says that public authorities at different government levels must allow, even encourage, the creation and the strengthening of a pluralist financial market, a market where different subjects can operate on a level playing field with regards to the specific objective of their activity. I am here thinking of mutual banks, ethical banks, ethical investment funds, etc. These are all institutions that not only do not offer their customers "creative finance" but that also play a complementary role, therefore also a balancing role, with the agents of speculative finance. Had the financial authorities loosened, over the past decades, all the regulatory constraints binding the agents of alternative finance, the current crisis would not have been as devastating as it has proved to be.

TOWARDS GLOBAL GOVERNANCE

The encyclical *Caritas in Veritate* deals powerfully with one extremely topical issue: the link between peace and integral human development. Paul VI popularized this topic in his *Populorum progressio* (1967) with the famous dictum: "Development is the new name of peace." In full agreement, Benedict XVI formulates a systematic argument that I here summarize as follows: a) peace is possible, because war is an event, not a state of things. War is therefore a transitory emergency, however long it may last, and not a permanent condition of human society; b) nonetheless, peace must be built, because it is not something spontaneous, rather it is the fruit of work aimed at creating institutions of peace; c) in this historical period, the most urgent institutions of peace are those that involve human development.

What are the institutions of peace deserving top priority today? To sketch out an answer, it is better to focus on some stylized fact of our age. The first is the scandal of hunger. It is well known that hunger is not a tragic novelty of our time; what makes it scandalous today, and thus intolerable, is that it is not the result of a "production failure" at global level, that is to say of the incapacity of the economy to produce enough food for each and all. It is therefore not a scarcity of resources, at global level, that is causing hunger and deprivation. Rather, the main cause is "institutional failure," that is to say the lack of adequate economic and legal institutions.

Just consider the following events. The extraordinary increase in economic interdependence over the past quarter-century means that a substantial part of the world population may be adversely affected, in their living conditions, by events in places far removed from where they live and about which they cannot do anything. Thus, today the well-known "depression famine" is coupled by "boom famine," as Sen has so abundantly demonstrated. Furthermore, the expansion of the market area—a phenomenon which is *per se* positive—means that a social group's access to food depends crucially on the decisions of other social groups. For instance, the price of a commodity (coffee, cocoa, etc.) that is the main source of revenue for a given community, can depend on what happens to the prices of other products, independently of any change in the conditions of production of the first good.

A second stylized fact is the changed nature of trade and competition between rich and poor countries. In recent decades the growth rate of the poorest countries has been higher than that of the richest countries: around 4 percent compared to 1.7 percent per year in the period 1980–2000. This is unprecedented, since in the past it had never happened that the poor countries had grown faster than the rich. This explains why, in the same period of time, there was for the first time in history a decrease in the number of absolutely poor people (people living with less than two dollars a day, taking into account purchasing power parities). Allowing for the increase in population, we can say that absolute poverty rate in the world fell from 62 percent in 1978 to 29 percent in 1998. (Needless to say, this remarkable achievement did not involve the various regions of the world equally. For example, in

Sub-Saharan Africa the number of absolute poor people went up from 217 million in 1987 to 301 million in 1998). At the same time, however, relative poverty, meaning inequality—according to such yardsticks as the Gini coefficient or of the Theil index—has increased strikingly since 1980. It is well known that the total inequality index is given by the sum of two components: inequality *between* countries and inequality *within* countries. As the important work by P. Lindert and J. Williamson points out, a good part of the increase in total inequality can be attributed to the increase in the second component both in populous countries with high economic growth rates (China, India and Brazil), and in the advanced Western countries.[4] This means that the redistribution effects of globalization are not univocal: not always do the rich benefit (be they countries or social groups) nor do the poor always lose out.

I also want to briefly address a third stylized fact. The link between people's nutrition and their capacity for work affects both the way food is distributed among family members—more specifically between male and female—and the way in which the job market works. Poor people possess only the potential for work; in order for this potential to be translated into actual labor power, the individual needs adequate nourishment. Now, undernourished people, when not appropriately helped, are not able to satisfy this condition in a free market economy. The reason is simple: the quality of the labor that a poor person can offer on the job market is not enough to "command" the food he or she needs for a decent standard of living. As modern nutritional science has shown, 60 percent to 75 percent of the energy an individual gets from food is used to keep the body alive; only the rest of that energy can be used to work or to carry out other activities. This is why in poor societies "true poverty traps" can emerge, destined to last for long periods of time.

What is even worse is that the economy can continue to feed those poverty traps even as aggregate income rises. For instance, it can—and does—happen that economic development, measured in terms of per capita GDP, encourages peasants to shift from growing grain to producing meat, raising more livestock, as the profits from the latter are higher than for the former. However, the consequent rise in the price of grain will worsen the nutritional levels of the poor, who have no access to meat anyway. The point is that an increase in the number of low-income individuals can aggravate the malnutrition of the poorest because of a

4. Lindert and Williamson, "Does Globalization Make the World More Unequal?"

change in the composition of the demand for final goods. Let us observe, finally, that the link between state of nutrition and labor productivity can be "dynastic": once a family or social group falls into the poverty trap, it is truly difficult for their descendants to get out of it, even when the economy as a whole is growing.

What conclusions should then be drawn? That awareness of a close linkage between "institutional failures" and the scandal of hunger and worsening global inequality reminds us that institutions are not—like natural resources—a natural fact, but instead the rules of the economic game fixed at political level. If—as was the case at the beginning of the twentieth century—hunger depended on a situation of absolute shortage of resources, there would be nothing to do but encourage fraternal sympathy and solidarity. Knowing, on the contrary, that it depends on the rules, that is to say on the institutions, which are in part outdated and in part wrong, cannot but drive us to intervene on the mechanisms and on the procedures for setting fixing and implementing those rules. The urgency of action in this direction is stressed in a passage from Norberto Bobbio showing, with rare efficacy, the link between liberty, equality and the struggle for power: "In human history, battles for supremacy alternate with struggles for equality. This alternation is absolutely natural since the fight for supremacy presupposes that there are two individuals or groups that have achieved a certain equality. The struggle for equality usually precedes the fight for supremacy . . . Before fighting for dominance, each social group must conquer a certain degree of parity with its rivals."[5]

The difficulty in carrying out institutional actions such as this is clear to everyone. This is precisely why the encyclical speaks of the urgency to give birth to a global political Authority, which must however be subsidiary and polyarchical. This implies, on the one hand, opposition to some kind of super state and, on the other hand, the political will to radically update the conclusions of the 1944 Bretton Woods Conference, where the new international economic order was shaped after a long period of wars.

En guise de conclusion

In *Weddings*, Albert Camus wrote the following: "If there is a sin against life, perhaps it is not so much to despair of it as to hope in another life and

5. Bobbio, *Destra e Sinistra*, 164.

so flee from the implacable grandeur of this one."[6] Camus did not believe in God, but he teaches us a truth: you must not sin against this life by discrediting and humiliating it. One must not, therefore, shift the center of his/her faith beyond the grave so that the present becomes meaningless; it would mean to sin against the Incarnation. It is an ancient option going back to the Fathers of the Church who called the Incarnation a *Sacrum Commercium* to highlight the relationship of profound reciprocity between the human and the divine and above all to underscore the fact that the Christian God is a God of men who live in history and who cares about, and is even moved by, their human condition. To love life is thus an act of faith and not only of personal pleasure. This opens us to hope, which concerns not only the future but also the present, since we need to know that our actions, besides a destination, have a meaning and a value here and now too.

The fifteenth century was the century of the first Humanism, a typically European phenomenon. The twenty-first century, from the very outset, powerfully demonstrates the need for a new Humanism. Then, the shift from feudalism to modernity was the decisive factor which pushed in this direction. Today, it is an equally radical epochal transition—from industrial society to post-industrial society, i.e., from modernity to post-modernity—that shows us the need for a new Humanism. Globalization, the financialization of the economy, new technologies, migration, the increase in social inequality, identity conflicts, the environmental question, international debt, are only a few of the keywords telling us about the "discontents" of today's "civilization," to cite Freud's seminal essay. In facing these new challenges, merely updating our old categories of thought or resorting to collective decision techniques, however refined, is not suitable for the purpose. We must have the courage to walk on new paths: this is essentially the heartfelt appeal of *Caritas in Veritate*.

6. Camus, *Weddings*.

6

The Paradoxical Nature of the Good

Relationality, Sympathy, and Mutuality in Rival Traditions of Civil Economy

Adrian Pabst

PARADIGMATIC SHIFTS

A CROSS DIFFERENT ACADEMIC DISCIPLINES, we are witnessing a fundamental and perhaps paradigmatic shift away from individuality towards relationality. Both natural sciences and humanities are seeing the emergence of different relational models that attempt to theorize the widespread recognition that reality cannot be reduced to self-generating, individual beings and that the outcome of interactions between various entities is more than the sum of parts (whether these be more atomistic or more collectivist). For instance, in particle physics it has been suggested that there are "things" such as quarks (subatomic particles) which cannot be measured individually because they are confined by force fields and only exist inside certain particles (hadrons) that are themselves bound together by a strong "substantial" interplay with other hadrons.[1]

Likewise, recent evidence from research in fields such as evolutionary biology and neuroscience shows that modern ontological atomism and the spontaneous spirit of possessive acquisitiveness are at odds with more holistic models of human nature. Indeed, the human brain is in some important sense organically connected to the world and responds unconsciously to the social environment within which it is embedded. Such an account of selfhood contrasts sharply with the dominant modern conception that the self is a separate, self-standing agent that makes conscious, rational decisions based on individual volition.[2] Linked to the naturally given social embeddedness of the self is the argument (substantiated by findings from a comprehensive, global survey) that fundamental moral distinctions are somehow "hard-wired" in human beings and that virtuous habits such as cooperative trust or mutual sympathy precede the exercise of instrumental reason or the interplay of sentimental emotions.[3]

Relational patterns and structures are also moving to the fore in a growing number of disciplines in the humanities and social sciences. For example, in anthropology it is argued that the idea of a purely self-interested *homo oeconomicus* in pursuit of material wealth (central to Adam Smith's *Wealth of Nations*) reduces the natural desire for goodness to a series of vague, pre-rational moral feelings (as set out in his *Theory of Moral Sentiments*). As such, it marks a radical departure from older ideas of man as a "political animal" in search of mutual social recognition through the exercise of virtues embodied in practices and the exchange of gifts—instead of a mechanical application of abstract values

1. The emphasis on relationality in particle physics can be traced to nineteenth-century "field theorists" like Michael Faraday and James Clerk Maxwell whose research shaped Einstein's theory of relativity. See Einstein, *Relativity*, Appendix V. Cf. Einstein, "The Mechanics of Newton," in *Ideas and Opinions*.

2. Hauser, *Moral Minds*. This needs to be complemented by the argument that a proper ethics surpasses the classically modern dichotomy between "right" and "wrong" in the direction of an outlook towards the virtue of justice and the transcendent reality of goodness. Such an outlook is a fusion of natural desire and supernaturally infused habit, as Christian Neo-Platonists in East and West have tended to argue.

3. In this context, Matt Ridley's claim in his influential book *Origins of Virtue* that human virtue is driven by self-interest and closely connected to the division of labor uncritically accepts the modern dualism of egoism and altruism and also the premise that morality is grounded in a purely immanent account of human nature.

and the trading of pure commodities.[4] For these (and other) reasons, individuals cannot be properly understood as separate from the relations that bring them into existence and sustain them in being. Instead, individuals are best conceived in terms of personhood, defined as the plural and composite locus of relationships and the confluence of different microcosms.

Similarly, in sociology, cultural studies, and cognate fields, the past decade or so has seen a growing body of research on human cooperation, creativity, and connectedness.[5] Closely related to these themes is a renewed interest in rival conceptions of ontology. Here the focus on social relationality in the social sciences coincides with a growing emphasis on metaphysical relationality in philosophy and theology. In turn, this is linked to a fresh concern with a theological metaphysics that rejects the late medieval and modern primacy of individual substance over ontological relation.[6]

Crucially for the present essay, the most innovative research in contemporary economics repudiates the modern, liberal separation of private and public goods in favor of relational goods and a renewed emphasis on the reciprocal bonds of sympathy that always already tie individuals together.[7] Closely tied to this is a critique of methodological individualism and a total mapping of individual preferences. Since neither is theoretically and empirically warranted, the entire edifice of modern political economy (after Adam Smith) and modern economic science (after Carl Menger) becomes unhinged. This casts doubt over key premises and concepts such as economics as a "value-free" and pure science, instrumental rationality, perfect information, the "rational

4. Polanyi, *Great Transformation*, 45–70; Hénaff, *Le prix de la vérité*, 351–80.

5. Donati, *Relational Sociology*; Shirky's books *Here Comes Everybody* and *Cognitive Surplus* suggest that contemporary social activity linked to the Internet and telecommunications refutes the modern idea that man is a utility-maximizing rational actor. Shirky also argues that technological innovation that harnesses human communication is in part a sign that the natural desire for relationality also shapes economic activity and political processes.

6. E.g. Desmond, *God and the Between*; Pabst, *Metaphysics*; Shults, *Reforming Theological Anthropology*.

7. Bruni and Zamagni, *Civil Economy*, 45–99; Halpern, *Hidden Wealth of Nations*, 56–123. The emphasis on relationality and sympathy develops ongoing research on the cooperative instincts of humans and (other) animals in a stronger metaphysical and political direction. It also qualifies cruder distinctions between "bonding" and "bridging" in the work of Robert Putnam and others.

expectations" hypothesis as well as the "efficient market" theory.[8] All this calls into question the conceptual foundations and empirical conclusions of both classical and neo-classical economics.

It is true that Smith himself sought to overcome the atomism of early modern political economy (as developed by Mandeville, Hobbes, and Locke) in the direction of a social philosophy and moral theory that accentuates universal moral sentiments of benevolence and fellow-feeling. His account replaces the idea of private vice and arbitrary divine power with the rival idea of enlightened self-interest and human agency. But he views the market as unconstrained by the strong bonds of interpersonal ties and in some sense prior to the sociality which market relations make possible. Only the liberty and equality of commercial society generates the trust on which fellow-feeling and social bonds depend.

In this manner, Smith introduces a double split: first, between the quest for happiness and the exercise of virtue; second, between private, moral virtues such as love and benevolence, on the one hand, and public, civic virtues such as prudence or justice, on the other hand. As such, he departs from the emphasis in the Neapolitan Enlightenment of Giambattista Vico, Paolo Mattia Doria, and Antonio Genovesi on the mutual sympathy that binds together what we now call civil society and the market—a civic economy wherein market exchange is embedded in relations of mutuality and reciprocity. For instance, Doria defines "commerce as 'mutuo soccorso', mutual assistance [. . . that] requires both liberty and security of contracts, which in turn depend on trust (*fede*) and justice."[9]

By contrast with the Neapolitan School and his friend Hume, Smith argues that the virtues of sympathy and benevolence only operate at the micro level of interpersonal relations, producing strong, thick bonds between individuals bound together by personal ties of family or friendship. Unlike the Neapolitan and Humean accounts,[10] sympathy and benevolence are absent from the macro level of weaker, thinner ties among individuals who are not bound together by personal bonds:

8. Screpanti and Zamagni, *Outline of the History of Economic Thought*, 43–71, 145–211.

9. Robertson, *Case for the Enlightenment*, 201–405 (quote at 334).

10. Hume's account of sympathy is not limited to the interpersonal and the social but encompasses the cosmic and metaphysical—"the coherence and apparent sympathy in all the parts of this world," as he writes in *Dialogues Concerning Natural Religion*, XII, 86. On this reading of Hume, see John Milbank, "Hume versus Kant."

"Men, though naturally sympathetic, feel so little for one another, with whom they have no particular connection, in comparison of what they feel for themselves; the misery of one, who is merely their fellow-creature, is of so little importance to them in comparison even of a small inconveniency of their own."[11]

Crucially, Smith is adamant that sympathy and benevolence are not important at all for the market; on the contrary, Bruni and Zamagni are right to conclude that for the Glaswegian professor of moral philosophy, "*the market* itself doesn't require them, and works even better without them (hence the praise of weak ties)."[12] Economic production and trade based on contract is sundered from mutual sympathy and concern for the personal well-being of fellow "economic actors" such as our butcher, brewer or baker. In turn, this gives rise to the notion of "cooperation without benevolence" that links Smith's moral philosophy in *The Theory of Moral Sentiments* to his political economy in *The Wealth of Nations*.[13]

As a result, exchanges in the marketplace are divorced from the practice of virtues, and agents treat economic relations as an instrument to attain self-interested objectives. Only God's intervention—the divine "invisible hand of the market"—can providentially blend self-interest and instrumental market relations with the pursuit of efficiency and public happiness.[14] Moreover, market relations are now seen as the precondition rather than the outcome of sociality: Smith writes that

> society may subsist among different men, as among different merchants, from a sense of its utility, without any mutual love or affection; and though no man in it should owe any obligation, or be bound in gratitude to any other, it may still be upheld by a mercenary exchange of good offices according to an agreed valuation.[15]

Thus, Smith's anthropology hovers halfway between Bernard Mandeville's dubious claim that public virtue is somehow the unintended consequence of private vice, on the one hand, and the Neapolitan insistence that the civic institutions and virtuous practices of civil life

11. Smith, *Theory of Moral Sentiments*, part II, sec. 2, ch. 3, 125.

12. Bruni and Zamagni, *Civil Economy*, 106 (emphasis original).

13. Smith, *Theory of Moral Sentiments*, part II, sec. 2, ch. 1-3, 112–32 and part VI, sec. 1-2, 307–48; Smith, *Wealth of Nations*, part I, sec. 2, ch. 2.

14. I have argued this at greater length in my "From Civil to Political Economy."

15. Smith, *Theory of Moral Sentiments*, part II, sec. 2, chap. 3, 124.

are indispensable for transforming the individual pursuit of self-interest into public happiness, on the other hand.

Contrary to the civic humanism of the Neapolitan Enlightenment, Smith severs the eighteenth-century link between material and spiritual well-being and redefines political economy away from the "science" of happiness towards the science of wealth. Indeed, the key shift in Smith is the argument that only the providential market order directs the pursuit of self-interest to the maximization of material welfare and public happiness. Once the market mechanism is stripped of the disciplining habit of practicing the virtues and equated with pure instrumentality, political economy becomes the science of individual, rational choice in conditions of resources scarcity (as the economists Menger, Marshall and Pigou saw it). On this account, the "doctrine" of marginal utility breaks any remaining link between economics, virtue and happiness. As such, the instrumentality of trading ties is enthroned as the norm that reconfigures all human relationships merely as means to maximize utility (a project already delineated by Jeremy Bentham and James Mill).[16] Just as human relationships are no longer seen as part of the diffusely distributed "common good," so economic goods are no longer viewed as "relational goods" but instead reduced to commodities that satisfy needs —rather than goods that help attain personal flourishing.

These theoretical transformations shaped the conception and institution of modern capitalism, just as changes in political and economic conditions led to new conceptual developments in modern economics. Smith's account of the market as the unique locus of human cooperation with divine providence serves to illustrate, first of all, the importance of theological structures of thought and practice for modern political economy, and, secondly, the mutual, inextricable interaction of ideational and material factors in explaining historical and contemporary transformations of politics and economics. The current crisis of global capitalism, coupled with the paradigmatic shift from the priority of individual to the primacy of relational ideas and practices, provides a unique opportunity to chart an alternative to the complicit collusion of sovereign individuals in the marketplace and the sovereign state that characterizes liberalism and modern political economy. In this perspective, the shift of

16. J. S. Mill's emphasis on cooperative structures in his *Principles of Political Economy* provides a corrective to the impoverished utilitarian primacy of market relations and the state in Jeremy Bentham and James Mill.

focus from individuality to relationality opens the way for transforming modern economics by reconnecting the post-Smithian legacy of political economy with the pre-Smithian tradition of civil economy. That is one of the main perspectives opened up by Pope Benedict's social encyclical.

No Humanism without God: Pope Benedict's Theological Metaphysics

In *Caritas in Veritate*, Pope Benedict XVI deploys a pre-secular metaphysics and anthropology in order to develop a post-secular humanism and political economy.[17] At the heart of the theological vision underpinning this remarkable document lies the uniquely Christian idea that human, social, and natural reality is irreducibly relational and that all is ordered by the divine "economy of charity" to the highest Good in God. In line with *Deus Caritas Est*, Pope Benedict argues in his social encyclical for a comprehensive new model of "integral human development" based on "charity in truth"—the recognition that "[e]verything has its origin in God's love, everything is shaped by it, everything is directed towards it." The call to love, for Benedict, is at the heart of human nature, "the vocation planted by God in the heart and mind of every human person."[18] In other words, love is a deep anthropological desire to enter into an economy of gift-exchange where gift-giving occurs in the real hope of a gift-return. So configured, love translates into practices of mutual help and reciprocal giving, thereby shifting the emphasis from the false dualism between egoism and altruism to the "radical middle" of trust, caring, and cooperation. Building on Balthasar's conception of love as the form of all virtues, the Pope views love as that which infuses all other virtues—theological and "classical," moral and civic. Without love, moral and civic virtues are deficient and lack ordering to their final end in God.

Drawing on Henri de Lubac's work, Joseph Ratzinger develops in his pre-papal and papal writings an integral humanism that underpins his call for a civil economy in *Caritas in Veritate*. At the heart of this humanism lies a theological anthropology that centers on the idea of relationality—the idea that human beings stand in mutually irreducible relations with each other and their transcendent source in God. By

17. Benedict XVI, *Caritas in Veritate*. Henceforth, references to the encyclical will be given parenthetically in the text.

18. Benedict XVI, *Deus Caritas Est*, 1.

contrast with Balthasar's focus on beauty, Benedict shifts the emphasis towards goodness, both at the level of philosophical theology and civil economy. This shift brings to the fore notions such as, first of all, the natural desire for the supernatural Good in God; secondly, the conflict between modern market capitalism and the natural law tradition; thirdly, the new theological imperative to view all production and exchange ultimately in terms of the idea of relational goods that outwits in advance the false, modern liberal dichotomy between private, individual goods, on the one hand, and public, social goods, on the other hand.

Crucially, Pope Benedict locates the logic of gratuitous gift-exchange and inter-personal trust at the heart of the economic system. Since Smith, the economy represents an increasingly autonomous and abstract space, consisting in market exchange based on formal contracts policed and enforced by the state and functioning according to the principle of "cooperation without benevolence," as I have already indicated. Benedict's insistence that the logic of contract cannot function properly without the logic of gratuitousness marks a radical departure from the legacy of Smith and his followers and a renewed engagement with the civil economy tradition of the Neapolitan Enlightenment.

Far from simply restoring this tradition, the Pope blends the Neapolitan Enlightenment with the Christian Neo-Platonism of the Church Fathers and Doctors and the Romantic Orthodoxy of nineteenth-century theology.[19] Central to Benedict's vision is the "re-hellenization" of Christianity, which he delineated in his groundbreaking Regensburg address.[20] In the context of *Caritas in Veritate*, "re-hellenizing" Christian theology serves to break with the dualism between "natural" contract and "supernatural" gift that is at the origin of both modern capitalism and modern economics. Indeed, the Pope eschews the Baroque scholasticism of Francisco Suárez in favor of the patristic and medieval synthesis of Augustine and Aquinas.[21] The latter two envision the ecclesial *corpus mysticum* as the highest community on earth, a profound and permanent spiritual union within the Church in the reciprocal love of the Holy Spirit, as Saint Paul wrote in the Letter to the Corinthians.

By contrast, Suárez contends that the mystical body refers to the sacraments and that the primary community is the nation or population

19. Rowland, *Pope Benedict XVI*, 9–47.

20. Pabst, "Sovereign Reason Unbound," 135–66.

21. Cf. Pabst, *Metaphysics*, ch. 7.

regulated by abstract, formal standards of rights and contracts—not the universal brotherhood of the Church governed by liturgical practices and the exercise of virtue. Linked to this is the Baroque scholastic separation of "pure nature" (*pura natura*) from the supernatural and the concomitant relegation of divine grace to an extrinsic principle that is superadded to the natural realm, rather than a supernaturally infused gift that deifies nature from within. Against Suárez's Baroque scholasticism, Benedict contends that love is received and returned through our participation in the universal eucharistic community of the Church that enfolds the social-political body of human society and directs it to the supernatural Good in God. Beyond the Old Testament, the New Testament fuses the commandment to love God with the commandment to love our neighbor. What underpins this is the mystical union with God as revealed in the eucharistic mystery that is both sacramental and social; the celebration of the Eucharist has traditionally been intimately linked to public processions and integral to the life of local communities and guilds.[22]

In turn, the Pope links this patristic and medieval legacy to modern Romanticism, notably their shared emphasis on natural intimations of the divine and human, artistic activity. It is this Romantic tradition that has helped sustain and create the high culture which Benedict champions and upholds against capitalist commodification that is predicated on the Baroque separation of supernatural grace from "natural," human culture:

> Let it not be forgotten that the increased commercialization of cultural exchange today leads to a twofold danger. First, one may observe a *cultural eclecticism* that is often assumed uncritically: cultures are simply placed alongside one another and viewed as substantially equivalent and interchangeable. This easily yields to a relativism that does not serve true intercultural dialogue; on the social plane, cultural relativism has the effect that cultural groups coexist side by side, but remain separate, with no authentic dialogue and therefore with no true integration. Secondly, the opposite danger exists, that of *cultural levelling* and indiscriminate acceptance of types of conduct and life-styles. In this way one loses sight of the profound significance of the culture of different nations, of the traditions of the various peoples, by which the individual defines himself in relation to life's fundamental questions. What eclecticism and cultural levelling have in common

22. Milbank, "Future of Love," 368–74; Bossy, "Mass as a Social Institution," 29–61.

> is the separation of culture from human nature. Thus, cultures
> can no longer define themselves within a nature that transcends
> them, and man ends up being reduced to a mere cultural statistic.
> When this happens, humanity runs new risks of enslavement and
> manipulation. (*Caritas*, 26; emphasis original)

Here the pontiff is much closer to the Christian socialism of Karl Polanyi and his Anglican friend R. H. Tawney than to the Marxism of liberation theology. The same vision also underpins his defense of traditional liturgy (including the Tridentine Mass) against the onslaught of "sacro-pop"—"parish tea party liturgies and banal 'cuddle me Jesus' pop songs," as Tracey Rowland puts it so aptly in her book *Ratzinger's Faith*. In this manner, Benedict retrieves and extends the patristic and medieval vision of the Church as the *corpus mysticum* which he has inherited from the *nouvelle théologie* of Henri de Lubac.

Beyond the liturgy, the pope's defense of Romanticism is also key to saving secular culture from itself. By rejecting both absolute instrumental reason and blind emotional faith, the Romantic tradition outwits the contemporary convergence of soulless technological progress and an impoverished culture dominated by sexualization and violence. More fundamentally, it opposes the complicit collusion of boundless economic *and* social liberalization that has produced *laissez-faire* sex and an obsession with personal choice rather than objective (yet contested) standards of truth, beauty and goodness—a concern shared by the Archbishop of Canterbury Rowan Williams in his seminal work on our cultural bereavement, *Lost Icons*.

All this runs counter to the tradition of Baroque scholasticism. By divorcing "pure nature" from the supernatural, this tradition introduces a series of dualisms into theory and practice such as faith and reason, grace and nature or transcendence and immanence. Such and similar dualisms are incompatible with the (theo)-logic of the Incarnation and undermine the continuous link between Creator and creation. Specifically, the idea that "pure nature" correlates with a purely secular (non-sacred) social space unaffected by divine grace is linked to the "two ends" account of human nature. According to this theory, human beings have a natural end separate from their supernatural end. Instead of participating in the Trinitarian communion of love by which we are perfected, human society and the economy operate independently and are ordered towards a different finality.

Concretely, this means that the market is viewed as morally neutral and committed to the promotion of human freedom—exactly the neo-Baroque position of influential contemporary Catholic commentators such as George Weigel and Michael Novak who unsurprisingly oppose those sections of the encyclical most critical about the unbridled "free market."[23] However, this is merely the *laissez-faire* liberal side of the modern coin whose reverse face is the socialist utopia of statism and collectivism. How so? Both uproot the market and the state from the communal and associationist networks of civil society, thereby severing production as well as exchange from the civic virtues that are embodied in intermediary institutions and from the moral sentiments that govern interpersonal relations. As such, Baroque Catholic scholasticism and Smith's Calvinist dualism of grace and contract are mutually reinforcing apologias for the primacy of commercial society over against political authority and civil autonomy.

For Benedict, by contrast, neither politics nor the economy are purely self-governing or self-sufficient realities. Instead, they either reflect some revealed cosmic order, like Augustine's *Civitas Dei* that is governed by theological virtues embodied in real, primary relations among its members (self-organized within communities, localities, and associations). Or else political and economic arrangements represent a human artifice built over against the inalterability of "given" nature, like the modern tradition of the social contract where ties between the state and the individual and also among individuals are determined by abstract standards like formal rights and proprietary relations (a vision which finds its original expression in the works of Hobbes and Locke). The aim of Catholic social teaching is to transform humanly devised political and socio-economic arrangements such that they ever more mirror the divinely created cosmic ordering towards the supernatural Good in God. As the universal community and sociality, the Church embodies this promise and through the eucharistic celebration offers a foretaste of the heavenly banquet in anticipation of the beatific vision.

23. Rowland, "A Tale of a Duck-Billed Platypus Called Benedict and His Gold and Red Crayons," this volume, ch. 2.

Mutuality and Sympathy: The "Metaphysical" Economy of Christian Neo-Platonism

By appealing to the Neapolitan tradition of civil economy, Benedict shifts the emphasis away from a more Aristotelian concern for individual substance towards a more Christian Neo-Platonist focus (in Augustine and Aquinas) on the self-diffusive Good that endows all things with goodness and makes them relational. In turn, this draws on Plato's argument that we have a natural desire for the transcendent Good that "lures" us erotically—the *Meno* paradox of desiring to know that which we do not as yet understand. It is the presence of the transcendent Good in immanent nature that directs human activity to the common good in which all can share. Concretely, the common good is neither purely publicly provided nor exclusively privately owned but instead distributed communally across the whole of societies and embodied in intermediary institutions and structures such as cooperatives, employee-owned partnerships, community banks, and civil welfare. For unlike the collectivist state or the unbridled free market, such and similar structures work for the social good open to all rather than exclusively nationalized ownership or purely private profit, as *Caritas in Veritate* reaffirms.

Benedict's appeal to Christian Neo-Platonism is significant for a relational politics and economics on (at least) seven accounts. First of all, it modifies existing genealogical accounts of the tradition of civil economy in the direction of a stronger recognition of the central significance of the Christian Neo-Platonist metaphysics of relationality. The opposition between an active, civic Aristotelian and Ciceronian humanism (associated with Coluccio Salutati and Leonardo Bruni), on the one hand, and an individualistic, contemplative Neo-Platonist and Epicurean humanism (wrongly ascribed to Pico della Mirandola and Marsilio Ficino), on the other hand,[24] must be qualified by linking the heritage of Dominicans like St. Thomas Aquinas (and his Neo-Platonist reading of Augustine) to the Neapolitan tradition of civil economy. Here the conceptual link is the idea of horizontal and vertical relationality of human beings. Metaphysically, patristic and medieval Christian Neo-Platonists reject the earlier radical Aristotelian idea of autonomous individual substance disconnected from the efficient causality of the Prime Mover by arguing that we are created in the image and likeness of the Trinitarian God whose creative activity sustains us in actuality. As such, being is situated

24. Bruni and Zamagni, *Civil Economy*, 27–99, esp. 45–57.

in the intermediary realm of "the between" (Plato's *metaxu*) where the original relation among the divine persons and the participatory relation between creation and creator intersect without however collapsing into one another. Humans can thus be described as relational substances participating in the substantive relationality of the triune Godhead.

Second, this vision resonates with Salutati's civic humanism and his vision of a horizontal, relational orientation of humanity that is nevertheless always already linked to its transcendent source in God: "The two sweetest things on earth are the homeland and friends [. . .]. Providing, serving, caring for the family, the children, relatives, friends, and the homeland which embraces all, you cannot fail to lift your heart to heaven and be pleasing to God."[25] This is also reflected in Genovesi's relational anthropology and "musical metaphysics," for example in his 1766 treatise *The Philosophy of the Just and Honest* where he writes that "[we are] created in such a way as to be touched necessarily, by a musical sympathy, by pleasure and internal satisfaction, as soon as we meet another man; no human being not even the most cruel and hardened can enjoy pleasures in which no one else participates."[26] Likewise, in his *Lectures on Civil Economy* (1765–67), he links the social nature of human animals to the principle and practice of reciprocity: "How is man more sociable than other animals? [. . .] [It is] in his reciprocal right to be assisted and consequently in his reciprocal obligation to help the others in their needs."[27]

In turn, inter-personal relationality at the metaphysical and anthropological level translates into an emphasis on shared, communal happiness and the mutual enjoyment of "relational" goods at the civil and economic level. In the *Lectures*, Genovesi argues that

> even among people that are corrupted by the luxury and bad custom there is no one, a chief of family or whatever person, who does not feel an inner pleasure in doing good things to other people, in making others happy [. . .] It is a characteristic of man of not being able to enjoy a given good without sharing it with somebody else. Some say that it is self-love or pride [*superbia*] to show our happiness to others. I do not think so: it seems to me that there is in us an inner need to communicate to each other our happiness.[28]

25. Coluccio Salutati, quoted in Bruni and Zamagni, *Civil Economy*, 47.

26. Genovesi, *Della diceosina*, 42.

27. Genovesi, *Lezioni di commercio*, part I, ch. 1, §17, 14.

28. Ibid., part I, ch. 16, §2, footnote.

In this manner, Genovesi links happiness to goodness and conceives both in terms that outwit in advance the modern, liberal separation of private happiness and individual commodities from public welfare and public, "relational" goods. The civil economy tradition combines an Aristotelian-Ciceronian emphasis on happiness and a Neo-Platonist-Epicurean insistence on the good.

Third, Genovesi's accentuation of metaphysical and anthropological relationality is neither naïve nor utopian but acknowledges the reality of human vice and sinfulness. Precisely because his account of civil economy is explicitly grounded in a conception of human nature, he recognizes that there are natural instincts (such as self-preservation, seeking comfort or distinguishing oneself)[29] that can direct us away from the quest for the common good towards the pursuit of self-interested wealth and utility. In this process, human vice that leads to practices such as usury "converts friendship and humanity into merchandise," and utility is divorced from the natural outlook towards the supernatural good.[30] Thus, the institutions and practices of civil society governed by both higher and lower virtues are required to correct human deviation from the natural law of seeking happiness that is itself relational: "[i]t is a universal law that we cannot make ourselves happy without making others happy as well."[31]

Fourth, Genovesi argues against the ontological atomism of Machiavelli, Hobbes, Locke, and Mandeville that neither the economy nor society can function properly without cooperation and trust and that in turn these require more than either egoism or altruism. Beyond this false divide, what is needed is a network of practices and institutions that blend the strive for utility with the quest for happiness and thereby direct man's ambivalent nature (virtue and vice, unsociability and sociality, etc.) to the pursuit of the common good in which all can participate. It is precisely the civic relations of civil society that constitute the nexus of relationships where individual interest and public welfare coincide without ever being fully identical.

This link between personal and public goods and happiness in the civil economy tradition can be traced to the Italian philosopher and

29. Ibid., II, ch. 13, §5, 195.

30. Ibid., II, ch. 13, §5, 196.

31. Genovesi, *Autobiagrafia e Lettere*, 449. Here Genovesi echoes Doria's 1710 book *On Civil Life* which begins with the following words: "without any doubt, the first object of our desire is human happiness."

historian Ludovico Antonio Muratori, another key figure of the Italian Enlightenment. Long before the discourse on happiness bequeathed to us by the American and French Revolutions, he wrote in 1749 that

> . . . the master desire in us, and father of many others, is our own private good, or our particular happiness [. . .]. Of a more sublime sphere, and more noble origin, is another Desire, that of the Good of Society, of the Public Good that is Public Happiness. The first is born of nature, the second has virtue for a mother.[32]

Once more, it is clear from such and similar texts that the patristic and medieval Neo-Platonist emphasis on man's natural desire for happiness and the supernatural infusion of virtue, which directs us to the common good, is at the heart of the civil economy tradition.

Fifth, Genovesi looks to early Renaissance civic humanism and also the legacy of Giambattista Vico, Celestino Galiani, and Paolo Mattia Doria in order to make the case that intentional human actions do indeed have unintentional consequences thanks to divine providence and grace, rather than fate and fortune as for Machiavelli and Mandeville. Here Vico and Galiani are particularly important, with the latter speaking of the "Supreme Hand" and the former writing that "Man has free will, though it be weak, to turn passions into virtue; but is helped by God with divine Providence and supernaturally with divine grace."[33] In this context, we are reminded of Augustine's *City of God*, notably the fusion of coercive and persuasive elements in the operation of public institutions. For the Neapolitans as for the Bishop of Hippo, state law, education, and civil life constrain self-interest and direct it towards the common good which is always more than the collective sum of its individual parts (*pace* Bentham) because it is eminently qualitative rather than merely quantitative—enhancing as it does the capacity of each individual and of the whole of society to actualize our potential to do good. The twin accentuation of virtuous practices and civil institutions provides the "civic" nexus between (private and public) happiness and the economy. This aspect is wholly absent from Smith's conception of the "invisible hand" metaphor that fuses a questionable understanding of theodicy with a similarly questionable account of human cooperation

---

32. Quoted in Bruni and Zamagni, *Civil Economy*, 73.

33. Giambattista Vico, *Scienza Nuova*, II, §7, quoted in Bruni and Zamagni, *Civil Economy*, 84.

with divine providence.[34] In part, this explains why Smith is suspicious of the intermediary institutions of civil society with which he associates cartel-like collusion and price-fixing.

Sixth, by contrast with Smith's more Calvinist separation of human contract from divine gift, Genovesi and the other members of the Neapolitan School view the institutions and practices of civic life as a supernatural dynamic that seeks to perfect the natural, created order and calls for human cooperative participation. Linked to this is the insistence upon public trust or faith (*fede pubblica*) as an indispensable condition for socio-economic and political development within the framework of civil life and cognate notions such as honor and "the mutual confidence between persons, families, orders, founded on the opinion of the virtues and religion of the contracting parties."[35] In this manner, Genovesi emphasizes the importance of social sympathy and reciprocity in economic contract, such that mutuality binds together contractual, proprietary relations, and gift-exchange. From its inception, the tradition of civil economy rejects any separation of the market mechanism from civic virtues and moral sentiments. That is why in *Caritas in Veritate*, Pope Benedict argues that the genuine flourishing of each person involves the fostering of human, social, economic, and political bonds as exemplified by practices of gift-exchange, mutual help, and reciprocal giving. As such, economics is entirely reconfigured, away from the demand- and supply-driven market production of individually consumed goods and services or the paternalistic state provision of uniform benefits and entitlements towards the co-production and co-ownership of relational goods and civil welfare (a key aspect of the encyclical to which I shall return).

Seventh (and finally), the Christian Neo-Platonist vision is not merely abstract and conceptual but on the contrary translates into real, concrete practices which we can also trace back to the Dominicans rather than the Franciscans. For example, the idea of a "just price" which reflects the true value and not simply the prevailing market equilibrium of demand and supply. This has a wide variety of possible applications today, from the practice of paying workers a "living wage" (as opposed to merely a minimum wage) to anti-usury legislation and limits on interest rates and also the introduction of asset-based welfare and employee-ownership. Coupled with Benedict's appeal to the ecclesial *corpus*

34. See my "From Civil to Political Economy."

35. Genovesi, *Lezioni di commercio o sia di economia civile*, II, ch. 10, §5, 132.

mysticum as the most universal human community and in some sense the condition for sociality, the emphasis in the Christian tradition of Neo-Platonism on relationality ties together the sacramentally ordered universal community of the Church with the network of overlapping intermediary institutions, businesses, and the so-called third sector which operate on the basis of reciprocity and mutuality. Ultimately, this shows just how artificial the old barriers between or across state, market and civil society really are.

As such, the Neo-Platonist metaphysics of relationality is closely correlated with the civil economy tradition of Genovesi's civic humanism. Taken together, they have the potential to transform the state, the market and civil society in such a way that state regulation and governmental welfare no longer play a merely compensatory role within the anarchism of "free-market" capitalism. Instead, state and market are re-embedded in a civil compact. The idea is to foster civic participation based on self-organization, social enterprise, reciprocity, and mutuality which help produce a sense of shared ownership around "relational" goods. This approach seeks to balance liberty and responsibility as well as rights and duties in a spirit of individual and communal "charism" where the talents and particular vocations of each person are mutually augmenting and beneficial to society as a whole. That is what *Caritas in Veritate* seeks to articulate.

BENEDICT'S CALL FOR A CIVIL ECONOMY

Perhaps the most striking aspect of Benedict's social encyclical is the clarity with which it links Christian Catholic social teaching to the ongoing worldwide debate on economy, ethics, technology, and ecology. By calling for economic and political arrangements that are re-embedded in civil society and sustain both human and natural life, the Pope proposes a model of economic democracy that transcends the old dichotomies of state *versus* market and left *versus* right. Against the secular settlement that has been dominant since the French Revolution, Benedict shifts the emphasis away from the complicit collusion of the sovereign individual and the sovereign state towards practices of mutuality and reciprocity at all levels of human relation and association—from the family, the neighborhood, and the local community to regions, nations, and the world. In line with the principle of subsidiarity, the Pope argues for coordination and cooperation in a spirit of sympathy and benevolence at the most appropriate level. To reconnect global finance to the real economy, action is required at the transnational level without however justifying a quasi-Suárezian unitary world government.

Following the civil economy tradition, *Caritas in Veritate* suggests that the commonly held belief that the left protects the state against the market while the right privileges the market over the state is economically false and ideologically naïve. Just as the left now views the market as the most efficient delivery mechanism for private wealth and public welfare, so the right has always relied on the state to secure the property rights of the affluent and to turn small proprietors into cheap wage laborers by stripping them of their land and traditional networks of support. This ambivalence of left and right masks a more fundamental collusion of state and market. The state enforces and polices the centralized and standardized legal framework that enables the market to extend contractual and monetary relations into virtually all areas and aspects of life, notably education, the family, and sex. In so doing, both state and market reduce nature, human labor, and social ties to commodities whose value is priced exclusively by the iron law of demand and supply. However, the commodification of each person and all things violates a universal ethical principle that has governed most cultures in the past: nature and human life have almost always been recognized as having a sacred dimension. Like other world faiths, orthodox catholic Christianity defends the sanctity of life and land against the subordination by the "market-state" of everything and everyone to mere material meaning and quantifiable economic utility.

The Pope repudiates equally the left-wing adulation of the state and the right-wing fetishization of the market because ultimately both collude at the expense of alternative forms of economic and political organization, legitimacy and authority. This is why the Pope writes that "the exclusively binary model of market-plus-State is corrosive of society, while economic forms based on solidarity, which find their natural home in civil society without being restricted to it, build up society" (*Caritas*, 39). Notably, Benedict does not simply endorse civil society in its present configuration precisely because the actors and institutions of civil society are currently subject to the administrative and symbolic order of the secular "market-state."

His call for "a true world political authority" (*Caritas*, 67) cannot be taken as an argument in favor of a unitary global government that would echo Suárez's primacy of the political community over and against the mystical body of the Church. Instead, the Pope argues for a new kind of settlement whereby both the centralized bureaucratic state and the un-fettered global free-market are transformed in order to serve the genu-ine needs and interests of persons, communities, and the environment. According to Benedict, more global coordination and cooperation is required in order to address worldwide issues such as capital flows and climate change. Far from generating greater centralization and concen-tration of power and wealth in the hands of the most powerful nations, the Pope invokes the twin principles of subsidiarity and solidarity that are among the core tenets of Catholic social teaching.[36] Since subsidiar-ity concerns action at the appropriate level to uphold human dignity and reciprocal relations, Benedict's insistence on greater transnational political authority is fully consonant with the imperative to re-localize global finance that is increasingly abstracted from the real economy but at the same time pervades all sectors and links them to the volatility of worldwide capital movements.

Indeed, the world economy moves in upward and downward spirals, a series of speculative booms and spectacular busts whereby a new and accelerating bubble cycle has supplanted the older, more "regular" busi-ness cycle. Since 1973, successive waves of neo-liberal reforms abolished regulation and control, expanding capital mobility on an unprecedented scale. New complex instruments such as derivative-trading inflated the overall volume of capital in search of lucrative opportunities. With de-clining profit margins in industry and manufacturing, money switched to finance, insurance and real estate (or FIRE). Thus the new economy was born. Reinforced by easy credit, the U.S., the UK and other coun-tries that emulated Anglo-Saxon capitalism (such as Ireland, the Baltic States, and Ukraine) went on a collective, reckless speculation drive and consumption binge financed by a growing mountain of personal, corpo-rate, and public debt. All of which led to artificially inflated and grossly overvalued asset prices: in the U.S. alone, the "dot-com" bubble in the 1990s built up 7 trillion dollars in fictitious value, while the total housing bubble in the 2000s amounted to a staggering 12 trillion dollars.

36. Pontifical Council, *Compendium of the Social Doctrine of the Church*, 93–101. Dorr, *Option for the Poor*.

Paradoxically, the sheer size of the virtual economy makes state regulation and intervention more, not less, necessary, as markets looks to states in order to enforce property rights and thereby validate the perennial process of "primitive accumulation" through expropriation and dispossession.[37] Here we can go further and suggest that self-regulating markets are inherently transnational and nevertheless require state authority. For just as unfettered markets descend into "panic, manias and chaos,"[38] so ballooning public debt during economic downturns exposes national states to global financial markets. Faced with sovereign debt crises (like the eurozone's current predicament), stability necessitates determined, large-scale intervention by a single sovereign—the kind of power that self-regulating markets themselves can never have. Lockean "market relations" amongst free, self-governing individuals requires a Hobbesian Leviathan after all. Once again, this underscores the complicit collusion of the strong state and the free market.[39] If the political framework of the eurozone does not suffice, how can the loose, disparate grouping of the G20 possibly fulfill such a role? So against the pre-eminence of finance and the primacy of economics over politics, Benedict is surely right to argue for a new world political institution that

> . . . would have to have the authority to ensure compliance with its decisions from all parties, and also with the coordinated measures adopted in various international forums. Without this, despite the great progress accomplished in various sectors, international law would risk being conditioned by the balance of power among the strongest nations. The integral development of peoples and international cooperation require the establishment of a greater degree of international ordering, marked by subsidiarity, for the management of globalization. (*Caritas*, 67)

To achieve a civil economy at the global and local levels, the Pope argues that state and market must be re-embedded within a wider network of social relations and governed by virtues and universal principles such as justice, solidarity, fraternity and responsibility. Throughout *Caritas in Veritate*, the pontiff blends the civil economy tradition with Catholic social teaching.

---

37. Perelman, *Invention of Capitalism*.

38. Kindleberger, *Manias, Panics, and Crashes*; Reinhart and Rogoff, *This Time Is Different*.

39. See my "Crisis of Capitalist Democracy," 44–67.

Concretely, Benedict encourages the creation of enterprises that operate on the basis of mutualist principles like cooperatives or employee-owned businesses. These businesses pursue not just private profit but also social ends by reinvesting their profit in the company and in the community instead of simply enriching the top management or institutional shareholders. Benedict also supports professional associations and other intermediary institutions wherein workers and owners can jointly determine just wages and fair prices. Against the free-market concentration of wealth and state-controlled redistribution of income, the Pope proposes a more radical program: labor receives assets (in the form of stakeholdings) and hires capital (not vice-versa), while capital itself comes in part from worker- and community-supported credit unions rather than exclusively from shareholder-driven retail banks (*Caritas*, 38). Tangible examples include, first of all, the Basque cooperative Mondragon which employs over 100,000 workers who produce manufactured goods, with an annual turnover of around 3 billion dollars; secondly, *Crédit Mutuel*, a mutualized bank which operates in several EU countries; thirdly, the employee-owned partnership of John Lewis in the UK.

Moreover, Benedict urges us to view profit and technological innovation no longer as ends in themselves but as means to secure the stability of businesses, their employees, and the communities hosting them. Like the "market-state," money and science must be re-embedded within social relations and support rather than destroy mankind's organic ties with nature. For example, the world economy needs to switch from short-term financial speculation to long-term investment in the real economy, social development and environmental sustainability.

Taken together, these and others ideas developed in the encyclical go beyond piecemeal reform and amount to a wholesale transformation of the secular logic underpinning the "market-state." Alongside private contracts and public provisions, the Pope seeks to introduce the logic of gift-exchange—giving, receiving, and returning gifts—into the economic process. Benedict's key argument is that market exchange of goods and services cannot properly work without the free, gratuitous gift of mutual trust and reciprocity so badly undermined by the global credit crunch. That's why he writes that "the principle of gratuitousness and the logic of gift as an expression of fraternity can and must find their place within normal economic activity" (*Caritas*, 36). Unlike the Smithian tradition, Benedict retrieves and extends the civil economy tradition of the

Neapolitan School by accentuating gratuitous gift-exchange and linking contract to gift. For all contracts involve trust among the contracting parties and trust (*pistis* or faith since Greek Antiquity) in the reasonableness of exchange (and the reality of products and services which exchange implies). Without the giving and receiving of trust, contractual relations require an ever-greater scope and intensity of control and enforcement, thus empowering the state and its agencies to the detriment of autonomous civil society. That's why the extension of commercial exchange into areas previously governed by (a higher degree of) gift exchange always already entails the expansion of central state powers.

Nor is Benedict's vision of gratuitous gift-exchange reactionary or nostalgic. To the contrary, he retrieves and extends the notion of "integral human development" first proposed by Pope Paul VI forty years ago. Socio-economic development can only be humane if it promotes relationships of reciprocal self-giving in love, which is "the principle not only of micro-relationships (with friends, with family members or within small groups) but also of macro-relationships (social, economic and political ones)" (*Caritas*, 2). The concrete experience of love alerts us to the truth that life itself is God's loving gift. Benedict, referring to *Deus est Caritas*, writes that "everything has its origin in God's love, everything is shaped by it, everything is directed towards it. Love is God's greatest gift to humanity, it is his promise and our hope" (*Caritas*, 2).

By placing charity and truth at the heart of the moral and ecological economy, the Pope argues that Christianity avoids the irreducible modern dualisms that dominate contemporary culture, politics and the economy. The hypostatic union of the human and divine in Jesus Christ alerts us to the divine intention and promise of a restoration of the created order in and through an ever-closer union with God. Knowledge of God's providence is neither confined to faith in scriptural revelation nor a reliance on natural reason alone. By contrast with the modern separation of reason and faith, catholic orthodox Christianity always viewed reason itself as a gift of God which is elevated by revelation and faith. As Pope Benedict suggested in his Regensburg address, faith habituates reason to see the effects of God in all things, just as reasoning helps faith seeking understanding by relating the natural desire for the supernatural Good in God to the whole of creation which reflects the Creator in diverse ways that no finite mind can ever be equal to. As such, faith upholds reason and broadens its scope while reason binds faith to cognition and thereby ties together perception and imagination (or "lower reason") with intellectual vision (or "higher reason"). Knowledge of the world (*scientia*) and knowledge of God (*sapientia*) converge and prepare man for the beatific vision in the life to come, so that "we evermore dwell in him and he in us" (1 John 4:12–13)—"for of him, and by him, and in him, are all things" (Rom 11:36). To love in truth is to encounter the relational Good that comes from God and infuses all things with goodness—the self-diffusive Good or *bonum diffusivum sui* in Christian theology from Boethius via Aquinas to the Cambridge Platonists.

Thus, *Caritas in Veritate* is a complex and thoughtful document that resists the misleading categorization of left- or right-wing and statist or free-market. Benedict's call for a civil economy that curtails the power of the centralized state and the unfettered global market in favor of persons, communities, and associations is in fact a quest for a way that cannot be charted on our current conceptual map. By broadening the idea of "integral development" centered on universal human aspiration such as interpersonal relationships and organic links with nature, the Pope proposes a vision centered on relationality, mutuality, and sympathy that redefines links between the religious and the secular and thereby transcends their violent separation since the French Revolution.

FOSTERING CIVIL ECONOMIES

The civil economy tradition which Pope Benedict draws upon to develop Catholic social teaching can be applied and extended in the following ways:

Dealing with the Debt Crisis

First of all, across the world governments and the private sector must consider the option of debt forgiveness for heavily indebted individuals, households, small- and medium-sized enterprise (SME) as well as certain financial institutions such as mutualized banks or regional credit unions. Led by religious groups and civil society actors, the Jubilee 2000 campaign in favor of debt relief for the world's poorest economies provides an important precedent and template. The combined disaster of personal bankruptcy, home foreclosures, the mass death of SME, and soaring unemployment matters far more than arguments about "moral hazard" or "rewarding bad behavior." Debt forgiveness is ethically imperative and economically egalitarian, as it breaks the vicious cycle of debt-deflation and puts a floor under the value of real assets like personal saving funds, homes as well as the human, social, and physical capital embodied in SME and other businesses. Ontologically, debt cancellation rejects the secular capitalist subordination of social relations, life, and land to the sacrality of market commodification. By tying money to real assets and binding material things to their symbolic meaning, it helps restore the primacy of real worth over abstract, nominal monetary valuation. Coupled with a cap on usurious interest rates, a jubilee can reconnect capital to the value of actual assets and interrupt the destructive spiral of exponential debt.

Second, the public and the private sector must enact debt conversion whereby the most short-term, high-interest government bonds, mortgages, and consumer loans are converted into longer-term, lower, and (in some cases) fixed-interest credit. Of course, some creditors will effectively forfeit some of their investment, but they stand much more to lose in the event of mass bankruptcy and a second debt crisis with mass foreclosure, which threatens countries as varied as the U.S.A. and Spain. Governments should urgently consider proposals to offer mortgage holders the option of replacing a share of their mortgage (20–50 percent) with a low-interest loan from the state, subject to a maximum amount. In the U.S.A. or Europe, for example, this could be up to 125,000 U.S. dollars and 100,000 euros respectively. The annual interest rate could be as low as 1–1.5 percent, and the loan would be amortized over a period of 20–30 years. Such a scheme would almost certainly help minimize home repossessions and stabilize the property market in which more than 60 percent of the UK's wealth is tied up (around 4 trillion pounds out of a total of approximately 7 trillion). This sort of state assistance should be made available not just to individual borrowers but also to housing associations, especially those that have formed joint ventures with building companies and are now facing an acute funding shortage—caused in large part by the scandalous refusal of commercial banks to increase their lending while still paying their top management big bonuses. Similar debt conversion programs could be extended to other sectors that are crippled by debt, including commercial real estate and consumer loans.

By contrast with the current credit squeeze where the risk of bankruptcy becomes a self-fulfilling prophecy, debt conversion alleviates the immediate debt burden. In addition to reducing private and corporate bankruptcy, the restructuring of debt can establish a floor under asset

prices, thereby interrupting the vicious circle of debt-deflation and reducing the risk of a double-dip recession. Moreover, lending will only
be properly restored when assets stop falling, and assets will only stop
falling when debt is brought under control through forgiveness and
conversion. This would reconnect debt to assets and re-localize finance,
something which Pope Benedict XVI, the new Patriarch of Moscow and
All Russia Kirill I, and the Anglican Archbishops of Canterbury and York
Rowan Williams and John Sentamu already called for in the autumn of
2008. Indeed, reconnecting debt to assets would prevent the destructive
bubble cycle whereby unrestrained, debt-financed speculation leads to
a huge hike in asset and commodity prices and creates trillions of dollars in fake wealth, with devastating consequences for the real economy
once the artificial bubble bursts and the edifice built on cheap credit
collapses—exactly what the global credit crunch brought about in 2008.
By enacting debt cancellation and conversion, governments and the
financial sector can address the problem of debt-deflation and put the
economy on a more balanced footing.

Monetary and Financial Reform

As the history of financial crises suggests,[40] an international financial
meltdown like the 2007–09 global credit crunch tends to be accompanied by the twin risk of debt-deflation and double-dip recessions. In
conditions of fiscal contraction in response to sovereign debt problems,
monetary policy expansion is one of the few tools to counteract deflationist pressure. However, with interest rates close to 0 percent (as is
currently the case), the only instrument at the disposal of central banks
is large-scale quantitative easing (QE), i.e., injecting liquidity through
mass purchase of securities and the creation of electronic money. But its
systemic risks are unknown and there is a clear possibility that attempting to cure deflation leads to the opposite disease of hyperinflation. As
such, the use of QE could perpetuate and even exacerbate the bubble
cycle of boom and bust that has subverted the more "natural" business
cycle. At the same time, QE seems to be one of the few policy options to
deal with the debt burden that affects the public and corporate sectors.
Extended to government bonds, QE has the potential to monetize the
public deficit and avoid any financial crowding out.

40. Kindleberger, *Manias, Panics, and Crashes*; Reinhart and Rogoff, *This Time Is
Different*.

Reigning in debt in itself is only one precondition for re-localizing global finance and transforming the world economy. In order to generate sustainable growth that benefits society as a whole, the world's leading economies must abandon the doctrine of monetarism—a key pillar of the neo-liberal orthodoxy built on liberalization, deregulation, and privatization.

Monetarism stipulates the pursuit of price stability by focusing exclusively on monetary policy instruments such as interest rates in order to control the money supply. Such a policy stance is reinforced by the neo-classical view that expansionary fiscal policy merely generates inflation and should therefore be aimed at balanced budgets and low levels of public debt.

Taken together, the preferred monetary and fiscal policy mix of monetarism amounts to an economic straightjacket with an inbuilt contractionary, deflationist bias that can trigger a double-dip recession. Historical precedents abound: in U.S. in 1936–37 or Japan in 1990, public spending was slashed before the recovery of private sector investment and consumption was sustained, thus strangling the economy and causing a death spiral of debt-deflation that ended only when the world went to war. European history offers particularly important lessons. The new British coalition government's commitment to public spending cuts risks repeating the same mistake as the Conservative-Liberal coalition in 1931, whose emergency budget was described by Keynes as "replete with folly and injustice." Likewise, Germany's austerity package of 80 billion euros over five years seems to replicate the same erroneous policy as Heinrich Brüning, the finance minister from 1930 to 1932, whose devotion to fiscal orthodoxy plunged the Weimar Republic into mass discontent that fuelled the flames of National-Socialism. As such, monetarism risks transmitting internationally a policy of national contraction that could plunge the world economy into a double-dip recession. By contributing to mass unemployment and social dislocation, monetarism also undermines the social cohesion on which free, truly democratic societies rely.

In addition to monetary policy reform, civil economies won't emerge and flourish unless international finance is transformed. Current efforts by the G20 merely aim to regulate global finance at the margins, with new minimum capital requirements, bank liquidity standards and limits on leveraging. Besides important technical details about how to define and measure such and similar new conditions, there are questions about effective implementation and political authority. Rather than aiming for a global regulatory regime that risks being too rigid and could be evaded (given the scope of the offshore economy),[41] it seems preferable to create pan-national arrangements within existing economic zones like the EU, ASEAN or new blocs such as the Eurasian Economic Community (EurAsEC). But it's far from clear whether the series of proposed regulations could prevent a repeat of 2007–08 or avoid a new bubble cycle of boom and bust fuelled by corporate and private debt.

Instead of merely reforming financial services, the imperative is to re-localize global finance and tie money to real assets—contrary to dubious instruments such as credit default options (CDO) or credit default swaps (CDS) that make money with money but are nevertheless secured ultimately against material resources (such as primary commodities) which are thereby destabilized. Beyond reforms, new restrictions and incentives must be introduced. This could include a ban on certain speculative practices and an anti-usury cap on interest rates (whether voluntary or statutory will depend in large part on the sector). In addition to the separation of retail from investment banking, what is needed is a set of new regulations that help limit systemic risk and put an end to the neo-liberal privatization of profits and the nationalization of losses.

Here religious ideas and practices are directly relevant, especially mutuality and trust and an emphasis on reinvesting profits for investive purposes at the service of the common good in which all can share. The prohibition of usury and certain forms of speculation like large-scale short-selling must be reinstated as ethical limits and economic principles. In terms of incentives, it is worth mentioning both Muslim and Christian ideas of ethical banking and social investment that emphasize the transfer of ownership (as in the case of Muslim mortgage schemes) and the link between assets and charity (as in the case of Christian investment funds where charitable activity is tied not just optionally to profit but integrally to assets themselves). This is directly linked to new investment and growth models that are discussed in the following section.

Alternative Investment and Growth Models

Christian visions for an alternative economy that is re-embedded in politics and social relations offer a refreshing alternative to the residual

---

41. Brittain-Catlin, *Offshore.*

market liberalism of both left and right (for example, the work of Karl Polanyi or G. D. H. Cole). In practice, an embedded model means that elected governments restrict the free flow of capital and create the civic space in which workers, businesses and communities can regulate economic activity. Instead of free-market self-interest or central state paternalism, it is the individual and corporate members of civil society who collectively determine the norms and institutions governing production and exchange. Specific measures include, first of all, extending fair-trade prices and standards from agriculture and the food industry to other parts of the economy, including finance and manufacturing. This could be done by strengthening the associative framework and giving different sectors more autonomy in determining how to implement a set of desirable goals debated and voted upon by national parliament, regional assemblies or city halls.

Second, replacing the minimum wage with a just, "living wage" that reflects the true value of labor. Here the example of London Citizens is very instructive—a network of different local communities and faith groups which are joined together in action by the principles and practices of Catholic social teaching and which have persuaded both City Hall and a growing number of corporate businesses to sign up voluntarily and pay their staff the "living wage."[42] By extension, groups of trading guilds with overlapping membership, in cooperation with local councils or regional governments, must be empowered to negotiate just wages for workers. Employee co-ownership, savings, and pension scheme could also be linked more closely to firms that self-organize as part of professional guilds.

Third, at the level of the G20 and pan-national blocs like the EU pushing for global capital controls in the form of the Tobin tax and bank levies (including voluntary caps on interest rates), coupled with new incentives to reconnect finance to the real economy by promoting investment in productive, human, and social investment. More specifically, the financial industry must eschew the dichotomy of public, nationalized and private, corporate models in favor of social sector solutions such as social investment banks, social grants or social impact bonds. The latter could encompass a wide range of areas such as projects devoted to restorative justice, local socio-economic regeneration, the environment, education or culture.

42. Ivereigh, *Faithful Citizens.*

In order to diversify the nature and range of financial services, governments and parliaments could put in place a series of positive incentives to promote cooperation between non-profit organizations, social entrepreneurs and government agencies. Beyond current attempts to channel financial into social capital, the key is to link investment to charity (and thereby bind contract to gift), such that charitable activities and social action are not just added on and play a compensatory role for financial capitalism. Instead, each new financial investment would always already involve new assets for social activities, and a share of the profits would automatically be reinvested in social enterprise. Such an organic connection between investment and charity would transform the very way global finance operates. The trillions of pounds which the now retiring generation of baby boomers have to invest can be tapped into as a source of capital. The overriding aim must be to preserve the sanctity of natural and human life and to promote human relationships and associations that nurture the social bonds of trust and reciprocal help on which both democracy and markets depend.

Welfare Reforms

In terms of social policy, there is now a unique opportunity not just to rebuild the economy but also to transform the welfare state away from state paternalism or private contract delivery towards civic participation and community organizing in conjunction with national collective activity and state investment. Centralized statist welfare plays at best a compensatory role in relation to *laissez-faire* economics and at worst is secretly complicit with the extension of the market into hitherto largely self-regulating areas of the economy and society. Indeed, the centralized and corporatized welfare *state* merely regulates the conflict between capital owners and wage laborers without fundamentally altering relations between capital and labor. Whilst it does provide some much-needed minimum standards, statist-managerial welfare subsidizes the affluent middle classes and undermines (traditional or new) networks of mutual assistance and reciprocal help amongst workers and within local economies. Today, by contrast, a renewed emphasis on the principles of reciprocity and mutuality can translate into policies that incentivize the creation of mutualized banks, local credit unions, and community-based investment trusts.

Indeed, Christian socialists like Karl Polanyi warn against the fallacy of appealing to a welfare model that traps the poor in dependency and redistributes income to the wealthy. At the hands of former Conservative Prime Minister Margaret Thatcher and the New Labour party of Tony Blair and Gordon Brown, the welfare state was first rationalized and then deployed to fashion "the freely-choosing reflexive and risking individual removed from the relational constraints of nature, family, and tradition," as John Milbank has rightly remarked in the present volume. At a time of fiscal austerity, ageing populations and the ballooning deficits of social security and pension systems, the social-democratic left must look beyond redistributive policies to asset-based welfare and decentralized models that foster human relationships of communal care and mutual help—rather than state paternalism or private contract delivery.

For example, Christians could advocate a system that combines universal entitlement with localized and personalized provision, e.g. by fostering and extending grassroots initiatives like "Get Together" or "Southwark Circle" in London that blend individual, group and state action. Both initiatives reject old schemes such as "befriending" or uniform benefits in favor of citizens' activity and community-organizing supported by local council—instead of being determined by central targets and standards. The link between different actors and levels is neither abstract, formal rights and entitlements nor monetarized, market relations but instead human relationships of mutuality and reciprocity. Citizens join welfare schemes like social care as active members who shape the service they become part of rather than being reduced to merely passive recipients of a "one-size-fits-all," top-down model. Southwark Circle works on the principle that people's knowledge of their neighborhood, community, and locality is key to designing the provision and delivery of welfare. Services are delivered involving civic participation, social enterprise (like the company Participle), and the local council.

By contrast, state paternalism or private contract delivery cost more to deliver less, and they lock people either into demoralizing dependency on the state or financially unaffordable dependency on outsourced, private contractors. The reason why civic participation and mutualism costs less and delivers more is because it cuts out the "middleman"—the growing layers of gatekeepers such as doctors, social workers, and bureaucrats who assess people's eligibility and enforce centrally determined standards and targets instead of providing services that assist genuine individual needs and foster human relationships. But since such models require upfront state investment and continuous involvement of the local council, the state is neither eliminated nor simply retrenched. Rather, the vision of civic participation and mutualism is inextricably linked to the decentralization of the state in accordance with the twin Catholic Christian principles of solidarity and subsidiarity (action at the most appropriate level to protect and promote human dignity and flourishing). A genuine alternative to the prevailing options must eschew both conservative paternalism and liberal *laissez-faire* in favor of something like an organic pluralism and a radical communitarian virtue ethics that blends a hierarchy of values with an equality of participation in the common good.

Specifically, different countries and economic regions could move towards a system of welfare that fuses subsidiarity with solidarity and universal provision with local delivery. As is well known, the principle of subsidiarity in Catholic social teaching does not entail the decentralization of public policy towards the lowest level but rather the most appropriate level for specific functions and services to promote the well-being of persons in relationship with other persons. Put differently, subsidiarity shifts the emphasis from the centralization of power to a proper balance between different levels of decision-making. Applied to cases as different as the U.S. or the European Union, subsidiarity involves the devolution of power to regions, localities, and neighborhoods as well as the delegation and pooling of sovereignty at the supra-national level. A proper European social policy, for example, does not imply a single, uniformized model or a supranational welfare state but instead a diversity of policies with some common, pan-European elements such as fully portable contributions and entitlements across the Union and a Europe-wide pension fund (in order to diversify risk and raise the rate of return for individual contributors). Likewise, the principle of solidarity does not imply the unilateral help for the needy but instead a complex web of mutuality and reciprocal relations which involves not just individual rights and abstract entitlements but communal responsibility, mutual duties, and a shared concern for the common good.

In this light, the task for pan-national economic zones is not to engage in piecemeal social engineering which results in a greater legislative and bureaucratic burden on member-states and their constituents but to provide a framework which ensures the universal provision of welfare for all citizens and residents and the decentralization of delivery to regional, local, and neighborhood levels—involving not just state agencies or market actors but also cooperatives and not-for-profit organizations from the voluntary sector, a I have already indicated.

Here we can go further and say that, first of all, welfare can no longer be fragmented and divided along artificial lines. On the contrary, institutions, governments, and socio-economic actors at all levels must find a governing concept that binds together all aspects of welfare aid, including unemployment, social security, health, housing, education, and training. Second, this requires abandoning the separation of economic from social policy in favor of a more integrated approach centered on the consequences of public policy for human development and flourishing. A first step is to complement GDP-based statistics with measures of well-being (e.g., the UN's human development index and General Well-Being or GWP instead of GDP). The next step must be to combine universal, objective ends or finalities with particular, personalized means or measures.

Third, welfare and social policy must put individual and communal capabilities at the center of attempts to eradicate absolute poverty and reduce income and asset inequality. This will have to involve supplementing individual property and other rights with a communal sharing of common resources such as land, real estate, and other proprietary forms. Here the unrealized potential of the Catholic tradition of distributism is perhaps most evident. As the work of the Catholic moral philosopher John Ryan and others shows, distributism is not just concerned with a wider spread of ownership or property but also extends to the crucial question of fair prices and just wages.[43]

Let me illustrate some of the preceding arguments in relation to the problem of pensions. Public pay-as-you-go schemes offer universal coverage but they are financially unsustainable and socially unacceptable because in the absence of permanently higher labor productivity an ageing population will either have to raise pension contributions or lower pension benefits. Likewise, private pension funds involve high transaction costs and managements fees (even a small annual fee can add up to over 20 percent over the lifetime of a private fund). By definition, a private scheme is not and can never be universal. As a result, the alternative is to have a universal, publicly funded scheme with an annual rate of return of up to 5 percent, via an "interest swap" which is secured by indexed government bonds. Such a scheme could be composed of two pillars, with a mandated defined benefits (DB) part and a voluntary

43. In addition to the works of G. K. Chesterton and Hilaire Belloc, see Ryan, *Living Wage*, and Ryan, *Distributive Justice*.

defined contributions (DC) part. Since a pension scheme with a DB element involves risk-sharing, pan-national economic zones like the EU or, in future, EurAsEC offer greater potential for risk-pooling than the national level (especially in the case of smaller, poorer nations where there is a strong incentive to save money privately for old age rather than to contribute to a public scheme).[44]

So based on the twin principle of subsidiarity and solidarity, a pan-national pension system would be most appropriate. Among other things, this would require the introduction of two new types of assets: first of all, bonds indexed on consumer price index (CPI) of member states and, secondly, assets indexed on aggregate nominal income of all participant countries. An active market for these two assets would provide a guideline for expected returns on such assets and an instrument for investment for funded pension schemes. In the absence of pan-national taxation, each member state could create bonds indexed on its own national income. One could then bring these bonds together into a fund that would thus be based on aggregate transnational income. These bonds would pool risks at the pan-national level, a possibility that is not available to each and every individual country.

The macroeconomic dimension is that additional savings and investment are required to facilitate the transition to a funded system and to smooth out the demographic hump as a result of the retirement of the "baby boomer" generation and the constraints it will impose on pay-as-you-go schemes. As long as more savings translate into more investment (with the appropriate tax and regulatory incentives), the pan-national economic area as a whole and all the participant countries would avoid Keynes' "paradox of thrift" whereby more savings stifle aggregate demand due to the negative income effect, thereby reducing employment, output and investment, and so on. Crucially, a pan-national socio-economic compact that includes a pension system along these lines requires more physical investment and thus creates the conditions for the sort of strong economic growth that neo-liberal finance capitalism has over the last thirty years precluded.

In addition to property distribution and a pan-national pension fund, the third element of a new welfare system is to establish asset-based welfare such as "baby bonds," i.e., a capital sum given to each child

---

44. Interestingly this is also true for a country as vast and populous as China where the absence of a welfare system explains the extremely high household savings rate—a phenomenon that unwittingly contributes to the scope of current global imbalances.

at birth which bearers would be free to draw from the age of 18 in order to pay for their tertiary education, vocational training or to help buy a house. As the economist and *Financial Times* columnist Samuel Brittan has argued, the crucial difference of asset-based welfare is that it changes the whole life-cycle income and assets of individuals and households. By contrast, welfare based on income (e.g., benefits) has a much more limited impact on peoples' perceived and real wealth. And in contrast to home ownership and pensions, asset-based welfare sets in at precisely the age where people would otherwise start running up debts.

Pan-national economic zones must urgently identify ways of creating mechanism that extend the benefits of asset-based welfare to their populations. In the current situation where soaring budget deficits and exponentially growing levels of public debt make any ambitious scheme based on unfunded expenditure a financial folly, one way of introducing asset-based welfare would be to use capital receipts from the sale of new licenses, for example in connection with carbon-trading or other green technology. What must govern all future attempts to reconfigure the welfare system are the twin principles of subsidiarity and solidarity and the twin imperatives of universal entitlement and local provision.

Conclusion

Since the origins of the dominant ideology and politics can be traced to the convergence of state and market and the collusion of left and right, what is required is a new politics that recovers earlier traditions and blends the best of Romantic conservatism with Christian guild socialism. This will have to be pursued elsewhere,[45] but this chapter has suggested a variety of ways in which the ideas of *Caritas in Veritate* and the civil economy tradition can be applied and extended in the direction of a new civil compact wherein the relations between individuals, the state, and the market are re-embedded in the overlapping networks of reciprocal human relationships of mutuality and sympathy.

45. I am currently writing *The Politics of Paradox*, a book on alternatives to capitalist democracy.

PART IV

Caritas in Veritate and Traditions of Christian Social Teaching

7

The Anthropological Unity
of *Caritas in Veritate*

Life, Family, and Development

David L. Schindler

INTRODUCTION

"The truth of development consists in its completeness: if it does not involve the whole man and every man, it is not true development."[1] This, says Pope Benedict in his new encyclical, is "the central message of [Paul VI's] *Populorum Progressio*, valid for today and for all time" (*Caritas*, 18). "Integral human development on the natural plane, as a response to a vocation from God the Creator, demands self-fulfillment in a 'transcendent

---

1. Benedict XVI, *Caritas in Veritate*, 18. Further references to this encyclical will be given parenthetically in the text.

humanism which gives [to man] his greatest possible perfection: this is the highest goal of personal development'" (*Caritas*, 18).[2]

According to Benedict, God-centered charity in truth is the key to "integral human development." "Everything has its origin in God's love, everything is shaped by it, everything is directed towards it" (*Caritas*, 1). Love is thus "the principle not only of micro-relationships (with friends, with family members or within small groups) but also of macro-relationships (social, economic and political ones)" (*Caritas*, 1). The call to love, in other words, stirs in the heart of every man. "The interior impulse to love" is "the vocation planted by God in the heart and mind of every human person," even as this love is "purified and liberated by Jesus Christ," who reveals to us its fullness (*Caritas*, 1). "In Christ, *charity in truth* becomes the Face of his Person" (*Caritas*, 1; emphasis original). The Church's social teaching thus, in a word, is "*caritas in veritate in re sociali*: the proclamation of the truth of Christ's love in society" (*Caritas*, 5). My purpose is to discuss the anthropological unity of the Catholic Church's social teaching suggested here, as manifest in the link between development, family, and life issues.

ON THE CONTRIBUTION OF *CARITAS IN VERITATE*
TO CATHOLIC SOCIAL TEACHING

First of all, it is important to see that the Church's social teaching does not claim to offer technical solutions with respect to economics and development (*Caritas*, 9). At the same time, by virtue of her sacramental embodiment of the truth of Christ as Creator and Redeemer, the Church does become an "expert in humanity,"[3] in the sense that she has "a mission of truth to accomplish, in every time and circumstance, for a society that is attuned to man, to his dignity, to his vocation" (*Caritas*, 9). Her social doctrine draws from the truth as found in all branches of knowledge, often in fragmented form, and assembles that truth into a unity.

On the one hand, then, the purpose of the Church is not to suggest a distinct economic system *as an economic system*. On the other hand, it *is* to propose principles that affect all human activities from the inside, including activities in politics and the public realm (*Caritas*, 56) and every

2. Paul VI, *Populorum Progressio*, 16.
3. Paul VI, *Discourse to the General Assembly*, 3.

phase of economic activity (*Caritas*, 37). In this connection, Benedict recalls the teaching of John Paul II, who, following the collapse of the economic and political systems of the Communist countries of Eastern Europe, said that a comprehensive new plan of development was called for, not only in these countries but also in the West; and Benedict states that this is "still a real duty that needs to be discharged" (*Caritas*, 23).

Regarding tendencies in the West, *Caritas in Veritate* rejects the reading of *Centesimus Annus* that would understand the three "subjects" of the social system—the state, the economy, and civil society—each to have an exclusive logic of its own, only extrinsically related to the others (*Caritas*, 38–40). As Cardinal Tarcisio Bertone states in an address to the Italian Senate: "This conceptualization, which [for example] confuses the market economy that is the genus with its own particular species which is the capitalist system, has led to identifying the economy with the place where wealth or income is generated, and society with the place of solidarity for its fair distribution."[4] *Caritas in Veritate* rejects this dichotomy between "subjects," which would undermine the call to love as integrative of every human activity and all development: of the whole man and every man. To paraphrase Cardinal Bertone, we must supersede the dominant view that expects the Church's social teaching, involving the centrality of the person, solidarity, subsidiarity, and the common good, to be confined, as it were, to social activities, while "experts in efficiency" would be charged with running the economy.[5] This of course does not mean that expertise and efficiency are unnecessary, but only that the integration of these is necessary for the functioning of the economy already in its wealth-producing activity, rightly conceived. In a word, "without internal forms of solidarity and mutual trust, the market cannot completely fulfill its proper economic function" (*Caritas*, 35).

Secondly, the main presupposition undergirding the argument of *Caritas in Veritate* is the universality of the vocation to love. We all know that we "are not self-generated" (*Caritas*, 68). This implies a sense of the Creator which Cardinal Ratzinger/Benedict describes in other writings in terms of *anamnesis*, the memory of God that is "identical with the foundations of our being."[6] This memory of God can be ignored or

---

4. Bertone, "Address of Cardinal Tarcisio Bertone, Secretary of State, During His Visit to the Senate of the Italian Republic," 3 (typescript).

5. Ibid., 4 (typescript).

6. Ratzinger, *Values in a Time of Upheaval*, 92.

denied but it is never absent from any human consciousness.[7] In a word, a dynamic tendency toward communion with God, and with other creatures in relation to God, lies in the inmost depths of every human being, and not only Christians. The encyclical's call for a new trajectory of thinking informed by the principles of gratuitousness and relationality, metaphysically and theologically conceived, takes its beginning from this universal *anamnesis* of love and God (cf. *Caritas*, 53, 55).

Thirdly, the integrated human development described in the encyclical involves a "broadening [of] our concept of reason and its application" (*Caritas*, 31). "Charity is not an added extra, like an appendix to work already concluded in each of the various disciplines: it engages them in dialogue from the very beginning" (*Caritas*, 30). This does not mean that one can legitimately bypass reason and its proper conclusions. The point is simply that "intelligence and love are not in separate compartments: *love is rich in intelligence and intelligence is full of love*" (*Caritas*, 30; emphasis original), and that love must animate the disciplines in a whole marked by unity and distinction (*Caritas*, 31). The problem today is an "excessive segmentation of knowledge" that results in an inability to "see the integral good of man in its various dimensions" (31). Thus, a recovery of the place of metaphysics and theology, especially in their integrative capacities in the realization of wisdom and as themselves integrated by love, "is indispensable if we are to succeed in adequately weighing all the elements involved in the question of development and in the solution of socio-economic problems" (*Caritas*, 31).

Fourth, *Caritas in Veritate* strongly re-affirms the idea of the common good. "To desire the *common good* and strive towards it," says Benedict, "*is a requirement of justice and charity*" (*Caritas*, 7; emphasis original). Concern for the common good involves the "complex of institutions that give structure to the life of society, juridically, civilly, politically, and culturally, making it the *polis*, or 'city' . . . " (*Caritas*, 7). Commitment to the common good shapes "the *earthly city* in unity and peace, rendering it to some degree an anticipation and a prefiguration of the undivided *city of God*" (*Caritas*, 7; emphasis original). Regarding economic activity, the Pope thus insists that it cannot resolve social problems simply through the application of *commercial logic*, but "needs to be *directed towards the pursuit of the common good*, for which the political community in particular must also take responsibility" (*Caritas*, 36;

7. *Catechism*, 31–38. See also *Compendium of the Social Doctrine of the Church*, 109.

emphasis original). "The *principle of gratuitousness* and the logic of gift as an expression of fraternity can and must *find their place within normal economic activity,*" as expressed in *commercial relationships* (*Caritas*, 36; emphasis original).

Benedict's emphasis on the common good bears two especially important implications. On the one hand, it entails rejection of the dualism between the temporal and the eternal that is a hallmark of liberal societies. Contrary to the view of John Locke, for example, Benedict insists that public, economic activity is not a matter exclusively of the temporal order, as though the eternal order, or the heavenly city, arrives only *after* life on earth, or in any case remains in this life something purely "private." Locke, for his part, recognizes that religion is important for morality and thus useful for the functioning of the earthly city, but he does so, in contrast to the view of Benedict, only as a *means* of maintaining *external public order*, and not as an *intrinsic good* for the civil community as such.

Caritas in Veritate thus also makes clear that the Church affirms the notion of the *common good*, rather than that of *public order*, as the proper purpose of political-economic activity. The encyclical, in other words, rejects the "juridical" idea of political and economic institutions that has been a prevalent reading, for example, of the Council's *Dignitatis Humanae*, as well as of John Paul II's *Centesimus Annus*: the idea, that is, which holds that these institutions are concerned with justice as procedural fairness (Rawls), in abstraction from justice as a matter also of the naturally given order and end of man.[8]

DEVELOPMENT, FAMILY, AND LIFE

The idea of humanity as a single family and of marriage and family, as well as life issues, play an important role in providing a foundation for, and in giving original form to, the principles of gratuitousness and relation, and indeed the logic of freedom and rights, that is implied by the common good, as outlined here.

First, and strikingly, Benedict says that "*the development of peoples depends, above all, on a recognition that the human race is a single family* . . ." (*Caritas*, 53; emphasis original), and that "the Christian revelation of the unity of the human race presupposes a *metaphysical interpretation*

8. On the common good as the end of the state, see *Catechism*, 1910. On the state's implication of a vision of man, see *Catechism*, 2244.

of the 'humanum' in which relationality is an essential element" (*Caritas*, 55; emphasis original). Here several points can be made:

(i) The idea that all human beings make up a single family derives from the common origin of each in the Creator. The unity implied in this idea does not submerge the identity of each person, but rather renders each transparent to the other within their legitimate diversity. The two persons becoming "one flesh" in marriage gives us a sense of how this may be so, as does Christian revelation itself, with its understanding of God as a Trinity of Persons in the unity of one divine Substance (*Caritas*, 54).

The idea of a single unified family deriving from a common relation to the Creator invites further reflections drawn from the theological anthropology of Joseph Ratzinger/Pope Benedict and Pope John Paul II, notably regarding the idea of sonship and filiality, in the former, and regarding the "original solitude" of man, in the latter. *Caritas in Veritate* emphasizes that love is first received by us, not generated by us. Already in his commentary on the anthropology of *Gaudium et Spes*, Ratzinger stresses the capacity for worship as the primary content of man's imaging of God. This is so because human beings are most basically "sons in the Son": they are images of God in and through Jesus Christ who is God precisely as the *Logos* who is from-and-for the Father (cf. Col. 1:15–18). As Ratzinger puts it succinctly elsewhere, "the center of the Person of Jesus is prayer."[9] Likewise, John Paul II affirms the primacy of man in his "original solitude," by which he means that man's relationality begins most radically in his "aloneness" before God. The point is thus not that man is originally without relation, but that man's relationality, his original being-with, is a being-with God before it is a being-with other human beings. Or better: man's being-with God, as creaturely, is first a *being-from*, in the manner of a child who participates in being only as the fruit of the radical generosity of the One Who Is.

Here, in what we may call the filial relation associated with the family, we find the root meaning of the encyclical's central category of relation as *gift*. Indeed, once we see the radicality of this relation, which originates in God as the Creator, we see that it must include not only all human beings, though especially and most properly these, but all creatures and thus also all of the natural, physical-biological entities of the cosmos. Thus Benedict says that

9. Ratzinger, *Behold the Pierced One*, 25.

nature expresses a design of love and truth. It is prior to us . . . and speaks to us of the Creator (cf. Rom 1:20) and his love for humanity. It is destined to be "recapitulated" in Christ at the end of time (cf. Eph 1:9–10; Col 1:19–20). Thus it too is a "vocation."[10] Nature is given to us . . . as a gift of the Creator who has given it an inbuilt order, enabling man to draw from it the principles needed in order "to till and keep it" (Gen 2:15). (*Caritas*, 48; emphasis original)

Indeed, we could say that, in its own analogical way, and with the help of man, nature thus participates in the prayer constitutive of the creature in its inmost filial movement toward the Creator.

A further implication regarding filiality: we teach our children to say "please" and "thank you." But, rightly understood, this is not a matter merely of manners. On the contrary, it is a matter of teaching them who and what they are in their deepest reality: gifts from God who are thus meant to be grateful, to act in gratuitous wonder, in *response to* what is first *given*, as *gift*. Here is the origin of that recognition of being as true and good and, indeed, beautiful—*qua given* and not simply *quia factum* or as a function of human making—which must lie at the basis of any healthy human society. Here is the root of the encyclical's call for new lifestyles centered around the quest for truth, beauty, goodness and communion with others (cf. *Caritas*, 51).

(ii) Of course, children are sons and daughters of God only through a human father and mother, and the child is born as itself apt for either fatherhood or motherhood. Further, the fruitfulness of the union of the father and the mother is a continuing sign and expression of the creative generosity of God. Ratzinger in his commentary on *Gaudium et Spes* refers to this spousal communion between a man and a woman as the immediate consequence (*Folge*) of the content (*Inhalt*) of man's imaging of God that lies first in man's "unitary" being as child of God.[11] John Paul II refers to this constitutive aptness for spousal union-fruitfulness as the "original unity" of man and woman. This aptness for spousal union, established first in man's and woman's common filial relation to God, is constitutive of the human being.[12] Each human being is a member of the single family of creatures under God, in and through membership

---

10. John Paul II, *Message for the 1990 World Day of Peace*, 6.

11. Ratzinger, "Commentary on the Introduction and Chapter 1," 122.

12. *Compendium*, 37, 110, and 147.

in a particular familial genealogy of his own. This is the ground for the encyclical's calling on the state to promote "the centrality and the integrity of the family founded on marriage between a man and a woman, the primary cell of society, and to assume responsibility for its economic and fiscal needs, while respecting its essentially relational character" (*Caritas*, 44).

(iii) The implications of the constitutive relationality affirmed in *Caritas in Veritate* are stunning: *no relations taken up by human beings in the course of their lives are purely contractual*, or simply the fruit of an originally indifferent act of choice (cf. liberal "contractualism"). Man is never, at root, "lonely," which is to say, in the language of *Caritas in Veritate*, never poor in the sense of "isolated" (*Caritas*, 53). On the contrary, his being is always a being-with.

Hence, *regarding human freedom*: freedom is an *act* of choice only as already embedded in an *order* of naturally given relations to God, family, others, and nature (cf. *Caritas*, 68). And *regarding human rights*: just as the juridical idea of rights presupposes a contractualist idea of freedom, so does a truthful order-bearing idea of rights presuppose a relational idea of the self. Just as the contractualist idea entails a priority of rights over duties, so does the relational idea entail a priority of duties over rights, though of course rights remain unconditionally coincident with this anterior responsibility (see *Caritas*, 43).[13] Rights, in a word, are properly invested in every man, but no man is a solitary agent who can be abstracted from relations. On the contrary, man as he exists, always and everywhere, is innerly ordained to God and others, is a child born into a family, is sexually differentiated and apt for fatherhood or motherhood, and is intrinsically related to the whole of humanity and of nature. An adequate idea of rights must take intrinsically into account this order of relations that is constitutive of each man.

The second main argument of this section is as follows: *Caritas in Veritate* says that Paul VI's encyclical, *Humanae Vitae*, is "highly important for delineating the *fully human meaning of the development the Church proposes*" (*Caritas*, 15; emphasis original). *Humanae Vitae* makes clear "the *strong links between life ethics and social ethics*, thus ushering in a new area of magisterial teaching that has gradually been articulated in

---

13. To be sure, "duties" are affirmed here in terms of a responsibility to love, hence in a sense quite different from the Kantian sense of duty that prevails in modern discussions of duties and rights.

a series of documents, most recently John Paul II's encyclical *Evangelium Vitae*" (*Caritas*, 15; emphasis original).

Once more, a number of points can be made:

(i) The Pope notes in this connection *Humanae Vitae*'s emphasis on the unitive and procreative meaning of sexuality, thereby locating "at the foundation of society the married couple [who] are open to life" (*Caritas*, 15). He suggests that the tendency to make human conception and gestation artificial contributes to the loss of "the concept of human ecology and, along with it, that of environmental ecology" (*Caritas*, 51). The point here, though not explicitly developed in *Caritas in Veritate*, is that *Humanae Vitae*, in its affirmation of the unity of the personal and the procreative meaning of sexuality, implies a "new" understanding of the body as a bearer of the objective order of love, in a way consistent with and instructive for *Caritas in Veritate*'s view that the nature of the physical-biological cosmos as a whole "expresses a design of love" (*Caritas*, 48).

(ii) Relative to the relation between life ethics and social ethics, the Pope notes the inconsistency of societies which, affirming the dignity of the person and justice and peace, tolerate the violation of human life when it is at its weakest and most marginalized (*Caritas*, 15). He thus insists that "*openness to life is at the center of true development*" (*Caritas*, 28; emphasis original), and that we need to broaden our concept of poverty and underdevelopment to take account of this question of openness to life. It is precisely in its increasing mastery over the origin of human life manifest, for example, in *in vitro* fertilization, the harvesting of human embryos for research, and the possibility of manufacturing clones and human hybrids, that we see "the clearest expression" of a supremacy of technology in contemporary society (*Caritas*, 75).

Caritas in Veritate takes up the complicated question of technology in its last chapter. "Technology enables us to exercise dominion over matter" and "improve our conditions of life," and thus goes to "the heart of the vocation of human labor" (*Caritas*, 69). The relevant point, however, is that "technology is never merely technology" (*Caritas*, 69). It always invokes some sense of the order of man's naturally given relations to God and others. Technology thus, rightly conceived, must be integrated into the call, indeed the covenant, implied in this order of relations (cf. *Caritas*, 69): integrated into the idea of creation as something first *given to* man, as *gift*, "not something self-generated" (*Caritas*, 68) or *produced by* man.

Here again we see the importance of the family. It is inside the family that we first learn a "technology" that respects the dignity of the truly weak and vulnerable—for example, the just-conceived and the terminally ill—for their own sake. It is inside the family, indeed the family as ordered to worship, that we first learn the habits of patient interiority necessary for genuine relationships: for the relations that enable us to see the truth, goodness, and beauty of others as given, and also to maintain awareness of "the human soul's ontological depths, as probed by the saints" (*Caritas*, 76). It is inside the family that we can thus learn the limits of the dominant social media of communication bequeathed to us by technology, which promote surface movements of consciousness and gathering of technical information, and foster *inattention* to man in his depths and his transcendence as created by God. It is in the family that we first become open to the meaning of communication in its ultimate and deepest reality as a *dia-logos* of love revealed by God in the life, and thus including also the suffering, of Jesus Christ (cf. *Caritas*, 4).

Conclusion

In light of the foregoing, we can see, in sum, why *Caritas in Veritate* insists that the social question today "*has become a radically anthropological question*" (*Caritas*, 75; emphasis original); why "*the question of development is closely bound up with our understanding of the human soul*" (*Caritas*, 75; emphasis original); and why "only a humanism open to the Absolute can guide us in the promotion and building of forms of social and civic life—structures, institutions, culture and *ethos* . . . " (*Caritas*, 78).

8

Integralism and Gift Exchange in the Anglican Social Tradition, or Avoiding Niebuhr in Ecclesiastical Drag

John Hughes

INTRODUCTION

I N THIS CHAPTER I would like to begin by asking what, from an Anglican perspective, is particularly interesting about *Caritas in Veritate*, before exploring what resonances its key theological ideas of "integral development" and charity as reciprocal gift exchange have within the Anglican Social Tradition(s). My argument will be that, first, Anglicans have been at the forefront of the recovery of Augustinian notions of charity as reciprocal gift exchange and the associationist application of such ideas to the social and economic sphere; and secondly, that, despite some recent evidence to the contrary, Anglicanism has particular ecclesiologico-political reasons to be sympathetic to this integralist social agenda and indeed may have some of its own resources to offer in understanding this position in the modern world.

A CONSERVATIVE ENCYCLICAL? DEVELOPMENT, SEX, AND RELIGION

First, what is significant in Benedict XVI's encyclical *Caritas in Veritate*? In terms of the international development agenda, this encyclical may well receive a negative reception in liberal Western circles. If one wishes to paint Benedict as a social conservative, undoing all the "advances" of Vatican II and pulling up the ecclesiastical drawbridges, then it is easy to focus on the way the encyclical introduces a significant new element upon the work of its predecessor, Paul VI's *Populorum Progressio*, whose anniversary it marks, by linking social and economic development with what in liberal society are usually seen as more private concerns such as sexual ethics, questions concerning reproduction and the beginning and end of life (contraception, abortion and euthanasia) and even with explicit Christian belief.

On this interpretation, the encyclical marks a withdrawal of the collaboration begun in the 1960s between the Roman Catholic Church and other development and aid organizations on the grounds that such organizations are now pursuing more aggressively secular agendas which are incompatible with Catholic moral teaching. Claims such as *"openness to life is at the centre of true development,"* or "The Church forcefully maintains this link between life ethics and social ethics" may seem reasonably uncontroversial in themselves.[1] But when this is followed by appeals to *Humanae Vitae*, with its rejection of artificial contraception, and *Evangelium Vitae*'s analysis of the contemporary "culture of death" (supposedly evident in IVF therapies, embryo research and euthanasia), alongside renewed papal condemnation of "the spread of an anti-birth mentality" (*Caritas*, 28) by certain development agendas through the promotion of contraception and abortion as forms of demographic control, liberal alarm bells start to ring.

Similarly, few should be surprised by *Caritas in Veritate*'s grounding of the Church's social teaching in Christian faith and doctrine, as in claims such as *"God is the guarantor of man's true development"* (*Caritas*,

1. Benedict XVI, *Caritas in Veritate*, 28, 15 (emphasis original). Further references to this encyclical will be given parenthetically in the text.

29; emphasis original). But when this is accompanied by the claim that the Church's social teaching and commitment to development is part of evangelization, or by the renewed rejection of religious indifferentism, syncretism or "practical atheism," it may seem to some that Benedict is allowing the question of development to be subordinated to his more usual concerns about the rise of relativism and its erosion of the uniqueness of Christian claims (cf. *Caritas*, 15, 55, 29). More explicitly, when the Pope refuses the "exclusion of religion from the public square," cites John 15:5 ("Apart from me you can do nothing") and insists that "A humanism which excludes God is an inhuman humanism" (*Caritas*, 78), it sounds to many liberals as if he has abandoned the Second Vatican Council's willingness to collaborate with all people of good will, regardless of their beliefs.

While some Anglican ethicists have been sympathetic to the papal analysis of the culture of death and contemporary relativism and secularism,[2] it would be true to say that many Anglican commentators, perhaps influenced in this respect as much by the recent ecumenical *froideur* between Anglicans and Roman Catholics as by substantive differences such as the question of contraception, share a broadly liberal, unsympathetic reading of *Caritas in Veritate*. At best, such liberal Anglicans may see it as an unhelpful muddying of the waters of Christian social teaching, by dragging in a number of highly divisive and not necessarily relevant questions of life-ethics or religious confession. At worst, it may be seen as the return to an authoritarian, isolationist, and exclusivist social agenda, which is founded upon the belief that it is the Catholic Church's job to rule the world, and which promotes policies that oppress the reproductive rights of women and encourage a dangerously irresponsible neglect of contraception, worsening both the AIDS epidemic and the approaching demographic crisis.[3]

CHARITY BEYOND JUSTICE: THE RADICAL AGENDA

But, if, to many European liberals (including many Anglicans), *Caritas in Veritate* looks like a typical piece of conservative Catholic carping

2. For Anglicans sympathetic to the Papal encyclical tradition, we could think of Oliver O'Donovan, Michael Banner and John Milbank.

3. See Tina Beattie's well-argued piece on the gender blind spots of the encyclical: "Church's idealisation of sexuality may be root of abuse."

about sex and religion when it should be talking about poverty, this is not the whole story. For, across the Atlantic, to many neo-liberal and neo-conservative Roman Catholics, this encyclical looks like a confused muddle, a papal sell-out to leftist European social democratic ideals.[4] It is important not to overlook this social and economic radicalism in *Caritas in Veritate*, which arguably goes further than any previous papal encyclical in this direction.

Markets, Ethics and the Environment

Caritas in Veritate starts from the (traditional Christian) presupposition that the economic sphere is not a neutral realm unconnected with theology and morality. "The economic sphere," we are told, "is neither ethically neutral, nor inherently inhuman and opposed to society" (*Caritas*, 36). This insistence that "*every economic decision has a moral consequence*" (*Caritas*, 37; emphasis original) may seem uncontroversial in Christian social teaching, but it is of course in direct opposition to neo-liberal free market ideas of the market as a morally neutral, self-regulating force for good (*Caritas*, 37). Profit, according to the Pope, cannot be an absolute end in itself, but must serve the common good, without which it "risks destroying wealth and creating poverty" (*Caritas*, 21). If the market must not be allowed to become "the place where the strong subdue the weak," then the "economy needs ethics in order to function correctly" and examples of socially responsible businesses, "fair-trade," consumer co-operatives, and "ethical" banking and finance are commended (*Caritas*, 36, 66, 45).

Traditional policies of Catholic social teaching are reiterated: the encouragement of unionization to protect the dignity of workers, the desire for stable employment for all, the insistence upon "food and access to water as universal rights of all human beings, without distinction or discrimination" (*Caritas*, 24 & 64, 32 & 63, 27). The Pope endorses the need to care for the world's resources and to recognize our "responsibility towards creation" to ensure that our natural environment can sustain life into the future (*Caritas*, 48-51). The political principle of subsidiarity, or encouraging responsible decision making at the most local level, is reasserted against bureaucratic state centralism in welfare provision and neo-colonial models of aid and development, which are both accused of

4. See e.g. Novak, "Pope Benedict XVI's Caritas," and Weigel, "Caritas in Veritate in Gold and Red."

encouraging disempowering dependency; while at the same time collaboration is encouraged at every level, right up to the establishment of a new international global consensus (*Caritas*, 58, 67).

Beyond these traditional planks of Catholic social thought, the encyclical seeks to bring up to date the agenda of *Populorum Progressio* by responding to contemporary crises, environmental and economic, and it is here that *Caritas in Veritate* is particularly radical. On the question of ecological concerns, particularly in relation to energy consumption and the damaging effects of this upon our planet, the Pope moves beyond simple platitudes about the need to care for God's creation. Philosophically, he rejects both the technocratic optimism which characterized much of the domination of nature in the last two centuries and the more recent neo-pagan rejection of humanity's unique position as the crown of creation (*Caritas*, 68-71). Practically, he insists (to the horror of American neo-conservatives!) that the "technologically advanced societies can and must lower their domestic energy consumption" and that we also need "a worldwide redistribution of energy resources, so that countries lacking those resources can have access to them" (*Caritas*, 49).

Globalization and the International Regulation and Redistribution of Capital

In response to the international financial crisis, the Pope condemns "badly managed and largely speculative financial dealing" and economic short-termism, and looks for the "regulation of the financial sector, so as to safeguard weaker parties and discourage scandalous speculation, and experimentation with new forms of finance, designed to support development projects" (*Caritas*, 21, 32, 65). He recognizes that many of the problems of the recent crises have arisen out of the new situation of globalization with the deregulation and rapid international movements of capital and labor. The analysis of globalization is balanced, acknowledging that "globalization, *a priori*, is neither good nor bad. It will be what people make of it," while also recognizing that "inequalities are on the increase" (*Caritas*, 42, 22). The task, therefore, as the encyclical sees it, is the moral ordering of the ever increasing international flows of trade, capital and labor "to promote a person-based and community-oriented cultural process of world-wide integration that is open to transcendence" (*Caritas*, 42). While some have seen globalization as the end of the role of the state, the Pope argues instead that "in terms of the resolution of the current crisis, the State's role seems destined to grow" (*Caritas*, 41) and that greater international co-operation is needed.

Here the Pope is reviving one of the more radical proposals of his predecessor John XXIII (again to the horror of American neo-conservatives): the "urgent need for a true world political authority," beyond merely the reform of the United Nations and international financial organizations, so that "the concept of the family of nations can acquire real teeth" (*Caritas*, 67). Here the Pope speaks also of the need for "disarmament, food security and peace" (*Caritas*, 67). In terms of global inequalities, the Pope raises the question of the waste of international aid through corruption and excessive bureaucracy and, in keeping with much post-colonial development thinking in the past thirty years, calls for aid which encourages the recipients to be able to participate themselves in the international economy, rather than simply to become permanently dependent upon aid (*Caritas*, 58, cf. 60, 47).

It is in this context, however, that the Pope raises again one of his most challenging calls to the wealthy nations of the world: "The processes of globalization, suitably understood and directed, open up the unprecedented possibility of large-scale redistribution of wealth on a world scale" (*Caritas*, 42, cf. 37, 49). This will involve opening up the protectionism by which the rich nations maintain their dominance over the poorer ones, such as high tariffs and "an excessive zeal for protecting knowledge through an unduly rigid assertion of the right to intellectual property, especially in the field of health care" (*Caritas*, 33, 22).

New Forms of Social Enterprise and Civilizing the Economy

As if talk of local and international regulation of finance, protection of the environment and even large-scale redistribution of wealth were not quite upsetting enough for the neo-conservatives, the encyclical goes on to speak sympathetically of new models and forms of business enterprise. These new models are based upon fraternal solidarity and the gratuity of reciprocal giving, and belong neither purely to the realm of the market and the logic of pure profit alone, nor to the sphere of state control and public duty (*Caritas*, 38–40). These new models often seem most at home in civil society, but they are not confined to it. They are often "based upon mutualist principles" and can encourage forms of greater "economic democracy," such as co-operativist stakeholder ownership, rather than purely shareholder ownership (38). Here the traditional distinction of profit and non-profit organizations seems to be breaking down. In an important passage, the encyclical notes the emergence in recent decades of an intermediate area which is not just a third sector but is having an impact upon the two traditional models of public and private enterprise:

> It is made up of traditional companies which nonetheless sub-scribe to social aid agreements in support of underdeveloped countries, charitable foundations associated with individual companies, groups of companies oriented towards social welfare, and the diversified world of the so-called "civil economy" and the "economy of communion." (*Caritas*, 46)

The Pope endorses these "hybrid forms of commercial behavior," with their renewal of responsibility and ethics, fraternal solidarity and reciprocal gratuity in commerce and industry as "civilising the economy" (*Caritas*, 38). This stress on mutualism and new forms of social economy rooted in solidarity and reciprocal gift exchange is not without some precedent in Catholic social thought, but the renewed emphasis on them in *Caritas in Veritate* is quite striking. In the light of this radical social and economic agenda, it simply will not do to continue to paint Benedict XVI as an economic conservative on the basis of his past conflicts with liberation theologians.

CHARITY AS GIFT-EXCHANGE AND INTEGRAL HUMAN DEVELOPMENT: THE THEOLOGICAL HEART OF *CARITAS IN VERITATE*

While some have argued that *Caritas in Veritate* is just a hopeless mix-ture of conservative and radical views (thus Weigel's ridiculous claim that one can separate all the "gold" bits written by Benedict, which of course he likes, from those written by the supposedly dreadful "red" lib-erals at the Pontifical Council for Justice and Peace), it is my claim that the "conservative" and "radical" elements of the encyclical are part of a thoroughly consistent outworking of a theological perspective, which, while building upon much of the tradition of Catholic social teaching, also develops a distinctly Augustinian theological voice which is very much Benedict's own. We can summarize this as the belief in charity as gift exchange and integral human development.

Charity as Gift-Exchange

Benedict XVI has already laid out his views on Christian charity in what we might think of as his manifesto encyclical *Deus Caritas Est*, to which he refers repeatedly in *Caritas in Veritate*. Benedict's view of charity is thoroughly Augustinian and Johannine in stressing the social, public and reciprocal nature of charity as a supernatural participation in the divine Trinitarian life, against more modern and Protestant individualistic notions of charity as unilateral, private, interiorized and sentimentalized. "Charity," he tells us, "is love received and given" and "has its origin in God" (*Caritas*, 5, 1). It cannot be confined to "subjective emotions and opinions" but is "gift, acceptance and communion" and therefore concerns the "macro-relationships (social, economic and political ones)" just as much as the personal (*Caritas*, 3, 2).

As gift, charity goes beyond the opposition of obligation and self-interest: "Gift by its nature goes beyond merit, its rule is that of superabundance" (*Caritas*, 34). "Love—*caritas*—is," according to the encyclical, "an extraordinary force which leads people to opt for courageous and generous engagement in the field of justice and peace" and "the principle driving force behind the authentic development of every person and of all humanity" (*Caritas*, 2, 1). From all this it follows that "Charity is at the heart of the Church's social doctrine," but this is the first time Benedict has spelled out what this means in concrete political and particularly economic terms (*Caritas*, 2). This vision of charity as reciprocal gift exchange is the basis of the encyclical's rejection of dependency models of welfare and aid, but also of its support for radical sharing and redistribution of international resources and wealth. This is not just a private matter for individual believers: "in commercial relationships the principle of gratuitousness and the logic of gift as an expression of fraternity can and must find their place within normal economic activity" (*Caritas*, 36).

Generosity and communion, the gratuitous actual sharing of real goods, is at the heart of the Gospel message about economics and development and this is a central theme of *Caritas in Veritate*. Here, "charity goes beyond justice, because to love is to give, to offer what is 'mine' to the other" (*Caritas*, 6). Yet at the same time it "never lacks justice"; rather, "charity demands justice" which is the "minimum measure" of charity (*Caritas*, 6). More precisely, we can say "charity transcends justice and completes it in the logic of giving and forgiving" (*Caritas*, 6). In this account of the supercession of justice by the gift of charity, Benedict is making a particular argument which brings us onto the question of his "integralism."

Integral Human Development

When Benedict writes that "the logic of gift does not exclude justice, nor does it merely sit alongside it as a second element added from without," he is manifesting his Augustinian "integralism," against the dualism of what has been called the "distinction of planes" model of Christian social thought (*Caritas*, 34).[5] In doing this he is also subtly developing the tradition of his predecessors John Paul II and Paul VI. While he does not of course accuse them of this, it is certainly possible to see a slightly different tendency in the social teaching of these earlier popes.

Acting perhaps out of an admirable desire to find common ground with non-believers, but also building upon the neo-scholastic distinctions of reason and faith, nature and grace, previous encyclicals had often spoken with two voices: firstly setting forth the demands of natural justice which should be evident to all reasonable people regardless of their faith, and secondly describing the supererogatory works of charity to which Christians might be particularly called over and above these minimal demands of justice. We can certainly see the attraction of this "distinction of planes" strategy in seeming to enable a minimal consensus for international collaboration across religious and cultural divides upon questions of poverty and development.

Yet at the same time such a model, with its naïve optimism about the ease of global consensus and its relegation of the heart of the Christian faith to an optional supplement, now seems dated at best. This is not least in response to a more militant secularism which seeks to exclude religious viewpoints from the task of development altogether, while at the same time being left with a minimal account of justice incapable of negotiating the complexities of contemporary problems.

This is what leads the Pope to make the following claim: "The sharing of goods and resources, from which authentic development proceeds,

---

5. The phrase "distinction of planes" comes from Gustavo Gutiérrez. See *Theology of Liberation*, 88–100, for his discussion of the development of this model by Maritain and others as a response to the collapse of Christendom, and his critique of this in favor of the more radical integralism of de Lubac and de Montcheuil. For an excellent summary of what is meant by "integral humanism," see de Lubac, *Catholicism*, 353–56.

is not guaranteed by merely technical progress and relationships of utility, but by the potential of love that overcomes evil with good" (*Caritas*, 9). Once again, we can see that it is the *same* integralist theological reasoning which leads the Pope to insist that faith is indispensable for development *and* that leads to the most radical distributivist and mutualist elements of his economic vision.

INTEGRALISM AND CHARITY AS GIFT-EXCHANGE IN THE ANGLICAN SOCIAL TRADITION

We turn now to see how this distinctive theological agenda of Benedict, driving his social and economic thinking, compares with Anglican social thought. Here we have to speak of "thought" or "tradition/s" rather than capitalized "Teaching," because, significantly, there is no one voice which could claim to speak authoritatively and finally on social matters for the Church of England, let alone the Anglican Communion, in the way that the Roman Magisterium does for the Roman Catholic Church. Yet this is not to say that Anglicanism has no social thought. On the contrary, it has a substantial body of writings, some from representative or authoritative bodies, such as Synodical reports or official statements by Church leaders, and some from respected Anglican thinkers, whose authority is more organic than formal. This polyphonic tradition certainly contains different voices, but we can also discern commonalities and developments, and in this we might note that our earlier analysis has suggested that such diversity and development can be detected even within the Roman magisterial tradition.

To focus our attention on the last half century or so of British Anglican social thought, we might well come to the conclusion that the dominant strand was closer to the "distinction of planes" model than to Benedict's integralism. We can call this strand of Anglican social thought "conservative liberalism" and its heyday was the period from the 1960s to the 1980s.[6] The most significant figure for this tradition is William Temple (1881–1944) who was successively Archbishop of York and of Canterbury and whose book *Christianity and Social Order* was enormously influential, although it is unclear whether Temple himself should be completely situated within this tradition which claims

6. Sedgwick, "Theology and Society," 290.

him.[7] The William Temple Foundation, based in Manchester, has been one of the strongholds of this tradition, particularly through the work of Ronald Preston, Professor at Manchester University, and John Atherton, at Manchester Cathedral.[8] We could also however include the work of John Habgood, Archbishop of York, David Jenkins, Bishop of Durham, Peter Selby, Bishop of Worcester, Peter Sedgwick, Principal of St Michael's College, Cardiff, and Richard Harries, Bishop of Oxford, as well as many of the publications of the national Board for Social Responsibility in this "conservative liberalism" category.[9]

All these authors are characterized by a basically liberal (Kantian-Weberian) analysis of modernity, with its increasing secularization and pluralism, while at the same time, in varying degrees, wanting to hold on to something of the Church of England's historic claim to be the conscience of the nation. As a result all tend to offer comment on contemporary politics and economics which seeks to speak in the categories of "natural reason," independent of specifically Christian claims, and therefore supposedly acceptable to all, regardless of their beliefs; while at the same time they end up offering at most only very modest critiques of the *status quo*. The appeal is to a certain form of English common sense, against what is seen as the pietism and absolutism of more integralist alternatives such as Catholic liberation theology or Evangelical communitarian thought.

It is difficult to miss the episcopal, establishment nature of this strand of Anglican social thought, and it has often been expressed through responses to government reports and interventions in the House of Lords. Amongst the many theological influences, the principle figure seems to be Reinhold Niebuhr and his "Christian realism." It is not difficult therefore

7. It is striking for example, that Temple does not shy away from the Christian nature of his economic and social vision, and also has an account of the co-inherence of justice and love, and of guild models of association, which is not so far removed from *Caritas in Veritate*. See Temple, *Christianity and Social Order*, 93, 76–77, and 106.

8. E.g. Preston, *Religion and the Ambiguities of Capitalism*; Atherton, *Christianity and the Market*.

9. E.g. Habgood, *Confessions of a Conservative Liberal*; Jenkins, *Market Whys and Human Wherefores*; Harries, *Is There a Gospel for the Rich?*; Sedgwick, *Market Economy and Christian Ethics*. In fairness we should note that there are of course shades of difference in this tradition: so, for example, the report *Faith in the City*, Selby and Jenkins all stand at the more radical end politically and economically, and, as we have indicated, Temple retains more of an explicitly Christian integralist agenda than many of his heirs would claim.

to see why Stanley Hauerwas has nicknamed this strand of Anglican social thought "Reinhold Niebuhr in ecclesiastical drag."[10]

"Conservative liberalism" was not however the only show in town. We can trace a second strand of thought with more in common with the radical integralism of Benedict XVI, more at home in the academy than on the episcopal bench, which has perhaps risen to ascendancy in recent times and, I will argue, can trace its roots back to earlier strands of Anglican social thought. For want of a more precise label, I will call this loose grouping the Catholic Socialists. They share a sense that the Christian faith does not need to be translated into middle axioms to contribute to political debate in a pluralist society, but rather *is* its own social, political and economic vision. They also share a commitment to radical critique of the status quo on this basis and to more mutualist, co-operativist, communitarian forms of socialism rather than to statist solutions. This tradition might include such diverse figures as Ken Leech, community theologian in East London, Tim Gorringe, professor at Exeter University, Michael Northcott, professor at Edinburgh, John Milbank, professor at Nottingham, Graham Ward, professor at Manchester and, arguably, Rowan Williams, the current Archbishop of Canterbury.

In differing ways, they have expressed a wariness towards liberalism and its alliance with free market capitalism, a strongly internationalist and environmentalist concern, along with a recognition that what is required is not simply state interventions on the basis of justice, but more fundamentally new forms of business and commercial practice to achieve transformation at the level of the economic base. This certainly sounds closer to the integralist thinking of *Caritas in Veritate*. This perspective has gained a new ascendancy through the influence of more post-liberal and communitarian thinkers, such as Stanley Hauerwas and Alasdair MacIntyre in recent years. Meanwhile their influence in turn can be connected with broader cultural shifts, such as the breakdown of a liberal consensus in the face of more extreme pluralism and the marginalization of religion through a more vigorous secularism, which has curiously led to a revival of theological self-confidence.

Furthermore, this integralist Anglican tradition can be seen as not just a recent maverick departure from the dominant "conservative liberal"

10. From a response to a question at the conference "A Particular Place," at Westcott House, Cambridge, September 16–18, 2009.

perspective, but in fact a return to elements of an earlier tradition of Anglican social thought. We can certainly trace direct precursors of the more communitarian, confidently Christian, politically radical analysis we have been describing in the Anglo-Catholic "Christendom group" in the early twentieth century, and slightly earlier in the work of Henry Scott Holland and the *Lux Mundi* school, including R. C. Moberly and Charles Gore. This latter group stand slightly closer to the "conservative liberals," and we might group with them the important writings of the Anglican economist R. H. Tawney, Michael Ramsey, Archbishop of Canterbury, and in fact certain aspects of Temple's own work (his more idealist and unapologetically Christian moments).

More broadly, we can see something which at the least is quite different from the "distinction of planes" model in the thought of the grandfather of Christian socialism, F. D. Maurice.[11] In particular, his ecclesiology, with its universal reach and refusal of clericalist distinctions of laity from clergy, his theology of communion, for which the Church *is* itself a social reality, and his theology of creation, with its sense of all creation as graced and his refusal of any notions of pure nature, seems remarkably close to the integralist position set forth in the mid-twentieth century by Henri de Lubac (which stands behind Ratzinger's theology and *Caritas in Veritate*).[12] This should not come as such a surprise when we recall that both were in differing ways influenced by patristic, Platonic philosophies (in Maurice's case, with a Coleridgean flavor; while for de Lubac in a more Augustinian mode) rather than the Aristotelianism which had influenced neo-scholastic ways of thinking.[13]

We can also suggest that Anglican ecclesiology and soteriology, from Maurice, back to Hooker and even in proto-form in someone like Tyndale, preserved, in common with the Orthodox churches, an earlier Carolinian/Byzantine model of Church and society, and a more deification model of grace and nature, unaffected by the Hildebrandine, Tridentine, neo-scholastic, and Vatican I developments which had made the distinction of planes model seem so appropriate to Roman Catholicism.[14]

11. See Morris, *F. D. Maurice*, 158–60.

12. Ibid., 128 n.149, 135, 149, 169, 173, 203.

13. Ibid., 37–43, 46–49.

14. See Ramsey, *Gospel and the Catholic Church*, chs. 11 and 13; Williams, *Anglican Identities*, chs. 1 and 3; Hooker, *Of the Laws of Ecclesiastical Polity*, Book V, chs. 1, 2, 55 and 56.

Such a lineage might make integralism seem a hopelessly old-fashioned Constantinian model unsuited to the challenge of the present day. However, we should not forget that Maurice and de Lubac were each already responding to the challenge of secularism and even the rise of atheism in ways which were not just about reasserting control, but in the confidence that nothing is beyond the limits of grace. Likewise we have seen how it is ultimately such an integralist position which in fact offers a *more* radical analysis and response to our contemporary situation. If this argument is correct, then it is the case that not only are there important similarities between the message of *Caritas in Veritate* and recent Anglican social thought, but also an Anglican perspective can help to rescue the encyclical from the stale conservative/liberal debate and reveal its radical theological heart. On the other hand, this reading of the encyclical can encourage Anglicans in moving on from the "Niebuhr in ecclesiastical drag" model of social thinking, towards something that is at once more Christian and more radical.

Beyond this, we can make an even more bold or perhaps just mischievous claim: that some of the key ideas of *Caritas in Veritate* have received their most fulsome treatments and indeed may even have partially originated within Anglican thought. We can note, for example, that John Burnaby, Oliver O'Donovan, and John Milbank have been amongst the most important defendants of the Augustinian notion of charity as reciprocal gift exchange, and in the latter case has applied this to the economic sphere.[15] We can also recall that mutualism, co-operatives and association were much discussed by Maurice, the Anglican legal and economic historians J. N. Figgis, and R. H. Tawney, and the British Christian "guild socialists".[16] Also that one of the key Roman Catholic exponents of distributivist ideas was the convert from the Church of England, G. K. Chesterton. Finally, that many of the basic ideas of the *ressourcement* movement which contributed to de Lubac's integralism and the position of *Caritas in Veritate*, such as the concern with historical development, or the return to the Fathers instead of neo-scholasticism, had some of their roots in another famous convert, John Henry

---

15. Burnaby, *Amor Dei*; O'Donovan, *Problem of Self-Love in St. Augustine*; Milbank, *Being Reconciled* and *Future of Love*.

16. Morris, *F. D. Maurice*, 143, Tawney, *Acquisitive Society*; see also Milbank, *Future of Love*, ch. 4.

Newman.[17] These converts may well have brought some of their intellectual "patrimony" with them, so that both traditions are already more ecumenically interdependent than they might realize. It seems then as if Anglicans may have more sympathy for this encyclical and more of a contribution to make concerning its interpretation and reception than many would think.

17. de Lubac, *Catholicism*, 431–33.

PART V

Distributism and
Alternative Economies

9

Common Life

Ethics, Class, Community

Jon Cruddas MP and Jonathan Rutherford

The economy needs ethics in order to function correctly.

—Benedict XVI, *Caritas in Veritate*

INTRODUCTION

THE BUILDINGS OF CANARY Wharf in east London are huge factories of information and communications that have grown out of the old industrial structure of the Docklands. There are no longer any cranes on West India Dock lifting heavy goods from the holds of ships, very few workers engaged in physical toil, and no trade routes from the workshop of the world to the four corners of empire. The hard lives this industrial economy sustained have been made redundant. The new engines of

Western capitalism are companies like Credit Suisse, HSBC, Citigroup and Morgan Stanley. The new trade routes are digital and they no longer need the labor of the old working class. Instead they often rely on cheap labor for cleaning and servicing. If you follow the A13 from Canary Wharf along the river you reach Dagenham, home to many of the low paid, migrant workers who service the financial elite.

Dagenham was once the cornerstone of London's manufacturing industry, dominated by the giant Ford plant. In the 1950s Ford was employing over forty thousand men and women, and turning out four thousand cars a week. But de-industrialization and growing competition from Asia caused a dramatic fall in production and profits. Barely five thousand now work across the whole Ford estate. Keith Dover worked on the assembly lines for fifteen years: "Going in there at the start of a shift, we were like the living dead. It was over and over, the same thing, eight hours a day." Harry Coleman is ninety years old and spent his working life in the plant: "I wouldn't know the place now," he says. "What's left today? Only the ghosts."[1] View Britain through the prism of Dagenham and you will find a defining story about our country.

Despite its proximity to the City, Dagenham has seen none of the opulent wealth it generated. Thirty years of globalization have ripped through its communities with the destructive force of a tornado. The extraordinary speed of its industrial collapse has left behind unemployment and the disorientating loss of a way of life. There followed demographic change so rapid that it defeats the ability of the census to measure it. Under-resourced public services buckle under the pressure of incoming migrants. There is deep, intractable poverty and a chronic shortage of homes. A disorganized, insecure class of low paid immigrants, single mothers, pensioners, benefit claimants, and casual workers, struggle to get by on a daily basis. Fear and racial tension resonate with the insecurities of large numbers of people who feel that they have been abandoned to live as strangers without a community.

Britain has become a country we do not yet know. In the last three decades, despite increasing wealth, our class divisions have become more entrenched. Inequality defines our society. Growing differences in culture and lifestyles and the breaking up of the UK into our constituent nations have dislocated our sense of identity and belonging. Private con-

1. Quotes from Dennis Ellam, "Ford's Dagenham Car Plant."

sumption is valued more highly than the consumption of public goods, and this is manifest in the absence of a public discussion of the common good. There exists an unresolved dilemma about what is the right balance between a collective sense of security and the pursuit of individual freedom. We have been governed in the manner of Mosaic UK, the marketing system which breaks people down into 155 types of individuals, sixty-seven different households and fifteen groups. Politics has been reduced to a form of management with battles between "suburban mindsets" and "elderly needs." The erosion of civic culture and social bonds has led to a loss of trust and a sense of disenfranchisement amongst the electorate. Many people want more authentic, self-fulfilling lives but this searching exposes us to what can feel like an unanchored and lonely existence, full of personal risk. The financial crisis has brought to an end an economic era, and we have now entered a period of transition.

THE AGE OF EXCESS

In the last three decades Britain has been experiencing a transition from an economy organized around industrial mass production to one organized around the new information and communication technologies. Radical innovations in the generation, processing and transmission of information, backed by financial capital are modernizing the whole productive structure. Ford is an example of the fate of the old industrial leviathans in this new economic age. It had become an automobile manufacturer dependent on its credit vehicle financing arm. Profit no longer lay in producing cars, but in selling credit to customers to buy them. The lease and loan payments of Ford Credit could be securitized and sold on to raise money on the capital markets. Its business model felt the strain in the financial crash of 2008, and it left Ford with 25.8 billion dollars of debt. The British economy suffers a similar predicament. Once a manufacturing nation, we have become indebted consumers over-reliant on financial speculation for growth. An economy of excess, driven by greed, has brought us to the brink of financial collapse.

The historic crisis of Britain's old model of mass industrial production and the systemic failure of capital accumulation in the 1960s provided an opportunity for the right to establish a new hegemony. The 1979 Conservative government of Margaret Thatcher broke the power of organized labor, deregulated and restructured the economy, and opened it up to global market forces. Chancellor Geoffrey Howe's 1981 "austerity budget" of public spending cuts and tax increases destroyed the post-war consensus of welfare capitalism. But it was the 1980 Housing Act and the "right to buy" your council house that helped win popular support for the Conservative Government and secured the thirty year hegemony of neo-liberalism.

In the name of a property-owning democracy, a new kind of popular compact between the individual and the market took shape. Home ownership aligned the modest economic interests of individuals with the interests of financial capital. This relationship between the individual and the market began to displace the old social welfare contract with the state and provided a foundational structure for the development of a new liberal market society of consumers. Commodification and market relations were extended into society. The public sector and civic institutions began to reconfigure their organizations into proxy and quasi-markets governed by cost efficiency and targets. Individual social relationships incorporated a larger element of the rational calculation of the market. This ideological transformation of culture and society was driven by a state that was itself being privatized, outsourced, and marketized. Where the nation-state had taken a moral responsibility for the welfare of its citizens, the new kind of market state promised them instead the economic opportunity to consume.

Economic growth depended on this compact. The housing market became the epicenter of a casino economy that turned homes into assets for leveraging ever-increasing levels of borrowing. The lives of millions were integrated into the global financial markets as their savings, pensions, and personal and mortgage-backed debt were expropriated by financial capital. In three decades GDP doubled, but it was a false prosperity disguising deep structural problems in the economy. Britain's boom was dependent on the imbalance between the huge trade surpluses of emergent economies and the deficits of the rich countries. The relocation of manufacturing to low wage economies was creating a new global division of labor and destroying working class jobs in Britain. In 1978, 7.1 million were employed in manufacturing, by 2008 this had fallen to 3 million.[2] The boom years brought replacement jobs in the public sector,

2. ONS, "Workforce Jobs by Industry."

retailing, restaurants and hotels, and in finance and business services.[3] But the City had little appetite for investing in economic development, and it was government that created jobs in former manufacturing regions. Despite the extraordinary growth of the financial sector, its business model did not spread wealth nor did it create a significant number of jobs. Between 2005 and 2006 the financial sector's share of UK GDP increased from 8.8 percent to 9.4 percent, in the same period income poverty began to rise again.[4]

The process of de-industrialization undermined the income base of the working class. The share of national wealth going to wages peaked at 65 percent in 1973, by 2008 it had dropped to 53 percent.[5] To sustain living standards, low and middle earning households increased their dependence on capital markets and borrowed. In 1997 the debt to income ratio was 91:1, by 2007 it had risen to 157:4.[6] The boom years of the neo-liberal economic order, both globally and nationally, transferred wealth and resources from labor to capital on a massive scale. Millions have been left economically inactive or working in casual, low paid and insecure employment. In contrast, the compact established a banking oligarchy which captured both the financial regulatory system and the political class. The business model of shareholder value aligned the interests of a business elite with the market value of their companies.

While business productivity failed to grow, the pay of company directors and the senior workforce of the financial houses soared. The credit they sold to middle earners fueled the highly lucrative market in debt securitization that generated bank bonuses. In 2007 these totaled 14 billion pounds. Gordon Brown, in his Mansion House speech that year, hailed "the beginning of a new golden age for the City of London." The following year house prices in Britain lost 13.3 percent of their value, HBoS bank and the Royal Bank of Scotland faced imminent bankruptcy and money markets froze. The neo-liberal compact worked in favor of the rich who were able to establish themselves as an oligopoly. The banking elite captured both the financial regulatory system and the political class.

3. Ibid.

4. See online: http://www.cpag.org.uk/povertyfacts/index.htm.

5. Lansley, *Unfair to Middling*, 7.

6. Ibid., 8.

Britain entered recession in September 2008 with levels of personal debt at 1.4 trillion pounds, of which 223 billion was unsecured.[7] In the five years between 2002 and 2007, during its period of maximum profiteering, the financial industries contributed 203 billion pounds in taxes.[8] Against this the IMF calculates that the direct cost to the taxpayer of the banking crash is 289 billion pounds. If the loans and guarantees are added in, the potential exposure to the taxpayer has been 1183 billion pounds.[9] The economy faces an uncertain future. The unchecked power of financial capital has left Britain with some of the highest levels of poverty and inequality in Europe. In 1976 the bottom 50 percent of the population owned 8 percent of the nation's wealth, by 2001 it had fallen to 5 percent.[10] In contrast, 1 percent of the population earn an average annual income of 220,000 pounds and own approximately 25 percent of marketable wealth. Within this group, a super rich elite of 0.1 percent earns an average of 780,000 pounds.[11] The neo-liberal compact provided unprecedented levels of consumer choice for millions, but it functioned to transmit money into the financial sector rather than create durable economic security. It provided a social structure for enabling new forms of capital accumulation and so helped in the resurgence of creative destruction.

Outside, Looking In

The middle earners of Middle Britain lost out to the wealthy who grew tax light and dynastically rich, but millions were excluded from the compact of cheap credit, consumerism and home ownership. As the economic boom came to an end in 2007–08, 13.5 million people, or 22 percent of the population were living in households on or below the poverty line of 60 percent of the median household income.[12] Of these, 5 million are surviving on 40 percent of median income, around 10,000

7. See online: http://www.creditaction.org.uk/september-2008.html.

8. CRESC, *Alternative Report on UK Banking Reform*, 31.

9. Ibid., 32. For details, see IMF, *State of Public Finances*.

10. See National Statistics, available online: http://www.statistics.gov.uk/cci/nugget.asp?id=1005.

11. Brewer, Sibieta, and Wren-Lewis, *Racing Away?*

12. See The Poverty Site, http://www.poverty.org.uk. For information about the median income, see http://www.statistics.gov.uk/cci/nugget.asp?id=285.

pounds a year—a little over two weeks income for the top one percent. The numbers in deep poverty are at the highest level since records began in 1979.[13] The "right to buy" has enriched many peoples' lives, but the failure to invest in housing for the next generation has left millions without a decent home.

In a society of consumers, inequality has created a new kind of cultural domination around lifestyle and the conspicuous consumption of status-enhancing goods. Consumer culture became a mass symbolic practice of individual social recognition distributing humiliation to those lower down the hierarchy. The shame of failing in education, of being a loser in the race to success, of being invisible to those above, cuts a deep wound in the psyche. Invidious comparisons between one's self and others and between one group and another create feelings of inferiority and chronic anxiety. Richard Wilkinson has shown how this kind of anxiety dramatically increases vulnerability to disease and premature death. Drawing on the findings of neuroscience he argues that "the variety of physiological processes affected by chronic anxiety mean that its health effects are in many respects analogous to more rapid ageing."[14] As he points out, violence is more common where there is more inequality because people are deprived of the markers of status and so are more vulnerable to the anxieties of being judged by others.

Inequality not only destroys the well-being and damages the life chances of people living in poverty, it increases levels of mental illness across society, undermining trust, and creating fear and intolerance. Despite the injustices of inequality, those who gained the least from the economic boom—the poor, welfare recipients, single mothers, immigrants, and young people—have all been made scapegoats for anxieties about social disorder and incivility. Economic deprivation has precipitated inter-generational self-destructive behavior, addictions, depression and mental illness, criminality and "conduct disorder," but these are symptoms of incivility, not its root causes. Recipients of welfare benefits have been subjected to a punitive rhetoric that recalls the harshness of the Poor Laws. The New Labour government revived a disciplinary approach to welfare concerned with controlling individuals rather than supporting them. Poverty became an issue about personal behavior and

13. See online: http://www.statistics.gov.uk/cci/nugget.asp?id=285.

14. Wilkinson, "Health, Hierarchy and Social Anxiety"; Wilkinson, "Impact of Inequality"; Wilkinson and Pickett, *Spirit Level*.

dependency rather than about economic inequality and justice.[15] The problem was not structure or environment but individual failing and dysfunction.

The compact and its ideology of self-reliance and individual market choice, not only undermined the welfare ethos, it eroded social ties and public civic culture, contributing to the breakdown in trust and an increasing fear of crime. Many people have become disaffected with representative democracy. They have lost confidence in political parties and have disengaged from the public realm. The institutions which have in the past given people access to political ideas and civic activity, such as trade unions, churches and political parties face steep membership-decline. The 2009 Ipsos Mori Annual Survey of Public Trust in Professions reveals the depth of this crisis of political representation. Only 13 percent trust politicians, down from 21 percent in 2008, and only 16 percent trust government down from 24 percent.

SOCIAL RECESSION

In the first decade of the new century, there were growing anxieties about the condition of society. In September 2006, *The Daily Telegraph* published a letter signed by over one hundred professionals and academics. "We are," they wrote, "deeply concerned at the escalating incidence of childhood depression and children's behavioural and developmental conditions." Their letter was prescient of a UNICEF report, *An overview of child well-being in rich countries*, published the following February.[16] It paints a bleak picture of British childhood. The summary of six dimensions of child well-being places the UK at the bottom of the league.

In 2004, the Nuffield Foundation published a study, *Time Trends in Adolescent Mental Health*.[17] It looked at three generations of fifteen year olds in 1974, 1986 and 1999 and identified a sharp decline in their mental health. Behavioral problems have more than doubled over the

15. For an example of Lawrence Mead's work, see his 1996 paper, "Poverty and Political Theory." See also the work of Charles Murray, e.g., *Bell Curve Intelligence*. Murray was invited to Britain by *The Sunday Times* and his ideas were taken up by the *Institute of Economic Affairs Unit* run by Digby Anderson. It has since been renamed *Civitas*.

16. UNICEF, *Overview of Child Well-being in Rich Countries*.

17. Collishaw, Maughan, Goodman, and Pickles, "Time Trends in Adolescent Mental Health," 1350–62; The Nuffield Foundation, *2004 Seminars on Children and Families*.

last twenty-five years. Emotional problems such as depression, anxiety, and hyperactivity have increased by 70 percent. What the study could not explain was the cause of this trend. It did note however that rising levels of adolescent mental illness coincided with improvements in economic conditions. Further studies suggested that these levels have reached a plateau. Causal explanations have ruled out family size. Nor can it be fully accounted for by the increases in single parent families and levels of poverty.[18] One study, by Stephan Collishaw et al., ends inconclusively with the statement that "trends in mental health might also be conceived of as a product of both 'beneficial' and potentially 'harmful' societal changes."[19]

Children and adolescents are an acutely sensitive measure of the well-being of a society. As they grow, the fabric of conscious and unconscious communications of their families, and more widely of culture and class, race and social relations are precipitated in them. They internalize these social relations that come to form the innermost being of individual personality. Problems we associate with individuals—stress, depression, bullying, violence—are dysfunctions that originate in their families and wider social networks. As John T. Cacioppo and William Patrick describe it: "The social environment affects the neural and hormonal signals that govern our behavior, and our behavior, in turn, creates changes in the social environment that affect our neural and hormonal processes."[20] Research in neuroscience has demonstrated how poor parenting impacts on the biochemistry of children's bodies, determining their capacity in adulthood to cope with life's stresses.[21] There is now a wealth of evidence that poor attachment or emotional trauma in childhood affects long-term health and life chances.[22] Similarly feeling excluded and socially isolated

18. Maughan, Collishaw, Meltzer, and Goodman, "Recent Trends in UK Child and Adolescent Mental Health."

19. Collishaw, Goodman, Pickles, and Maughan, "Modelling the Contribution of Changes in Family Life to Time Trends in Adolescent Conduct Problems."

20. Cacioppo and Patrick, *Loneliness: Human Nature and the Need for Social Connections*, 11.

21. For an excellent introduction see Gerhardt, *Why Love Matters*.

22. Caserta, O'Connor, Wyman, Wang, Moynihan, Cross, Tuc and Jin, "Associations between Psychosocial Stress and the Frequency of Illness"; see also the article "Stressed Parents Equals Sick Kids." There are also two reports from the Sainsbury Centre for Mental Health: *Childhood Mental Health and Life Chances in Post-war Britain* (2009), and *Chance of a Lifetime* (2009).

undermines people's resilience, optimism and self-esteem and increases their levels of fear, anxiety and hostility.

In recent years the importance of social and relational life has been recognized in government and policy-making circles. However, the official perception of the problem has been framed by the concept of "social capital" which tends to reproduce a neo-liberal understanding of the individual and social experience. The exemplary and oft-quoted work in this field is Robert Putnam's book *Bowling Alone*. Putnam seeks to understand the trends in civic disengagement in U.S. society in the last third of the twentieth century. But he does not develop an account of the relations of subordination and domination that structure the social relations of a capitalist economy, and his methodology neutralizes differences of power in gender, race, and class relations. As a consequence, it fails to fully grasp the social and economic causes of civic disengagement.

Putnam, like Collishaw et al., is left with an enigma. He offers lists by way of explaining the slump in social capital and civic engagement: busyness, time pressure, financial pressure, financial anxiety, urban sprawl, mobility. In the end he can only surmise that the cause is generational and intensified by new communication technologies: "television and its electronic cousins are willing accomplices in the civic mystery."[23] The problem with the concept of social capital is its ideological affinity with the neo-liberal *status quo*. As a consequence the overall tendency of official policy-making has been to ignore the structural determinations of class and the changing means of production and consumption and their impact on human relationships, family life, and culture. Instead the focus has been local, encouraging networks and associations in neighborhoods to develop thick, bonding, and bridging capital. It is an approach which reproduces existing relations of power by transferring risk to those the policies claim to be helping. The causes of poverty and deprivation are shifted downward and relocated in the behaviors and values of the poor themselves. In the name of "self-empowerment," responsibility for change can be invested with them. The realities of power and subordination and the issue of redistributing wealth and resources are left unquestioned.

The theoretical failings of the social capital concept is symptomatic of the wider crisis of governance in the post-financial crash period. The role of the social—social relationships, association, mutualism—in

23. Putnam, *Bowling Alone*, 246.

economic development was addressed by separating it out from political economy. The "social" was treated as if it were a discrete, internally undifferentiated category, unconnected to class relations and to the capitalist reorganization of consumption and production. It offered an understanding of society which focused on a few trees separated out from the wood. Looking through the prism of Dagenham, we need a radically new approach to understanding the kind of society we are living in and the place of individuals within the complex ensemble of political, economic and cultural forces.

COMMON LIFE

In the wake of the financial crash, the neo-liberal contract that promised freedom through individual market choice no longer commands popular confidence. The sense of a shared national cultural life has been losing its hold over the popular imagination for several generations. The old nation-state's social welfare contract is in tatters, its safety net gravely damaged. What now is the ethical relationship of individuals to one another and to society? The current political and technocratic elites have no answers. Their intellectual capital was informed by the neo-classical tradition of economics. Social experiences and occurrences are accounted for in terms of what individuals think, choose and do. Individuals are treated as maximum utility-seekers governed by economic self-interest. This idealized model of human interaction suited the governance model of market choice. But it is devoid of reciprocity and it leaves individuals with no meaningful relationship to one another. In its depoliticized world, history is silent, and the dynamics of oppression are absent. A range of disciplines—sociology, psychoanalysis, epigenetics, complexity theory, and neuroscience—all show us how this understanding of human nature undermines well-being, destroys social connections, and impoverishes human potential.

The problem is not simply about mistakes in social policy, it is about the fundamental issues of political economy and philosophical principle. We need to create a politics that values the social goods that give meaning to people's lives: home, family, friendships, good work, locality, and imaginary communities of belonging. In our affirmation of ordinary, everyday life we will discover an ethics of the common good. This politics would begin with us as individuals relating to others and producing in society. Marx criticized classical economists like Ricardo and Mill who saw the individual as history's point of departure rather than its historic result. The modern epoch that produces the isolated individual is also the epoch of the most developed social relations. In the Introduction to *Grundrisse*, he argues that human beings can only individuate themselves in "the midst of society."[24] The sociologist Norbert Elias, in his 1939 essay "The Society of Individuals," provides a sociology of this individuality and dismisses the view that individuals are self-contained, "closed personalities." The pursuit of independence as an individualistic project, subject only to rules of just conduct, is an illusion. Human beings are social and emotional beings who are dependent upon other people throughout their lives. As Elias remarks, what shapes, binds and gives meaning to an individual's belonging is "the ineradicable connection between his desires and behaviour and those of other people, of the living, the dead, and even, in a certain sense, the unborn."[25]

Hannah Arendt provides some philosophical substance to Elias's sociology. She is interested in the fate of our common world. "To live together in the world means essentially that a world of things is between those who have it in common." She likens the "world of things" to a table around which people sit and which orders their relationships with one another. In the same way a common life both relates people to one another and separates them: "The public realm, as the common world, gathers us together and yet prevents our falling over each other, so to speak. The loss of this realm means that individuals no longer share a concern with the same 'world of things.'" Rather than leading to a diversity of identities and experiences, the consequence is the loss of "things essential to a truly human life." "Men have become entirely private, that is, they have been deprived of seeing and hearing others, of being seen and heard by them. They are all imprisoned in the subjectivity of their own singular experience."[26] The problems created by the neo-liberal economic order confront us with the need to remake a common life.

This understanding of the interdependency of individuals was anticipated by the New Liberals of the late nineteenth century. Leonard Hobhouse wrote: "Society exists in individuals. When all the generations through which its unity subsists are counted in, its life is their life,

---

24. Marx, "Introduction," in *Grundrisse*.
25. Elias, *Society of Individuals*.
26. Arendt, *Human Condition*, 52, 58.

and nothing outside their life."[27] Like Marx, for whom the individual was a category of relations, Hobhouse described "man [as . . .] the meeting point of a great number of social relations." In his 1898 essay "The Ethical Basis of Collectivism," he argues that a progressive movement must have an ethical ideal and it must be abstract in that it is not yet realized and embodied in social institutions. One element of this ideal must be liberty but it must find a synthesis with equality, "since it stands for the truth that there is a common humanity deeper than all our superficial distinctions."[28] For Hobhouse, social progress is the development of a society in which "the best life of each man is and is felt to be bound up with the best life of his fellow-citizens."

Hobhouse's social liberalism finds modern-day counterparts in the ethical socialism of Paul Ricoeur and Charles Taylor. For Hobhouse politics is "rightfully subordinate to ethics," it exists for the sake of human life. For Ricoeur there must be an "ethical intention" central to a politics of socialism. It is "the desire to live well with and for others in just institutions." By living well he means for each person to follow their "good life" or their "true life" which he describes in terms similar to those of Charles Taylor, as "the nebulus of ideals and dreams of achievements with regard to which a life is held to be more or less fulfilled or unfulfilled."[29] Charles Taylor argues that the ethical value of self-fulfillment has entered deep into modern Western consciousness, but the conditions for its realization do not yet exist. It is, he says, a new phenomenon: "There is a certain way of being human that is my way. I am called upon to live my life in this way, and not in imitation of anyone else's. But this gives a new importance to being true to myself. If I am not, I miss the point of my life, I miss what being human is for me."[30] The concern for one's own identity and self-esteem is social rather than individualistic. It involves the right of everyone to achieve their own unique way of being human. To dispute this right in others is to fail to live within its own terms.

Ethical socialism does not subordinate the individual to the community, nor does it fabricate community where it does not exist. It is about the structure of relations between individuals, which shape both our psyche and our place in the order of things. It does not pitch the

27. Hobhouse, *Social Evolution and Political Theory*, 85.

28. Hobhouse, "Ethical Basis of Collectivism," 141, 145.

29. Ricoeur, *Oneself as Another*, 172, 179–80.

30. Taylor, *Ethics of Authenticity*, 28–29.

individual against society, but sees individuals as constituted in society. Society has its own kind of regularity, but it is nothing more than the relationships of individuals. There is no "I" without first a "we" that is historical and forged out of culture and society. The anthropologist Ruth Benedict writes: "Society is never an entity separable from the individuals who compose it. No individual can arrive even at the threshold of his potentialities without a culture in which he participates."[31] A people subjected to cultural destruction lose their defense against more dominant cultures that seek to re-describe them. The image of "the chav" and the concept of "an underclass" are both examples of how a dominant class culture imposes its meanings on another.

Ethical socialism addresses the material conditions which give form to individual being. It is a politics of equality founded in the belief that individuals are of equal worth and it is governed by an ethic of reciprocity: "do not do to others what you would not like to be done to you." It recognizes that the task of living necessitates interdependency with others and that this interdependency leads to the question of equality and justice. Equality is the precondition for freedom. Not simply the negative freedom from the compulsion of others, but a positive freedom toward self-fulfillment. Paul Ricoeur describes equality as the ethical core of justice. "The unjust man is the one who takes too much in terms of advantages or not enough in terms of burdens." Justice requires not just a singular equality, but the pursuit of equalities around relations of class, sexuality, race and gender. There is no barrier between the individual and society that prevents the transition of ethics from interpersonal life to the social and political realm. Ethical socialism originates in the sphere of interpersonal relationships and extends upward into the wider social realm and into the political community that governs the distribution of resources. Ricoeur argues that equality "is to life in institutions what solicitude is to interpersonal relations." Justice holds persons to be irreplaceable and so adds to the solicitude of living with and for others, "to the extent that the field of application of equality is all of humanity."[32]

31. Benedict, *Patterns of Culture*, 182.

32. Ricoeur, *Oneself as Another*, 202.

A New Political Economy

Ethical socialism alone is not sufficient to realize a new society. It must animate radical change in the organization of the economy and its relations of control and ownership. We need an ethical economy which is people centered. The financial crisis should herald a progressive moment for the left. But it has struggled to confront its historical defeat in the 1980s and it has been floundering in the ideological vacuum left in the wake of New Labour. It has neither the alliances across civil society, nor the collective political agency to secure a new electoral agenda. It lacks a story that defines what it stands for. The ideology of liberal market capitalism might have lost its credibility, but it remains the only story of economic life on offer. We must apply our principles to developing an analysis of contemporary capitalism and a new political economy. Nowhere is the intellectual failing of the center left more acute than in the realm of political economy. The financial crisis and the discrediting of neoclassical economics has left an intellectual void in policy-making.

Renewal of the left must begin with a new ethical political economy. Britain has to make the transition from casino capitalism to a low-carbon, more equitable, and balanced form of economic development. The transition demands an economics whose principles are ecologically sustainable wealth creation, durability, recycling, cultural inventiveness, equality, and human flourishing. The fundamental logic of this new economy must be ecological sustainability. Climate change, peak oil, the need for energy, and food security are all core green issues at its heart. Social movements, single-issue campaigns, and civil society organizations will be essential to this developmental process, but they are not enough. A plural politics of alliances capable of achieving transformative economic and political change and of countering the destructive forces of capitalism requires a systemic theoretical and philosophical grounding and organizational coherence. Only by developing our traditions of socialism will we be able to create a new hegemonic politics.

In the decade ahead new forms of production and consumption will continue to reshape society and social relationships. Technology is facilitating new cultural practices and at the same time opening up opportunities for capital to commodify them. New kinds of property and property relations are being created. Just as early industrial capitalism enclosed the commons of land and labor, so the ICT-driven post-industrial capitalism of today is enclosing the cultural and intellectual commons (both real and virtual), the commons of the human mind and body, and the commons of biological life. Government must take on a new strategic authority and act as the dynamic builder of the green industrial economy of the future, facilitating a new techno-economic paradigm across markets and sectors.

We need to develop a democratized, redistributive, social activist, intra-nation state capable of setting limits to the scope of capital accumulation, regulating markets, and asserting the public interest in the wider economy. It will need to be decentralized and responsive to individual citizens and small businesses. The advocacy roles of civil society organizations, including the trade unions, need to be strengthened. We must make capitalism accountable to workers and citizens through regulation, economic democracy and forms of common ownership. Markets need re-embedding in society and the ethic of reciprocity reestablished within their contractual affairs. The economy must work for the common good. It needs an epochal shift from financial capital to production capital in order to spread wealth more evenly across the country. Banks as public utilities will need to play a major role in building homes and in the coming green industrial revolution by directing investment into new markets and into technological innovation and employment. In place of unfettered shareholder value, we must establish new relationships between finance and industry that foster long-term investment and real improvements in productivity. Regulation should discourage short-term financial gain. The privileging of finance capital has led to the country becoming dangerously exposed to its speculative activities. In the event of another financial crisis, the sheer scale of bank assets and liabilities will put the British state and economy in jeopardy. We literally can't afford the City to operate as a law unto itself. The first task of building a new economy is the wholesale reform of the banking sector and its business model of shareholder value.

In the future the effervescent quality of wealth creation will demand secure social foundations. The welfare system will have to respond to a flexible and fragmented employment market. There must be a non-punitive, publicly funded welfare system run in partnership with local, non-profit agencies that puts claimants at its center. We have to recover the principle of universal benefits and social insurance in the form of a citizens' pension, part of which can be accessed at different stages of life. In the longer term this can be connected up to child benefit and the child trust fund and developed into a citizens' income payable to each individual as a right of citizenship. This would be an unconditional, non-withdrawable income that guarantees access to the necessities of life.[33]

Alongside the productive economy we need to develop the care economy. A public service of childcare and support for parents, centered on the emotional development of children, and working to reduce child poverty is essential for both children and for greater social equality. Older people need a care system that affords them the same substantive freedoms as others in society. Careers need proper financial support. There are new emerging markets and needs around the third age, well-being and health, social care and education. On current trends this social economy will become the biggest sector by value and employment. We will need to develop novel ways of linking the formal and informal economy. The state needs to be capable of interacting with the complexity and values of social and community organizations, and devolving real power and decision making to workers and users.[34] Democratizing public services can avoid the problems of the market and bureaucracy and create new spaces of innovation and social development. Achieving a balance between freedom and security, efficiency and conviviality for both workers and users will be difficult, but essential.

A new political economy grounded in human welfare needs a revival of democracy in order to bring vested interests and elites to account. The introduction of proportional representation in local and national elections is essential in order to reflect the plural nature of Britain. A new system of party funding will remove the influence of rich individuals and interests. We need an elected House of Lords and the revival of local government tax raising powers in order to deepen and extend democracy through society. These changes will be met by fierce resistance, not only from the vested interests of finance capital and big business, but also from sections of society who fear they might lose out in a more egalitarian society. Our strength will lie in making deep and enduring alliances and building broad popular movements for change. Despite the disillusionment with political parties, there is an extraordinary level of political, cultural and community activism in our society. Politics has become more individualized, ethical, and rooted in a diversity of beliefs, lifestyles, and localities. This is stimulating a search

33. See the work of the Citizen's Income Trust at www.citizensincome.org.
34. Murray, *Danger and Opportunity.*

for new kinds of democratic political structures and cultures that will re-connect institutions of political power with social movements and political constituencies.

The birth of a real political alternative will require radical open thinking, insightfulness and inventive forms of organization. Nothing is guaranteed, the right will seek to maintain the power of capital over labor, and the political elite will strive for a return to business as usual. Areas of the country like Dagenham might face dark times ahead. But the opportunities for a more ethical and radical politics of the common good and social justice are real. The goal of center left politics is a strong and responsive democracy, a restoration of trust and reciprocity in public life, and an ethical and ecologically sustainable economy for human welfare and equality. It will be the great challenge of our time.

10

Equity and Equilibrium

Why Distributive Justice Is Necessary for Economic Science

John Médaille

INTRODUCTION

THE PREMISE OF THIS collection is that "there is a 'middle' position between an exclusively religious and a strictly secular perspective" on economics. But it seems to me that a "middle position" must, by definition, compromise the truths of both religion and economics. Indeed, such a premise accepts what is one of the primary problems with modern economics, namely, the belief in the so-called "equity/efficiency" trade-off. That is, the belief that an economic system can be equitable or it can be efficient, but it cannot be both.

What we should seek, I believe, is not a compromise, but a connection. What we must show is that not only is there no conflict between equity and efficiency, but, on the contrary, the latter is dependent on the former, and that if one reaches the opposite conclusion, then one has misunderstood either justice, or economics, or both. And I believe that at the root of this confusion is a misunderstanding about what kind of science economic science is. However, it is not enough merely to assert the connection; the connection must be demonstrated in terms that even the most rigorous economist could accept. Without this, ethics appear as mere platitudes, to be rightly rejected by the man of science. For as (then) Cardinal Ratzinger observed: "A morality that believes itself able to dispense with the technical knowledge of economic laws is not morality but moralism. As such it is the antithesis of morality. A scientific approach that believes itself capable of managing without an ethos misunderstands the reality of man. Therefore it is not scientific."

What is implied by this statement is that there is a dialogic relationship between theology, the Queen of the Sciences, and economics, or indeed with every other science. However, since each science is the master of its own methods, theology must speak to each science in terms intelligible to that science. This places a double burden on the theologian to learn his own language and to be able to translate it into another tongue. However, it is a burden that theology cannot refuse; she must comment on the mundane affairs of the world in terms intelligible to the world, or she must abdicate her responsibilities and lose her social utility. Theology must, on the one hand, exercise sovereignty over the other sciences, and on the other hand, humbly learn from every other science. This *sovereign humility* is a burden theology cannot refuse without making the gospel of no effect in the world, without reducing it to a mere academic curiosity.

What I will attempt to show is that economic order—that is, the rough balance between supply and demand known as equilibrium—is dependent upon equity. Indeed, it is the very lack of equity that makes equilibrium impossible and *in*efficiency *in*evitable, and the failure to recognize this makes economic science impossible. Three things are necessary for a scientific and ethical economics: first of all, to situate economics, or rather, political economy, in its proper place in the scientific hierarchy; secondly, to show why distributive justice is necessary to economic order; thirdly, to show that property, the most basic of economic relationships, lies at the root of distributive justice. Taken together, these three points add up to the economic philosophy known as "distributism." However, I wish to point out that this "distributism" is not some new theory of economic order, not another ideology, not an alternative "ism" in a marketplace of "isms," but rather an historic reality that occurs over and over again, and occurs today. Our task is not one of invention, but of discovery; it is not to invent new systems, but rather to discover the roots of economic order that are always operative, and to apply them to new situations. Our originality comes not from invention, but from application. Indeed, political economy is the practical science *par excellence* and is hence governed by the practical reason, which has as its first principle that "the good is to be done and evil avoided." And since it is a practical science, our first task is to locate political economy within the scientific hierarchy.

SCIENCE, NORMATIVE AND POSITIVE

Some wag somewhere has remarked that economists suffer from "physics envy." Sciences like physics have no need for concepts like "justice." Hence, if one attempts to model the movement of markets in the same way as the movement of molecules, then terms like "justice" can only be an embarrassment that can only compromise the purity of the science, while equity could only compromise the efficiency of markets. Since economists are human, they are often willing to allow such compromises, to allow the trade-off of some efficiency against a certain degree of equity. But equity in such cases will always be an interloper in good economic order, and any concessions to it will be made grudgingly.

Underlying such a discussion is the so-called "positive-normative" duality, but this duality poses a false dichotomy. Every science, insofar as it is a science, must be *both* positive *and* normative. Every science, insofar as it is a science, must be "normalized" to some criteria of truth. These truths will arise from two sources, an internal and an external source. The internal criteria involve the proper subject matter and methodology of a science. But these criteria are insufficient to found any science *qua* science. In addition, there must be external criteria of truth, and these truths can only come from one or more of the higher sciences. In the absence of such an "external" check, the "science" will merely be circular, dependent on nothing but its own axioms and unconnected to the hierarchy of truth. Thus, for example, biology is responsible to chemistry and chemistry to physics. No biologist can violate the laws of chemistry, and no chemist can reach a conclusion contrary to physics. Thus every science is responsible to its own methodology (and therefore "positive") and to the higher sciences (and therefore "normative"). Every science has, therefore, both its own proper autonomy, based on its subject matter and methodology, and its own proper connection to the near sciences, based on the hierarchy of truth.

Without submitting itself to this hierarchy of truth, no truth can be called a "scientific" truth. Without this proper *scientific humility*, no study can find its proper place in the hierarchy. Merely being mathematical, or empirical, or axiomatic is not enough—no matter how precise the mathematics, how careful the observations, or how certain the axioms. An astrologer, for example, will make observations as precise as you like, will draw charts as complex as you like, and make predictions as specific as you like. And all of it will be consistent with astrology's own axioms. However, these axioms are never subject to the judgment of any other science; lacking the requisite scientific humility, astrology cannot be science. It may be, for all I know, God's own truth; it can never be man's own knowledge. It must be accepted or rejected *sola fide*; no scientific judgment can ever be made because it can never be science.

So the proper question is not whether economics is positive or normative; since it is a science it is both. The question is: "To which of the higher sciences is it subject?" The physical sciences normally terminate in physics, but the humane sciences—the sciences of human relations— terminate in some view of man and particularly in some view of justice. It is justice that regulates human relationships, not only in the moral sense, but in the practical sense as well. That is, an economics that has no sense of justice will make no sense at all; it simply will not work. Justice is not some arbitrary "value" imposed on the science, but a principle of practical reason that keeps things reasonable. Therefore, some theology must be the ultimate source of truth for economics with some intermediate stops at psychology and sociology. It would seem to be self-evident that a complete view of man would involve the sources of knowledge about man, yet this view is not at all universally (or even generally) accepted by economists.

How is it possible that a humane science can cut itself off from these indispensable sources of knowledge about humans? The answer is: it can't. It is not possible to theorize about human actions without some theory of humans. The selection of an economic system is also the selection of an underlying ethical system. The task is not to bury the ethical assumptions under the pretense of "objectivity," but to make those assumptions explicit—where they can be examined by all. What actually happens is that neoclassical and Austrian economists accept as a purely *economic* truth that which is, in fact, a purely philosophic stance, namely that of Jeremy Bentham's utilitarianism, and its various descendents. This philosophic assertion has become a pseudo-scientific dogmatism, placed beyond all question and critique and hence the science has become less scientific and more dogmatic.

Having said that, it is now incumbent on me to make plain my own ethical assumptions, at least those that lie nearest to the economic question. My primary ethical assumption concerns distributive justice, and by that I mean something very specific with a very specific economic signature. The specific meaning is that the output of production is divided proportionally to the contribution to production; that is, one takes no more than what one contributes. And the specific signature of distributive justice is that the returns to wages and capital are normalized to each other, that is to say, one cannot earn much more by investing than one could by working, which implies that there will not be great differences of wealth and poverty, that the income gradient will be relatively flat. This is the technical requirement for the condition of equity. But a further question immediately arises: why should this condition, this distributive arrangement, be vital to economic equilibrium?

EQUITY AND ECONOMICS

Equity and Equilibrium

When people come together in families or firms to produce things, they add wealth to the economy; in fact, this is the only *economic* way to add wealth. If they and others also get an equitable share of the output, or the wealth they create, there will be enough purchasing power in the economy to buy all the things the firms produce. This is the much-maligned "Say's Law of Markets," which states that "supply creates its own demand." Say's Law is much criticized because if you examine it closely, it says that recessions are impossible; there will always be enough purchasing power to clear the markets. Clearly, we purchase things in terms of other things. The total number of things created equals the total number of things that can be used for purchasing the other things. And yet, recessions *do* happen, quite obviously. Long ones. Deep ones. Serious ones. And they happened more so in Say's day, the heyday of the *laissez-faire* economy, than in ours. So, what is wrong with Say's "Law"?

To understand the problem, we have to look at the sources of demand in a money economy: wages and profit. Wages are, of course, the rewards of labor and profit the reward of capital. In another sense, however, these are the same rewards, since capital is merely "stored-up" labor, or things produced in one period to be used to continue production in the next period. For example, if a farmer wishes to have a crop next year, he must save some seed-corn from this year's crop. Now, the corn he consumes and the corn he saves are the same corn from the same crop. But by saving some corn for seed, it becomes "capital." Hence, the return on this capital is really a return on his prior-period labor, just as his wages are a return to current-period labor. Clearly the returns to capital and labor, profit and wages, spring from the same source (labor). Capital, then, ought to have roughly the same rewards as labor, plus some premium for saving.

If wages and profits are normalized to each other, economic recessions are unlikely to be protracted or serious. There will be enough purchasing power distributed equitably to clear the markets. In capitalist economies, the vast majority of men are not capitalists; that is, they do not have sufficient capital to make their own livings, either alone or in cooperation with their neighbors, but must work for wages in order to live. And since the vast majority of men and women work for wages, then the vast majority of goods will have to be distributed through wages. In conditions of equity, this will not be a problem; so long as there is equity, there is likely to be equilibrium, and periods of disequilibrium are likely to be brief. But it may happen, and quite often does, that profit and wages are *not* normalized to each other. Usually, this means that capital gets an inordinate share of the rewards of production. This, in turn, means that the vast majority of men and women will not have sufficient purchasing power to clear the markets, and the result will be a disequilibrium condition, that is, a recession.

At this point, the neo-classical economist might object that the division of rewards doesn't matter, since there will still be the same amount of purchasing power in the economy; even if capital gets more and labor less, there will still be the same amount of money, and hence of purchasing power. Alas this is not true. The CEO or Managing Director may get five hundred times what the line worker gets, but he cannot wear five hundred times the shoes, eat five hundred times the food, or live in a five hundred-bedroom manor. Nor can he productively invest the excess, because the very fact of receiving the excess narrows the market, which is always measured by the number of solvent consumers in that market. Hence, instead of productive investment, the investor finds no use for his money and he turns to speculative instruments like the CDOs, MBSs, CDSs, and the whole alphabet soup of financial gambling instruments with which we have become all too familiar. Thus, both purchasing power and investment funds leach out of the economy to produce structural shortfalls. When this happens, societies look to *non-economic* ways of restoring equilibrium.

Non-Economic Equilibrium

The major non-economic means of restoring equilibrium are charity, government spending, and consumer credit (that is, usury). Each of these methods transfers purchasing power from one group, which has an excess, to another, which has a deficit. The first method, charity, will always be necessary to some degree because even in the most equitable economies, there will always be people who are incapable of making a decent living, perhaps because of mental impairment, moral deficiency, or physical handicap. One hopes that there is enough generosity and benevolence in society to voluntarily cover these needs. However, when low wages become widespread, and when self interest becomes the dominant motivation in society, it is likely that charity will be insufficient, and other means must be used.

The second non-economic method is government spending, by which the government seeks to re-establish equilibrium conditions either by supplementing the income of some portion of the population, or simply by increasing its spending to create more jobs and thus add more purchasing power to the economy. This strategy is at the heart of Keynesian economics. Despite the fact that Keynesian transfers now consume a huge portion of the public expenditures, these transfers have been, for some years now, insufficient to balance supply and demand, and for some time now the economy has depended chiefly on the third method, usury or consumer credit. This is the plastic economy, an economy based on credit cards. And to the extent that an economy depends on consumer credit, it is, quite literally, a house of cards, and will be as unstable as those structures usually are. In fact, usury is the most destructive way of increasing demand, since a borrowed dollar used to increase demand today must be paid back tomorrow and hence decrease demand in a future period by that same dollar—plus interest. This requires more borrowing, which of course only makes the problem worse. Eventually, the system falls of its own weight, as credit is extended to an increasingly weakened consumer, and a credit crisis results.

POWER, PROPERTY, AND JUSTICE

The "Standard" Model

If the relationship between equity and equilibrium is so obvious, why have most economists missed it entirely? The truth is, they haven't missed it, but they use a different model of "fairness" in wages. Without going too deeply into this model, we can note that it states that in a perfectly competitive, free-market environment, wages would tend to reflect accurately the productivity of both labor and capital, and that each side would get the wealth it actually produced, and so equilibrium would be reached. The most famous proponent of this theory, called "marginal productivity," was J. B. Clark, who put it this way: "*Where natural laws have their way, the share of income that attaches to any productive function is gauged by the actual product of [that function].* In other words, free competition tends to give labor what labor creates, to capitalists what capitalists create, and to *entrepreneurs* what the coordinating function creates."[1]

Another way to state this theory is to say that wages determined by free-market bargaining will be "just wages," and equilibrium conditions will be satisfied. While time does not permit a complete critique of this theory, we can note that it depends on treating all things as commodities manufactured for the market with a supply regulated by the price. But labor (that is, human beings) is not a "commodity" whose supply is regulated by price—*pace* Thomas Malthus. However, the theory of marginal productivity is very easy to test empirically. According to the theory, wages should rise with productivity. And occasionally, this actually happens. But not always, and not even generally.

1. Clark, *Distribution of Wealth*, 3 (emphasis original).

For example, over the last thirty years in the United States, productivity has exploded in all categories of labor, but the median wage has not changed since 1973. Hence, the marginal productivity theory is falsified in practice. Clearly, workers are producing more, but they are not getting any of the benefits; the rewards of increased productivity are going to a few people at the top, while the mass of men have seen no improvement. However, it is obvious that if people are producing more but earning the same, they cannot from their earnings consume all that they produce, and hence the economy will have to rely on the non-economic sources of demand; usury and welfare will replace economic justice as the means to equilibrium.

Why doesn't free bargaining produce equitable wages? Adam Smith gave the answer a century before Clark proposed the theory. Concerning any dispute over wages, Smith writes that "It is not, however, difficult to foresee which of the two parties must, upon all ordinary occasions, have the advantage in the dispute, and force the other into a compliance with their terms. The masters, being fewer in number, can combine much more easily . . . In all such disputes, the masters can hold out much longer . . . Many workmen could not subsist a week, few could subsist a month, and scarce any a year without employment."[2]

In other words, Smith recognized that it was *power*, and not productivity, that determines the outcome of wage negotiations, and power will generally favor "the masters." But if it is power that is arbitrated in a wage contract, then the solution is to redress the balance of power between the parties. To do this, we must look at the primary source of economic power, namely property.

Property: The Source of Economic Power

Property relations are the most basic economic relations, and all other economic outcomes will depend in large measure on the nature of the basic property relations. As Daniel Webster noted, "Power follows property," and this is a simple truism that cannot be denied. We tend to take the modern form of property for granted, but in fact it is a relatively recent innovation, dating back to 1535 and the seizure of the monasteries, an act that created a new form of property. This modern form of property was not codified in law until 1667 in the Statute of Frauds, and

2. Smith, *Wealth of Nations*, 70.

the dominant form of modern property, the limited-liability corporation, did not gain its current status and powers until 1886, in a bit of
U.S. Supreme Court legislation known to history as *Southern Pacific v.
Santa Clara County*, a decision which made the corporations practically
independent and sovereign nations.

Before the reign of Henry VIII, property tended to be a widespread
condition throughout society. Technically, only the king was a property-
holder, in our sense of the term, while everyone else was a tenant, either
a tenant-in-chief (a duke or other great lord) or a sub-tenant. We associate "tenants" with "renters," people who normally have only thin, contractual, and precarious rights to the property they occupy, and who pay
for these limited privileges the highest amount that the market will bear,
an amount called "economic rent." But this was not so then. Rights in
tenancy were nearly as strong as outright ownership is today, and rents
were not "economic," but customary. That is, they were not related to
the economic value of the land, but to the value of the services provided
to the land, defense, improvements, courts, etc. They were more like a
tax than a rent, and did not vary from year to year. We tend to think of
a fifteenth-century peasant as powerless and perhaps starving, a mere
serf (or even a slave). But that was not the case. Wages were, in fact,
quite high. An artisan could provision his family with ten weeks of work,
while a common laborer could do so in fifteen—wage levels that were
not seen again until the late nineteenth century.[3]

However, after the seizure of the monasteries, wages collapsed so
that, at the close of the sixteenth century, it took an artisan thirty-five
weeks and a laborer forty-two weeks to provision his family.[4] The seizure
of the monastic lands and the enclosure of commons had dispossessed
most of the peasantry of their traditional lands and rights. They became
landless proletarians crowding into cities, which often could not provide
them with sufficient work, or brigands on the highway, stealing to support their families. Rents became economic, with landlords squeezing
out the last penny of value from the now weakened renters. This brief
history shows the power of property to completely change wage relationships. Men who have property—that is, the means of production—are
free to negotiate a wage contract, or not, as they wish. But a man with no
other means of support must accept the terms offered. In this latter case,

3. Rogers, *Six Centuries of Work and Wages*, 390.

4. Ibid., 390.

the wage contract becomes *leonine*, that is, based on the inequality of the parties, and leonine contracts are always about power.[5]

We should be careful to note here that the issue is not about private property *per se*, but about the form and extent of that property. Property is natural to man, we might even say it is *proper* to him. It is as natural for a man to say, "This is my house" or "This is my land," as it is for him to breathe. Indeed, when a man cannot say, "This is mine," then he really is less of a man; he might even find it difficult to breathe, or at least draw a free breath; his rights and freedoms have been truly compromised. The socialists correctly analyzed the problem in terms of property, but they analyzed it in the wrong direction. Having ascertained that there were too few owners, they tried to ensure that there would henceforth be no owners. But the distributist takes the problem in the other direction; he wishes to make the mass of men more properly human by giving them what is proper to a man, namely property.

Restoring Distributive Justice

The primary justification for private property is that it ensures that each man gets what he produces. As R. H. Tawney put it, "Property was to be an aid to creative work, not an alternative to it."[6] But when property becomes aggregated into a relatively few hands, when only a few control the means of production, property loses its proper function, and "owner-ship" becomes divorced from use. In our day, "ownership" is frequently in the form of a corporate share, which loses most of the qualities of actual ownership to become attenuated to a mere lien on a certain portion of the profits, or not, as the managers decide.[7] Oddly enough, this puts not only the worker, but the investor at a disadvantage, as power passes to a new group, the *über*-managers, who sit on each other's boards and set each other's salaries. As John Bogle, the founder of the Vanguard investment funds, notes: the managers take an increasing share of the profits, leaving scraps for those who actually put their money at risk.[8] The result is that the returns to both kinds of labor, actual labor and the stored-up labor of capital, are reduced, while "management" and speculation get the lion's share of the profits.

5. Belloc, *Servile State*, 111.

6. Tawney, *Acquisitive Society*, 59.

7. Ibid., 62.

8. Bogle, *Battle for the Soul of Capitalism*.

The whole point of distributism is the restoration of distributive justice to its proper place in economic science, and this means, at the practical level, the wider distribution of property. Only a man who has his own property—the land, tools, and training to make his own way in the world—only such a man can fairly negotiate a wage contract. If he has alternatives to what is being offered, then the resulting contract is likely to be fair, that is, to fairly represent his contribution to the productive process. Nor is this conclusion really at odds with standard neo-classical economic theory, if only the economists would take their own theory seriously. For at the base of all the standard economic theory stands the "vast number of firms" assumption, which presumes that the production of any commodity is spread over a vast number of firms such that none of them has any pricing power. They should all be *price-takers* and not *price-makers*. But the precondition of the "vast number of firms" assumption is that property be widely dispersed throughout society; without the latter you cannot have the former. If economists took their own assumptions seriously, they would be the first to protest in front of firms like Wal-Mart or Exxon. But they do not take their own theories seriously, because if they did they would become distributists or something very like it. Indeed, they would note the obvious: that the modern corporation has collectivized production beyond the wildest dreams of any Stalinist bureaucrat.

CONCLUSION

In this chapter, I have attempted to situate economics in its proper place in the hierarchy of knowledge, a place that subordinates it to the other humane sciences, and ultimately to some theological vision of man. The question here is not, I believe, whether this happens, but how it happens. The predominant economic orthodoxy depends on a very specific view of man, but rather than explicitly examining that view, hides its theological and philosophical roots under the rubric of "science," thereby placing it beyond any actual examination or verification. In other words, the science becomes unscientific at its very core, just as Cardinal Ratzinger said it would.

I have attempted to show the connection between justice and economics, and specifically to show that justice is not some external restraint, but rather the practical principle which makes political economy possible, which gives it a standard of action and enables it to be a rational discipline and overcome the absurdity of the "equity/efficiency" trade-off. And I have attempted to show that the question of justice cannot be divorced from the question of property, and that distributive justice, as a purely practical matter, rests upon a proper understanding and division of property.

But my overriding point concerns not so much the practice of economics as it does the practice of theology. For the Queen of the Sciences cannot remain a prisoner in her own palace. Rather, she must make a progress through her provinces, and speak to her people as both their sovereign and their subject. Theology, to properly fulfill her role, must be out in the world, even in its most mundane corners. And the theologian must accept this burden of learning both his own language and someone else's. This requirement of learning the language of her subjects I call the *sovereign humility* of theology. This sovereign humility encounters scientific humility to form the two poles of a dialogue undertaken in perfect confidence, for science is the master of its own methods, while theology is the mistress of the practical reason. Theology cannot resign its sovereignty, any more than science can abandon its proper methods. But the sovereign listens to the judgment of the methods, while the methods are subject to the sovereign, not as to some outside conqueror or interloper, but as the force which guarantees the very validity and meaning of the science.

Finally, there is an old platitude that says: "If you wish for peace, you must work for justice." The economic equivalent is: "If you wish for equilibrium, you must work for equity," for equilibrium is economic peace and equity is economic justice, and you will never see the one without the other.

Bibliography

Church Documents

Catechism of the Catholic Church. 2nd ed. Vatican: Libreria Editrice Vaticana, 2000.

Pontifical Council for Justice and Peace. *Compendium of the Social Doctrine of the Church.* Vatican: Libreria Editrice Vaticana, 2004.

Primary Sources and Secondary Literature

Arendt, Hannah, *Imperialism.* San Diego: Harcourt Brace, 1976.

———. *Human Condition.* Garden City: Doubleday, 1958.

Aristotle. *Ethics.* Translated by J. A. K. Thomson. Harmondsworth, UK: Penguin, 1978.

Armstrong, Scot. "Truth and Freedom in the Anthropology of Benedict XVI." PhD registration paper, John Paul II Institute, Melbourne, Australia, 2009.

Arrighi, Giovanni. *The Long Twentieth Century: Money, Power, and the Origins of Our Times.* London: Verso, 1994.

Atherton, John. *Christianity and the Market.* London: SPCK, 1992.

Badiou, Alain. *Saint Paul: The Foundation of Universalism.* Translated by Ray Brassier. Palo Alto, CA: Stanford University Press, 2003.

Baranzini, Mauro, and Roberto Scazzieri. *Foundations of Economics: Structures of Inquiry and Economic Theory.* New York: Blackwell, 1986.

Bauman, Zygmunt. *Legislators and Interpreters: On Modernity, Post-modernity and Intellectuals.* Cambridge: Polity, 1987.

Baumier, Matthieu. *La démocratie totalitaire: Penser la modernité post-démocratique.* Paris: Renaissance, 2007.

Bazzicchi, Oreste. *Alle radici del Capitalismo: medioevo e scienza economica.* Turin: Effatà, 2003.

Beattie, Tina. "Church's Idealisation of Sexuality May Be Root of Abuse." *Irish Times.* November 3, 2009.

Belloc, Hilaire. *An Esssay on the Restoration of Property.* Norfolk, VA: IHS, 2002.

———. *The Servile State.* New York: Cosimo, 2007.

Benedict, Ruth. *Patterns of Culture*. London: Routledge, 1961.

Benedict XVI/Ratzinger, Joseph. *Behold the Pierced One*. Translated by G. Harrison. San Francisco: Ignatius, 1986.

———. *Caritas in Veritate: Charity in Truth*. Dublin: Veritas, 2009.

———. *The Church, Ecumenism and Politics: New Endeavors in Ecclesiology*. New York: Crossroad, 1988.

———. "The Church and Economy: Responsibility for the Future of the World Economy." *Communio* 13:3 (1986) 199–204.

———. "Commentary on the Introduction and Chapter 1: The Dignity of the Human Person." In *Commentary on the Documents of Vatican II*, edited by Herbert Vorgrimler, vol. 5. *Pastoral Constitution on the Church in the Modern World*, 115–63. New York: Herder & Herder, 1969.

———. "Erster Hauptteil: Kommentar zum I." In *Lexikon für Theologie und Kirche 14: Das Zweite Vatikanische Konzil*, edited by H. Vorgrimler et al., vol. 3. Fribourg: Herder & Herder, 1968.

———. *God and the World: Believing and Living in Our Time. A Conversation with Peter Seewald*. Translated by H. Taylor. San Francisco: Ignatius, 2002.

———. *God Is Love: Deus Caritas Est*. San Francisco: Ignatius, 2006.

———. Interview with the Italian Catholic Agency SIR. Rome, May 7, 2004.

———. *Introduction to Christianity*. Translated by J. R. Foster. San Francisco: Ignatius, 2004.

———. *On the Way to Jesus Christ*. Translated by M. J. Miller. San Francisco: Ignatius, 2005.

———. *A Turning Point for Europe? The Church in the Modern World: Assessment and Forecast*. Translated by B. McNeil. Harrison, NY: Ignatius, 1994.

———. *Values in a Time of Upheaval*. Translated by B. McNeil. San Francisco: Ignatius, 2006.

Bertone, Cardinal Tarcisio. "Address of Cardinal Tarcisio Bertone, Secretary of State, during His Visit to the Senate of the Italian Republic." July 28, 2009. Online: http://www.vatican.va/roman_curia/secretariat_state/card-bertone/2009/documents/rc_seg-st_20090728_visita-senato_en.html.

———. *The Ethics of the Common Good in Catholic Social Doctrine*. Vatican City: Libreria Editrice Vaticana, 2008. Online: http://www.acton.org/press/economic_globalization_and_social_consensus.php.

Black, Antony. *Guilds and Civil Society in European Political Thought from the Twelfth Century to the Present*. London: Methuen, 1984.

Blond, Phillip. *Red Tory: How Left and Right Have Broken Britain and How We Can Fix It*. London: Faber & Faber, 2010.

Bobbio, Noberto. *Destra e Sinistra*. Rome: Donzelli, 1999.

Bogle, John. *The Battle for the Soul of Capitalism*. Rev. ed. New Haven: Yale University Press, 2007.

Boltanski, Luc, and Laurent Thévenot. *On Justification: Economies of Worth*. Translated by Catherine Porter. Princeton: Princeton University Press, 2006.

Boltanski, Luc, and Eve Chiapello. *The New Spirit of Capitalism*. Translated by Gregory Elliott. London: Verso, 2007.

Bossy, John. "The Mass as a Social Institution." *Past & Present* 100 (1983) 29–61.

Braverman, Harry. *Labor and Monopoly Capital: The Degradation of Work in the Twentieth Century*. New York: Monthly Review, 1974.

Brenner, Robert. *Merchants and Revolution: Commercial Change, Political Conflict and London's Overseas Traders 1550–1653*. London: Verso, 2003.

Brewer, Mike, Luke Sibieta, and Liam Wren-Lewis. *Racing Away? Income Inequality and the Evolution of High Incomes*. London: The Institute of Fiscal Studies, 2008. Online: http://www.ifs.org.uk/publications.php?publication_id=4108.

Brittain-Catlin, William. *Offshore: The Dark Side of the Global Economy*. Basingstoke: Picador, 2006.

Brooks, David. *Bobos in Paradise: The New Upper Class and How They Got There*. New York: Simon & Schuster, 2001.

Bruni, Luigino. "Common Good and Economics: Toward an Agapic Economy." Translated by N. Michael Brennan. Online: http://dipeco.economia.unimib.it/perone/bruni/brunihp.

Bruni, Luigino, and Stefano Zamagni. *Civil Economy: Efficiency, Equity, Public Happiness*. Bern: Peter Lang, 2007.

Burnaby, John. *Amor Dei*. Norwich: Canterbury, 1991.

Cacioppo, John T., and William Patrick. *Loneliness: Human Nature and the Need for Social Connections*. New York: Norton, 2008.

Carlyle, Thomas. *Past and Present*. London: Chapman & Hall, 1899.

Caserta, Mary, Thomas O'Connor, Peter Wyman, Hongue Wang, Jan Moynihan, Wendi Cross, Xin Tuc, and Xia Jin. "The Associations between Psychosocial Stress and the Frequency of Illness, and Innate and Adaptive Immune Function in Children." *Brain, Behaviour, and Immunity* 6 (2008) 933–40.

Cavanaugh, William T. "From One City to Two: Christian Reimagining of Political Space." *Political Theology* 7:3 (2006) 299–321.

———. *Theopolitical Imagination: Christian Practices of Space and Time*. Edinburgh: T. & T. Clark, 2003.

Chesterton, G. K. *Collected Works*. San Francisco: Ignatius, 1987.

———. *The Outline of Sanity*. London: Dodd, Mead & company, 1927.

Clark, J. B. *The Distribution of Wealth: A Theory of Wages, Interest, and Profits*. New York: Augustus M. Kelly, 1899.

Clarke, Peter. *Keynes: The Twentieth Century's Most Influential Economist*. London: Bloomsburg, 2009.

Claudel, Paul. *Le Soulier de Satin*. Paris: Gallimard, 2000.

Collishaw, Stephan, Barbara Maughan, Robert Goodman, and Andrew Pickles. "Time Trends in Adolescent Mental Health." *Journal of Child Psychology and Psychiatry and Allied Disciplines* 45:8 (2004) 1350–62.

Collishaw, Stephan, Robert Goodman, Andrew Pickles, and Barbara Maughan. "Modelling the Contribution of Changes in Family Life to Time Trends in Adolescent Conduct Problems." *Social Science and Medicine* 65 (2007) 2576–87.

Connolly, William. *Capitalism and Christianity, American Style*. Durham, NC: Duke University Press, 2008.

Crouch, Colin. *Post-Democracy*. Cambridge: Polity, 2004.

CRESC. *An Alternative Report on UK Banking Reform*. Manchester, UK: University of Manchester, Centre for Research on Socio-Cultural Change, 2009. Online: http://www.cresc.ac.uk/publications/documents/AlternativereportonbankingV2.pdf.

Davidson, Paul. *The Keynes Solution: The Path to Global Economic Prosperity*. London: Macmillan, 2009.

Day, Dorothy. *The Long Loneliness*. New York: Harper & Row, 1952.

Derrida, Jacques. *Edmund Husserl's Origin of Geometry: An Introduction.* Translated by J. P. Leavey Jr. Lincoln: University of Nebraska Press, 1989.

Desmond, William. *God and the Between.* Oxford: Wiley-Blackwell, 2007.

Dickson, David. *The Politics of Alternative Technology.* New York: Universe, 1975.

Donati, Pierpaolo. *Relational Sociology: A New Paradigm for the Social Sciences.* London: Routledge, 2010.

Dorr, Donal. *Option for the Poor. A Hundred Years of Vatican Social Teaching.* Maryknoll, NY: Orbis, 1992.

Eagleton, Terry. *Reason, Faith, and Revolution.* New Haven: Yale University Press, 2009.

———. *Terry Eagleton Presents Jesus Christ and the Gospels.* New York: Verso, 2007.

Eichengreen, Barry. *Globalizing Capital: A History of the International Monetary System.* 2nd ed. Princeton: Princeton University Press, 2008.

Einstein, Albert. *Ideas and Opinions.* New York: Bonanza, 1954.

———. *Relativity: The Special and General Theory.* New York: Crown, 1961.

Elias, Norbert. *The Society of Individuals.* London: Continuum, 1991.

Ellam, Dennis. "Ford's Dagenham Car Plant: Eighty Years of a British Giant." *Daily Mirror.* January 3, 2009. Online: http://www.mirror.co.uk/news/top-stories/2009/03/01/ford-s-dagenham-car-plant-80-years-of-a-british-giant-115875-21161458/.

Ellul, Jacques. *The Technological Society.* Translated by J. Wilkinson. New York: Vintage, 1964.

Elshtain, Jean Bethke. *God, State and Self.* New York: Basic, 2008.

Eschmann, I. T. "St Thomas on the Two Powers." *Medieval Studies* 20 (1958) 177–205.

Fager, Charles. "Small Is Beautiful, and So Is Rome: The Surprising Faith of E. F. Schumacher." *Christian Century* (April 6, 1977) 325–28.

Ferguson, Adam. *An Essay on the History of Civil Society.* Cambridge: Cambridge University Press, 2003.

Fiedler, Leslie. *Waiting for God.* New York: Harper Perennial, 2001.

Florida, Richard. *The Rise of the Creative Class.* New York: Basic, 2003.

Foucault, Michel. *The Birth of Biopolitics.* Translated by Graham Burchell. London: Palgrave Macmillan, 2008.

Frank, Thomas. *One Market Under God: Extreme Capitalism, Market Populism, and the End of Democracy.* New York: Doubleday, 2001.

Franks, Christopher A. *He Became Poor: The Poverty of Christ and Aquinas's Economic Teachings.* Grand Rapids: Eerdmans, 2009.

Friedman, Thomas. *The Lexus and the Olive Tree.* New York: Farrar Straus & Giroux, 1999.

Fukuyama, Francis. *The End of History and the Last Man.* New York: Free Press, 1992.

Genovesi, Antonio. *Autobiagrafia e Lettere.* Milan: Feltrinelli, 1963.

———. *Della diceosina o sia della filosofia del giusto e dell' onesto.* Milan: Marzorati, 1973.

———. *Lezioni di commercio o sia di economia civile.* Critical edition. Edited by M. L. Perna. Naples: Instituto Italiano per gli studi filosofici, 2005.

Gerhardt, Sue. *Why Love Matters: How Affection Shapes a Baby's Brain.* New York: Brunner-Routledge, 2004.

Giddens, Anthony. *The Third Way.* Cambridge: Polity, 1998.

Gill, Eric. *Sacred and Secular.* London: Dent, 1940.

Glasman, Maurice. "Landed and Maritime Markets in Ancient Rome: The Polanyi Paradigm Reconsidered." Unpublished paper.

———. *Unnecessary Suffering: Managing Market Utopia.* London: Verso, 1996.

Godbout, Jacques. *Ce Qui Circule Entre Nous: Donner, Recevoir, Rendre.* Paris: Seuil, 2007.

Godbout Jacques, and Alan Caillé. *The World of the Gift*. Translated by Donald Winkler. Montreal: McGill-Queen's University Press, 1998.

Goodman, Paul, and Percival Goodman. *Communitas: Means of Livelihood and Ways of Life*. Chicago: University of Chicago Press, 1947.

Guardini, Romano. *Letters from Lake Como: Explorations in Technology and the Human Race*. Introduction by Louis Dupré. Translated by Geoffrey W. Bromiley. Grand Rapids: Eerdmans, 1994.

Gutiérrez, Gustavo. *A Theology of Liberation*. London: SCM, 2001.

Habgood, John. *Confessions of a Conservative Liberal*. London: SPCK, 1988.

Halpern, David. *The Hidden Wealth of Nations*. Cambridge: Polity, 2010.

Harries, Richard. *Is There a Gospel for the Rich?* London: Mowbray, 1992.

Harvey, David. *The Enigma of Capital and the Crises of Capitalism*. London: Profile, 2010.

―――. *The New Imperialism*. Oxford: Oxford University Press, 2005.

Hauser, Marc D. *Moral Minds: How Nature Designed Our Universal Sense of Right and Wrong*. London: Ecco, 2006.

Hayek, F. A. *The Road to Serfdom*. 2nd ed. London: Routledge, 2001.

Heidegger, Martin. "The Question Concerning Technology (1954)." In *Basic Writings*, edited by David Krell, 307–42. New York: Harper Collins, 1977.

Hénaff, Marcel. *Le prix de la vérité: Le don, l'argent, la philosophie*. Paris: Seuil, 2002.

Henrici, Peter. "Response to Louis Dupré." In *Catholicism and Secularization in America*, edited by David L. Schindler. Notre Dame, IN: Communio, 1990.

Henwood, Doug. *After the New Economy*. New York: New Press, 2003.

Hilton, Boyd. *The Age of Atonement: The Influence of Evangelicalism on Social and Economic Thought, 1785–1865*. New York: Oxford University Press, 1986.

Hirst, Paul. *Associative Democracy: New Forms of Economic and Social Governance*. Cambridge: Polity, 1996.

Hirst, Paul, and Veit-Michael Bader, editors. *Associative Democracy: The Real Third Way*. London: Routledge, 2001.

Hobhouse, Leonard. "The Ethical Basis of Collectivism." *International Journal of Ethics* 8 (1898) 137–56.

―――. *Social Evolution and Political Theory*. New York: Columbia University Press, 1922.

Hooker, Richard. *Of the Laws of Ecclesiastical Polity*. London: Dent, 1954.

Hume, David. *Dialogues Concerning Natural Religion*. New York: Hafner, 1948.

Husserl, Edmund. *The Crisis of the European Sciences and Transcendental Phenomenology*. Translated by David Carr. Evanston, IL: Northwestern University Press, 1970.

Hutton, Will. "What I Told the Pope about How to Shape the New Capitalism." *The Observer*. June 1, 2008.

Illich, Ivan. *Tools for Conviviality*. New York: Harper & Row, 1973.

International Monetary Fund. *The State of Public Finances: A Cross-Country Fiscal Monitor*. IMF Staff Position Note. July 30, 2009. Online: http://www.imf.org/external/pubs/ft/spn/2009/spn0921.pdf.

Ivereigh, Austen. *Faithful Citizens: A Practical Guide to Catholic Social Teaching and Community Organising*. London: Darton Longman & Todd, 2010.

John Paul II. *Teachings of John Paul II*. Vatican: Libreria Editrice Vaticana, 1995.

Jenkins, David. *Market Whys and Human Wherefores*. London: Cassell, 2000.

Johnson, Kelly. *The Fear of Beggars: Stewardship and Poverty in Christian Ethics*. Grand Rapids: Eerdmans, 2007.

Johnson, Simon, and James Kwak. *13 Bankers: The Wall Street Takeover and the Next Financial Meltdown*. New York: Pantheon, 2010.

Judt, Tony. *Ill Fares the Land*. London: Allen Lane, 2010.

Kindleberger, Charles P. *Manias, Panics, and Crashes: A History of Financial Crises*. 5th ed. Hoboken, NJ: Wiley, 2005.

Lansley, Stewart. *Unfair to Middling*. Touchstone Pamphlets. Online: http://www.tuc.org.uk/touchstonepamphlets

Latour, Bruno. *Nous n'avons jamais été modernes: essai d'anthropologie symétrique*. Paris: Editions La Découverte, 1991. English translation: *We Have Never Been Modern*. Translated by Catherine Porter. New York and London: Harvester Wheatsheaf, 1993.

——. *Pandora's Hope: Essays on the Reality of Science Studies*. Cambridge: Harvard University Press, 1999.

Lindert, Peter H., and Jeffrey G. Williamson. "Does Globalization Make the World More Unequal?" In *Globalization in Historical Perspective*, edited by Michael D. Bordo, Alan M. Taylor, and Jeffrey G. Williamson, 227–76. Chicago: University of Chicago Press, 2003.

Long, D. Stephen. "Usury: Avarice as a Capital Vice." In *Calculated Futures: Theology, Ethics and Economics*, by D. Stephen Long, Nancy Ruth Fox, Tripp York, 139–64. Waco, TX: Baylor University Press, 2007.

Lubac, Henri de. *Catholicism: Christ and the Common Destiny of Man*. San Francisco: Ignatius, 1988.

——. *The Eternal Feminine: A Study on the Text of Teilhard de Chardin*. New York: Harper & Row, 1972.

MacIntyre, Alasdair. *After Virtue: A Study of Moral Theory*. 2nd ed. London: Duckworth, 1985.

——. *Against the Self-Images of the Age: Essays on Ideology and Philosophy*. South Bend, IN: University of Notre Dame Press, 1978.

——. *Marxism: An Interpretation*. London: SCM, 1953.

Marx, Karl. *Capital: Critique of Political Economy*. Translated by S. Moore and E. Aveling. London: Lawrence & Wishart, 1983.

——. "Introduction." In *Grundrisse*. London: Penguin, 1993. Online: http://www.marxists.org/archive/marx/works/1857/grundrisse.

Massingham, H. J. *The Tree of Life*. London: Jon Carpenter, 2003.

Mathewes, Charles. *A Theology of Public Life*. Cambridge: Cambridge University Press, 2007.

Maughan, Barbara, Stephen Collishaw, Howard Meltzer, and Robert Goodman. "Recent Trends in UK Child and Adolescent Mental Health." *Social Psychiatry and Psychiatric Epidemiology* 43:4 (2008) 305–10.

McCabe, Herbert. *Faith Within Reason*. New York: Continuum, 2007.

——. *God, Christ, and Us*. New York: Continuum, 2003.

——. *God Matters*. New York: Continuum, 2005.

——. *God Still Matters*. New York: Continuum, 2001.

——. *The Good Life: Ethics and the Pursuit of Happiness*. New York: Continuum, 2005.

——. *Law, Love, and Language*. New York: Sheed & Ward, 1968.

——. *On Aquinas*. New York: Continuum, 2008.

McCarraher, Eugene. *The Enchantments of Mammon: Corporate Capitalism and the American Moral Imagination*. Forthcoming.

McNabb, Vincent, O.P. *The Church and the Land*. Norfolk, VA: IHS, 2003.

McNally, David. *Against the Market: Political Economy, Market Socialism, and the Marxist Critique*. New York: Verso, 1993.

Mead, Lawrence. "Poverty and Political Theory." Online: http://www.nyu.edu/gsas/dept/
politics/faculty/mead/Research/Pov_and_Pol_Theory.pdf.

Milbank, John. *Being Reconciled: Ontology and Pardon*. London: Routledge, 2003.

———. "The Future of Love. A Reading of Benedict XVI's Encyclical *Deus Caritas Est*."
Communio: International Catholic Review 33:3 (2006) 368–74.

———. "Hume versus Kant: Faith, Reason and Feeling." *Modern Theology* 27 (2011)
Forthcoming.

———. "Were the 'Christian Socialists' Socialists?" In *The Future of Love: Essays in
Political Theology*, 63–74. Eugene, OR: Cascade Books, 2009.

———. *The Word Made Strange: Theology, Language, Culture*. Oxford: Blackwell, 1997.

Morris, Jeremy. *F. D. Maurice and the Crisis of Christian Authority*. Oxford: Oxford
University Press, 2005.

Mumford, Lewis. *The Myth of the Machine: Vol. I, Technics and Human Development*. New
York: Harvest, 1967.

———. *The Myth of the Machine, Vol. II, The Pentagon of Power*. New York: Harvest,
1970.

Muralt, André de. *L'unité de la philosophie politique. De Scot, Occam et Suárez au libéral-
isme contemporain*. Paris: Vrin, 2002.

Murray, Charles. *The Bell Curve Intelligence and Class Structure in American Life*. New
York: Free Press, 1994.

Murray, Robin. *Danger and Opportunity: Crisis and the New Social Economy*. NESTA,
2009.

National Statistics. Online: http://www.statistics.gov.uk/cci/nugget.asp?id=1005.

Nell-Breuning, Oswald von. *Kapitalismus—kritisch betrachtet*. Basel: Herder, 1974.

Noble, David F. *Progress Without People: In Defence of Luddism*. Chicago: Charles H.
Kerr, 1993.

Novak, Michael. "Pope Benedict XVI's Caritas." *First Things Online* (August 17 2009).
Online: http://www.firstthings.com/onthesquare/2009/08/pope-benedict-xvis-
caritas-1.

———. *The Spirit of Democratic Capitalism*. New York: Simon & Schuster, 1982.

———. *Toward a Theology of the Corporation*. Washington, DC: American Enterprise
Institute Press, 1990.

The Nuffield Foundation. *2004 Seminars on Children and Families: Evidence and Implications*. Online: http://www.nuffieldfoundation.org/fileLibrary/pdf/2004_seminars_
childern_families_adolescents_and_wellbeing001.pdf.

Odonis, Gerald. *Tractatus de contractibus*. Translated by Giovanni Ceccarelli and Sylvain
Piron. "Gerald Odonis' Economics Treatise." *Vivarium* 47:2–3 (2009) 164–204.

O'Donovan, Joan. "The Theological Economics of Medieval Usury Theory." *Studies in
Christian Ethics* 14 (2001) 48–64.

O'Donovan, Oliver. *The Problem of Self-Love in St. Augustine*. New Haven: Yale University
Press, 1979.

Office of National Statistics. "Workforce Jobs by Industry." Online: http://www.statistics
.gov.uk/downloads/theme_labour/LMS_FR_HS/WebTable05_2.xls.

Oliver, Simon, editor. *The Radical Orthodoxy Reader*. London: Routledge, 2009.

Olivi, Peter John. *De emptionibus et venditionibus, de usuris, derestitutionibus*. In *Un trat-
tato di economia politica francescana*, Giacomo Todeschini. Rome: Instituto storico
per il medioevo, 1980.

Pabst, Adrian. "The Crisis of Capitalist Democracy." *Telos* 152 (2010) 44–67.

———. "From Civil to Political Economy: Adam Smith's Theological Debt." In *Adam Smith as Theologian*, edited by Paul Oslington, 106–24. London: Routledge, 2011.

———. *Metaphysics: The Creation of Hierarchy*. Grand Rapids: Eerdmans, forthcoming.

———. "Modern Sovereignty in Question: Theology, Democracy and Capitalism." *Modern Theology* 26 (2010) 570–602.

———. "Sovereign Reason Unbound: The Proto-Modern Legacy of Avicenna and Gilbert Porreta." In *The Grandeur of Reason: Religion, Tradition and Universalism*, edited by Peter M. Candler Jr. and Conor Cunningham, 135–66. London: SCM, 2010.

Perelman, Michael. *The Invention of Capitalism: Classical Political Economy and the Secret History of Primitive Accumulation*. Durham, NC: Duke University Press, 2000.

Polanyi, Karl. *The Great Transformation: The Political and Economic Origins of Our Time*. Boston: Beacon, 2000.

———. *Primitive, Archaic and Modern Economies*. Edited by George Dalton. New York: Anchor, 1968.

Preston, Ronald. *Religion and the Ambiguities of Capitalism*. London: Pilgrim, 1993.

Putnam, Robert. *Bowling Alone: The Collapse and Revival of American Community*. New York: Simon & Schuster, 2000.

Rahner, Karl. *Faith in a Wintry Season: Conversations and Interviews with Karl Rahner in the Last Years of His Life*. New York: Crossroad, 1991.

Rajan, Raghuram G. *Fault Lines: How Hidden Fractures Still Threaten the World Economy*. Princeton: Princeton University Press, 2010.

Ramsey, Michael. *The Gospel and the Catholic Church*. Peabody, MA: Hendrickson, 2009.

Reinhart, Carmen M., and Kenneth Rogoff. *This Time Is Different: Eight Centuries of Financial Folly*. Princeton: Princeton University Press, 2009.

Reynolds, Susan. *Fiefs and Vassals. The Medieval Evidence Reinterpreted*. Oxford: Oxford University Press, 1994.

Ricoeur, Paul. *Oneself as Another*. Translated by Kathleen Blamey. Chicago: University of Chicago Press, 1994.

Ridley, Matt. *The Origins of Virtue*. London: Penguin, 1996.

Robertson, John. *The Case for the Enlightenment: Scotland and Naples 1680–1760*. Cambridge: Cambridge University Press, 2005.

Roepke, Wilhelm. *The Social Crisis of Our Time*. Translated by William F. Campbell. Brunswick, NJ: Transaction, 2009.

Rogers, J. E. T. *Six Centuries of Work and Wages: The History of English Labour*. New York: Putnam, 1884.

Rousselot, Pierre. *The Problem of Love in the Middle Ages*. Translated by Alan Vincelette. Milwaukee: Marquette University Press, 2006.

Rowland, Tracey. *Pope Benedict XVI: A Guide for the Perplexed*. Edinburgh: T. & T. Clark, 2010.

———. *Ratzinger's Faith: The Theology of Pope Benedict XVI*. Oxford: Oxford University Press, 2008.

Rozsak, Theodore. *Where the Wasteland Ends: Politics and Transcendence in Postindustrial Society*. New York: Doubleday, 1972.

Ruskin, John. *Unto This Last and Other Writings*. New York: Penguin, 1997.

Rüstow, Alexander. *Die Religion der Marktwirtschaft*. Münster: LIT, 2004.

Ryan, John A. *Distributive Justice: The Right and Wrong of Our Present Distribution of Wealth*. Reprint. Whitefish, MT: Kessinger, 2008.

———. *A Living Wage*. Reprint. Whitefish, MT: Kessinger, 2007.

Sainsbury Centre for Mental Health. *Childhood Mental Health and Life Chances in Post-War Britain*. 2009. Online: http://www.scmh.org.uk.

———. *The Chance of a Lifetime*. 2009. Online: http://www.scmh.org.uk.

Schall, James V. "Certain Fundamental Truths." *Ignatius Insight*. October 6, 2009.

Schindler, David L. "Religious Freedom, Truth and American Liberalism: Another Look at John Courtney Murray." In *Heart of the World, Center of the Church: Communio Ecclesiology, Liberalism and Liberation*, 1–16. Edinburgh: T. & T. Clark, 1996.

Shults, F. LeRon. *Reforming Theological Anthropology: After the Philosophical Turn to Relationality*. Grand Rapids: Eerdmans, 2003.

Schumacher, E. F. *Good Work*. New York: Harper & Row, 1979.

———. *A Guide for the Perplexed*. New York: Harper & Row, 1977.

———. *Small Is Beautiful: Economics as If People Mattered*. New York: Harper & Row, 1973.

Screpanti, Ernesto, and Stefano Zamagni. *An Outline of the History of Economic Thought*. Oxford: Oxford University Press, 2005.

Sedgwick, Peter. *The Market Economy and Christian Ethics*. Cambridge: Cambridge University Press, 1999.

———. "Theology and Society." In *The Modern Theologians: An Introduction to Christian Theology in the Twentieth Century*, edited by David Ford, 286–310. Oxford: Blackwell, 1997.

Sen, Amartya. "Adam Smith's Market Never Stood Alone." *Financial Times*. March 11, 2009.

———. *The Idea of Justice*. London: Allen Lane, 2009.

———. "Open and Closed Impartiality." *The Journal of Philosophy* 99 (2002) 445–69.

———. "What Do We Want from a Theory of Justice?" *The Journal of Philosophy* 103 (2006) 215–38.

Seneca. "On Benefits." In *Moral Essays III*. Translated by John Basore. Cambridge: Harvard University Press, 1989.

Shirky, Clay. *Cognitive Surplus: Creativity and Generosity in a Connected Age*. London: Penguin, 2010.

———. *Here Comes Everybody: How Change Happens When People Come Together*. London: Penguin, 2009.

Shults, F. LeRon. *Reforming Theological Anthropology: After the Philosophical Turn to Relationality*. Grand Rapids: Eerdmans, 2003.

Skidelsky, Robert. *Keynes: The Return of the Master*. London: Allen Lane, 2009.

Smith, Adam. *An Inquiry into the Nature and Causes of the Wealth of Nations*. London: Random, 1991.

———. *The Theory of Moral Sentiments*. New York: Prometheus, 2000.

Stein, Ben. "In Class Warfare, Guess Which Class Is Winning." *New York Times*. November 26, 2006.

Stein, Edith. *Knowledge and Faith*. Translated by Walter Redmond. Washington, DC: ICS, 2000.

Tarde, Alfred de. *L'idée de juste prix*. Paris: F. Alcan, 1907.

Tawney, R. H. *The Acquisitive Society*. New York: Harcourt Brace, 1920.

———. *Equality*. London: G. Allen & Unwin, 1931.

———. *R. H. Tawney's Commonplace Book*. Edited by J. M. Winter and D. M. Joslin. Cambridge: Cambridge University Press, 1972.

———. *Religion and the Rise of Capitalism*. New York: Mentor, 1954.

Taylor, Charles. *The Ethics of Authenticity*. Cambridge: Harvard University Press, 1997.

Temple, William. *Christianity and Social Order*. Harmondsworth, UK: Penguin, 1956.

Tilly, Charles. *Big Structures, Large Processes, Huge Comparisons*. New York: Russell Sage, 1984.

UNCTAD. "The Global Economic Crisis: Systemic Failures and Multilateral Remedies." Online: http://www.unctad.org.

UNEP. "Dead Planet, Living Planet: Biodiversity and Ecosystem Restoration for Sustainable Development." Edited by Pavan Sukhdev. Online: http://www.unep.ch.

UNICEF. *An Overview of Child Well-Being in Rich Countries*. United Nations Children's Fund, 2007. Online: http://www.unicef.org/media/files/ChildPovertyReport.pdf.

Vico, Giambattista. *Scienza Nuova*. English translation: *The New Science*. Translated by Thomas Goddard Bergin and Max Harold Fisch. Ithaca: Cornell University Press, 1948.

Villey, Michel. *La formation de la pensée juridique moderne*. Paris: Presses Universitaires de France, 2003.

Weigel, George. "*Caritas in Veritate* in Gold and Red: The Revenge of Justice and Peace (or So They May Think)." *National Review Online*. July 7, 2009. Online: http://article .nationalreview.com/399362/icaritas-in-veritatei-in-gold-and-red/george-weigel.

Weil, Simone. "Factory Work." Translated by Felix Giovanelli. *Politics* 3:11 (1946) 369–73.

———. *Oppression and Liberty*. Translated by Arthur Wills and John Petrie. Amherst: University of Massachusetts Press, 1973.

———. *Simone Weil: Selected Essays 1934–1943*. Edited by Richard Rees. New York: Oxford University Press, 1962.

White, Lynn. "The Historical Roots of Our Ecologic Crisis (1967)." In *The Dynamo and the Virgin Reconsidered: Essays in the Dynamism of Western Culture*, 75–94. Cambridge: MIT Press, 1973.

Wicker, Brian. "Justice, Peace, and Dominicans, 1216–1999: Viii-*Slant*, Marxism, and the English Dominicans." *New Blackfriars* 80 (1999) 436–43.

Wilhelmsen, Frederick. *Christianity and Political Philosophy*. Atlanta: University of Georgia Press, 1982.

Wilkinson, Richard. "Health, Hierarchy and Social Anxiety." In *Annals of the New York Academy of Sciences*, edited by N. Adler, M. Marmot, B. McEwen, J. Stewart. 1999. Online: http://povlibrary.worldbank.org/library/view/4541.

———. "The Impact of Inequality: Empirical Evidence." *Renewal* 14:1 (2006) 20–26.

Wilkinson, Richard, and Kate Pickett. *The Spirit Level: Why More Equal Societies Almost Always Do Better*. London: Allen Lane, 2009.

Williams, Raymond. *Culture and Society 1780–1950*. New York: Harper & Row, 1958.

Williams, Rowan. *Anglican Identities*. London: Darton Longman & Todd, 2004.

———. "Face It: Marx Was Partly Right about Capitalism." *The Spectator*. September 27, 2008.

———. *Lost Icons: Reflections on Cultural Bereavement*. Edinburgh: T. & T. Clark, 2000.

Wood, Barbara. *E. F. Schumacher: His Life and Thought*. New York: Harper & Row, 1984.

Žižek, Slavoj. *The Puppet and the Dwarf: The Perverse Core of Christianity*. Cambridge: MIT Press, 2003.

———. "Self-Deceptions: On Being Smug and Intolerant." 2001. Online: http://www .lacan.com/zizek-self.htm.

Žižek, Slavoj, and John Milbank. *The Monstrosity of Christ: Paradox or Dialectic?* Cambridge: MIT Press, 2009.

Index